flat-woven rugs of the world

Kilim, Soumak, and Brocading

Valerie Sharaf Justin

VAN NOSTRAND REINHOLD COMPANY

New York   Cincinnati   Toronto   London   Melbourne

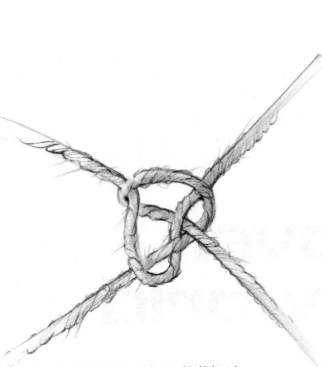

Printed in the United States of America
Designed by Loudan Enterprises

Published in 1980 by Van Nostrand Reinhold Company
A division of Litton Educational Publishing, Inc.
135 West 50th Street, New York, NY 10020, U.S.A.

Van Nostrand Reinhold Limited
1410 Birchmount Road, Scarborough, Ontario MIP 2E7, Canada

Van Nostrand Reinhold Australia Pty. Limited
17 Queen Street, Mitcham, Victoria 3132, Australia

Van Nostrand Reinhold Company Limited
Molly Millars Lane, Wokingham, Berkshire, England

16 15 14 13 12 11 10 9 8 7 6 5 4 3 2 1

Library of Congress Cataloging in Publication Data

Justin, Valerie.
    Flat-woven rugs of the world.

    Bibliography: p.
    Includes index.
    1. Kilims. 2. Soumaks. 3. Rugs.
    4. Tapestry. 5. Wall hangings. I. Title.
NK2800.J87   746.7'2   78-26836
ISBN 0-442-24211-5

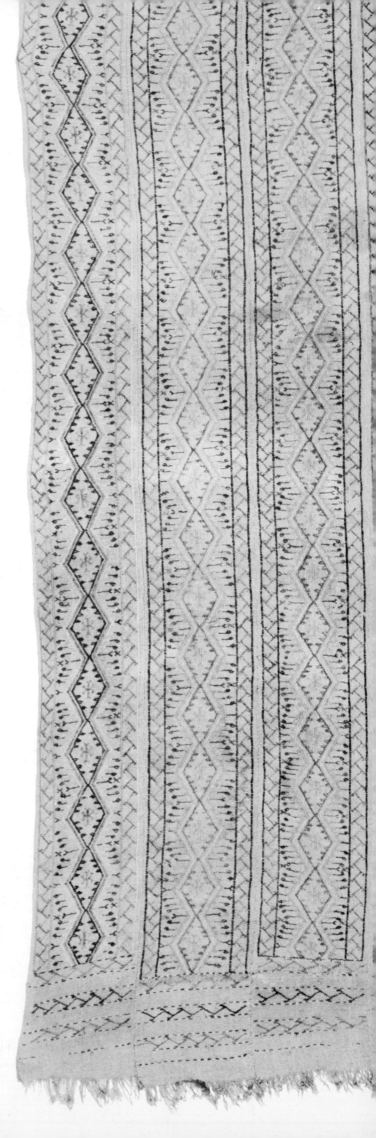

contents

acknowledgments

I am grateful for the encouragement of Robert Bartlett Haas, former director of Arts/Extension, UCLA, and for his reading of the manuscript. Special gratitude to Anthony N. Landreau, Curator of Education, Museum of Art, Carnegie Institute, whose comments on the manuscript resolved many questions. My thanks to Mary Jane Leland, Cal. State Univ. Long Beach for her help with weaving definitions and to Joyce Winkel for information about Eastern European textiles.

Museum personnel, individual collectors and dealers, anthropologists, and art historians have contributed generously. I owe thanks to the Southwest Museum and the Los Angeles County Museum of Art for material loaned, and to UCLA for the use of its fine libraries.

Except when otherwise credited the photographs are by Grant Taylor, whose complete cooperation I truly appreciate. All diagrams are by Carol Bowdoin Gil.

All the rugs and weavings not otherwise credited are the property of the Pillowry, New York and Los Angeles. It is due to Majorie Lawrence, my partner in the Pillowry and an energetic and peripatetic textile expert, that I became an enthusiast of the kilim, and it is because of the years of collecting and trading in tribal weavings at the Pillowry that this work was possible.

foreword

Weaving is one of the important chapters in the story of civilization and one of the oldest of the crafts and arts. In the view of Goethe weaving "is the most magnificent art which truely distinguishes mankind from the animal."[1]

Weaving was developed so far back in prehistory that almost every culture has attributed its invention to a god or goddess,[2] and some have elaborate mythologies surrounding it.[3] In Mexico, where many beliefs linked the weaving process with fertility and the need for rain,[4] the invention of spinning and weaving was attributed to the Aztec goddess Xochiqueotzal. In medieval Europe spinning was invariably associated with Eve.[5] A Navajo legend tells how Spider Woman instructed the women to weave on a loom that Spider Man had made for them (see Chapter 15). In Greece one of the many forms of the goddess Pallas Athena was that of Ergane, or working woman, patron of spinners and weavers. The epithet "Palas" is also used in the Caucasus and in northern Iran by some Turkmen tribes to refer to a class of flat-woven rugs (see Chapter 6); this suggests that some link between Palas the rug and Pallas Athena the goddess might be found.

History indicates that weaving probably developed independently in different places physically and temporally distant from one another. This is not to say that cultural diffusion did not also exist: certainly trade among different peoples thrived even in prehistoric times. Questions concerning weaving's early years are perhaps too remote in history to be answered. Since ordinary textiles cannot survive underground as can materials worked from metal or carved from stone, there are not many early examples left.

The looms and techniques of the ancient Egyptians seem to have been indigenously developed.[6] In Egyptian tombs excavators have found woven linen from the Badaric era (which lasted until 3400 B.C.), and fine linens of the Middle and New Kingdoms (3000–700 B.C.) were found in tombs near the desert where the air was so dry that it did not rot the cloth, as did the damp air of other climates.

Peruvian woven fabrics dating from 2000 ·B.C. to 1476 A.D. survive in quantity because they were entombed in graves in the extremely dry coastal desert. The stunning achievement of these Peruvian weavings in terms of structural complexity, use of color, and variety of design equals that of any other era in textile history.

Some fragments of woven linen fabrics from the late Stone Age, found in mud-buried Swiss Lake Dwellings (Irgenhaussen) were worked in a complex brocading technique. Woven fragments from Bronze Age graves found in Denmark (Skrydstryp, Borwn Aehej) were of very simply patterned wool, as were other European examples from those periods.[7]

Although no specimens survive, elaborately designed Babylonian and Assyrian wall hangings and clothing, woven of wool, linen, and silk, were all documented by observers of the period.[8]

From those early cultures developed ornamental patterns, the fabled animal and floral motifs that led to the heraldic style of European textiles in the Middle Ages. (Perhaps the exposure to the animal carpets made in Turkey at that time also had an influence.)

Literature is filled with descriptions of textiles in early cultures. Textiles were among the tribute paid by conquered peoples to the conqueror in every period and were among the gifts presented to and from the mighty. As such they were recorded: the names of what they were and lists of details about them survive, but in most cases examples of the textiles themselves and the techniques in which they were executed are lost. It is possible that one day more specific information can be extracted from the mass of written material available in many languages.

Of known knotted rugs there is one that preceded all the others by a thousand years. Almost complete, it was found by Soviet archaeologists in Southern Siberia and is known as the Pazaryk Carpet after the valley where it was preserved in a grave of ice. It is hard to imagine that from its tentative date (3rd century B.C.) to the 13th century when rugs recently found in Turkish mosques

were made there was a discontinuation in the obviously established tradition of rug making. The opposite must be the case. References to rugs woven by Persian tribes occur in works by geographers as early as the 9th and 10th centuries, and various forms of the words *bisat* and *farsh,* meaning "carpet," appear repeatedly in the works of Arab writers from the 8th century on.[9] The gap is certainly in our knowledge of the rugs, not in the tradition itself.[10]

The earliest forms of ornamentation and patterning consist of simple geometric figures, banded areas, and large blocks of colors. Along with intellectual and artistic development more complex ornamentation in the use of plants, animals, and the human figure usually occurs.[11] Naturalistic, conventionalized, or geometric treatment of that ornamentation reflects not only the spirit of the times but also the nature and level of the culture, as seen, for example, in the differing art produced by Shiite Moslems and Sunnite Moslems throughout the Middle East, described in later chapters.

The flat-woven rugs discussed in this book are direct descendants of those early weavings. Most fit into the tradition of geometric patterning. They do not seem to be affected by major stylistic changes. It is possible that they come from a once cohesive set of ancient tribal symbols with specific meanings, the knowledge of which may be lost today or known, in part or in essence, only by some tribal weavers.

Until recently these weavings were made of necessity and for the weaver's own use. Some have been traded in market towns and city bazaars, and in the 20th century some work has been done for purely commercial purposes. In various places peasants and tribal people have executed work designed by others outside of their own tradition. A few of the rugs in this book are examples. But, generally speaking, the work done by the weavers was done in a continuous tribal tradition. As Charles Grant Ellis points out, "The true value of the kilim lies in its consistency and continuity—in this regard the pile rug so frequently has been deficient. The kilim has maintained its integrity. Of course it could do so because until quite recently it has never been commercially produced."[12]

The rugs are called by different names in different areas and in different languages, depending on their use or their technique. The best-known of these names is "kilim," which is often used to mean any flat-woven rug. A kilim is technically a tapestry-woven rug originating in the Near East; tapestry-woven rugs from other areas have other names, and related flat-woven rugs made in varying techniques and in different areas have still other sets of names.

The way in which simple weavings are made has not changed since early history. Now, as then, the animal must be pastured for its wool, shorn, the wool spun, the loom strung, and the shuttle passed back and forth again and again in the hand of the weaver, who often sits on the ground in front of a tent or small village hut. The tent or hut has no furniture as we know it: the weavings provide the furnishings. Rugs are used on the floor and hang across the entrance. Woven bags of different sizes and shapes are used for storage and supplies—to hold bedding during the day and for seating. The tents of the Turkmen people are decorated with woven tent bands that serve useful and decorative functions. The intricacy of the weaving in the bags and covers can match in skill the most sophisticated textiles of East or West, and the beauty of many of the rugs can match in aesthetic achievement a fine easel painting.

introduction

Flat-woven rugs are hand-loomed textiles with a flat surface—without pile—which present a relatively two-dimensional surface. Their basic structure is a plain weave which results when warp and weft elements are interlaced on a loom. When weft elements, closely packed to hide the warp elements, are used in defined areas for patterning, the term tapestry weave is applied to the technique.

This volume covers countries in which tapestry weaving and related techniques have been used to produce rugs for floor use in the context of nomadic, tribal, and peasant traditions. The countries of the Near and Middle East, the oriental rug-producing areas, predominate.

An oriental rug is generally understood to be a carpet of eastern design with a hand-knotted pile introduced as the plain-weave base is woven.[1] Oriental rugs were appreciated in the West as long ago as the 13th century when the Venetian traveler Marco Polo described them. Trade between the Aegean and Mediterranean ports of the Ottoman Empire and the Italian city-states brought them to the attention of the Ottoman Empire and the countries of Europe, where they were prized for their bold designs and colors. Knotted rugs from Egypt had reached Spain and England by the 12th century.

A great flowering of Persian carpet making developed under the influence of three monarchs of the Saffavid dynasty. The most famous carpets in western museums and those that established the superiority of the Persians as designers and weavers of oriental rugs were produced during the reigns of Shah Tahnasp and Shah Abbas. By 1722 the Saffavid line had ended, and fine carpets were either not made or not recorded. It has been estimated that 1,500 carpets, including fragments, from the 15th through the 17th century still exist.[2] In the middle of the 19th century Persian rugs found their way into the West in large quantities. By the late 19th century there were copies and adaptations

of the great early designs. The building of the Russian Trans-Siberian railroad at the turn of the 20th century opened additional rug-producing areas to travelers. Rugs of the Turkmens, for example, became popular in Russia, the rest of Europe, and America.

As rug collecting became more popular and the value of fine rugs appreciated, a multitude of books on oriental rugs appeared. Later, as techniques of scholarship developed, more accurate books were published. The bibliography in Kurt Erdman's *Oriental Carpets—An Account Of Their History* contains more than 620 titles. All these works concentrate on knotted rugs, with only occasional mention of flat-woven rugs.[3]

Flat-woven rugs have been generally ignored by writers, collectors, and the general public. In 1966 *From the Bosporus to Samarkand,* an exhibition of flat-weave rugs, the first of its kind in this country, opened at the Textile Museum in Washington, D.C., and a book based on the exhibition was published. The authors analyzed the flat-woven pieces in terms of structure and developed a classification system according to technique that allows for a precise description of flat-woven rugs.[4]

In subsequent years a group of scholars with common defined goals has worked in rug-producing areas, collecting, analyzing, and documenting pile and flat-weave rugs alike. In Turkey Anthony Landreau[5] and Dr. May Beattie[6] have worked extensively, as has Belkis Acar, Curator of the Rug Museum of the Sultan Ahmet Camii in Istanbul.[7] Walter Denny, Professor of Art History, University of Massachusetts at Amherst, has defined a method for studying Anatolian rugs. His suggestions are followed here; at least as far as Turkish spelling and terminology are concerned.[8] In Iran John Wertime and Amadeo de Franchis have investigated tribal weavings,[9] as has Jenny Housego.[10] All have published valuable studies, referred to in later chapters. A recent exhibition and catalog called *Yörük, the Nomadic Weaving Tradition of the Middle East,* is a result of the collaboration of some of these researchers.[11] Social anthropologists William Irons of Pennsylvania State, G. P. Fazel, University of Massachusetts, and Daniel Bates of Hunter College, working in areas of the Middle East, have also loaned the present author ethnographic material.

This book is a survey that attempts to bring together many examples of flat-woven rugs from various areas, with accurate information about their size, material, technique, and, where possible, origin. There is also found information about the cultures from which they come and about the people who made them.

Because many of the rugs discussed were not acquired at their source, attribution has often been difficult. The changes of national boundaries, with resultant movement of people, complicated by the patterns of nomadic migration, have added to this problem. When facts of origin were not known, pieces were studied in terms of design details, structure, and materials and compared to examples of known origin.[12] The comparison of related examples from a specific flat-weave-producing area is important in amplifying differences and similarities. Weavings are often identified in terms of the market or market area in which they were acquired. Knowledge of migratory patterns results in a knowledge of such markets and helps define real origin.

It is hoped that readers will respond to the information on provenance or attribution presented in this book with critical opinions of their own and with supporting information. The author will in turn share photographic material and other information from her own research files.

This volume attempts to include examples from most areas in which a tradition of flat-woven rugs is known to exist. These include:
1. areas in which flat weaves were produced by tribal people for their own use
2. areas in which settled village people have made flat-woven rugs in a continuing tradition
3. areas in which flat weaves are made in workshop conditions if the work is in the tribal or peasant tradition
4. areas in which fine weaving in the techniques covered in this volume flourished, although rugs were not made.

The rugs are covered by country, using contemporary names and current boundaries. Such a classification by national boundaries causes some awkward place-hopping. The USSR, for example, the world's largest nation, contains many diverse peoples. From a purist's point of view a Ukrainian kilim and a Kirghiz felt tent rug are not logically connected, although here they are in the same chapter because the origin of both is the USSR.

In order to utilize a system of classification for the material, flat-woven pieces are referred to in this volume according to these major categories:
1. kilims (tapestry-woven rugs)
2. Soumak rugs
3. brocaded rugs
4. embroidered rugs
5. compound-weave rugs
6. mixed-technique rugs[13]
The equivalent in the language of origin for each weaving term (kilim, soumak, brocaded, embroidered) appears when first mentioned if such an equivalent is known.

the kilim and its cousins

Flat-woven rugs are being shown, discussed, and collected; kilims, a characteristic example of which is shown in color plate 1 (page 193), are timely. Fine examples should be prized and protected, for the older kilims will soon become scarce. It is hoped that many will enter museum collections and be displayed so that they may be seen at first hand by a large public.

The shrinkage of our planet caused by post–World War II technology and advances in transportation and communication has increased our appreciation of other cultures by making their art and their works available. This appreciation coincided with a climate of social change in America. In an escape from conventional life patterns, Americans (mostly young) streamed to faraway places. Among the patterns that they were escaping from were the plastic, mass-produced flotsam of the industrialized western world. They responded to tribal weaving traditions where they encountered them and related to the idea of nomadic life. These self-made nomads acquired tribal weavings. They brought back kilim and soumak rugs, saddlebags, and animal trappings to western Europe and the United States in abundance. This phenomenon is one that presents a particularly contemporary problem. Will such popularity cause a void at the source? Another possible case of consumerism gobbling up the would-be cherished object in a glut of appreciation?

While the members of the flower generation were discovering tribal traditions in far-reaching parts of the world, their parents, grandparents, and contemporaries at home were altering their lifestyle. In areas where no attention had been paid to ethnic crafts and clothes people of all ages put on African beads and Afghan shirts; women wore the native costumes of Greek peasant women and Kuchi nomads. Baskets from all over the world were used as home accessories. Of the import shops that opened in shopping malls across America many had beautiful examples of the arts and crafts of many diverse people, never before available to touch and to have.

The fact is that kilims look wonderful in contemporary settings, as is shown in the architectural interiors in Color Plate 37 (page 224). They give a residence a flattering richness without the formality of an oriental rug. They imbue an institutional setting with warmth. On the long wall behind tellers' cages in a bank they give respite to waiting depositors. They mix well on walls hung with hard-edge graphics and easel paintings, under glass or exposed on linen stretchers.

As opposed to knotted rugs, which have an "establishment" cachet (Kurt Erdmann wrote that the possession of a "genuine Persian" was de rigeur for his grandparents),[1] kilims are considered "the other Oriental rug," *outside* the establishment. There have always been class distinctions among oriental rugs. Arthur Upham Pope suggests that a court rug be called "high style," that fine rugs made for provincial khans and tribal chieftains would be designated "middle style," and rugs made for tribal and village use "low style."[2] The author of *Formes et Symboles Dans Les Arts Du Maroc* contrasts the popular arts of Morocco with the dominant influence of European elite culture. He feels that the reality of North African life rests with the folk culture (low style): "Imagination, the creativity and spirit of initiative, are the primary materials possessed by a people."[3]

The regional differences, the diversity of peoples, the variety of articles made to embellish their own lives, are the dialects of the language of art. The kilim has a folk integrity, free from the influence of high style and commercialism. The regional kilims of this book speak in dialects that we can understand.

2

materials

Rugs are fabrics woven from yarn, which is made of fibers. Fibers can be of natural origin (animal, plant, mineral) or man-made. The fibers used in the rugs discussed in this book are:

1. Animal—external skin products
   a. sheep wool
   b. goat hair
      (1) mohair from Angora goats (Asia, Asia Minor)
      (2) cashmere from Tibetan goats
      (3) mountain-goat hair (Asia Minor, Turkestan, Central Asia).
   c. camel hair
      (1) hair of two humped Asian bactrians
      (2) hair of one humped Arabic dromedary
   d. hair of cameloids
      (1) llama
      (2) alpaca
      (3) vicuna (wild)
      (4) guanaco (wild and domesticated)
   e. occasional use of dog hair; human hair; rabbit, rat, and mouse fur; shells sometimes used for ornament
   f. silk—the filament secreted from the cocoons of the cultivated silkworm and wild silk from similar undomesticated caterpillar moths[1]
2. Plant—fibers and floss surrounding the seeds of the herbaceous cotton and other plants
   a. cotton—native to Egypt; West, East, and Central Africa; Iran; Afghanistan; India; the Americas
   b. leaf fibers
      (1) sisal (also known as ixtle and maguey)
      (2) yucca
   c. plant stems
   d. flax (the source of linen, the oldest plant fiber in use)[2]
   e. hemp, jute
   f. grasses, reeds (some leaves as well as stems)[3]

3. Mineral
   a. metals
      (1) gold and silver threads
      (2) wire thread and ribbons[4]
      (3) coins
      (4) disks
   b. clay beads
   c. glass beads

Of the above materials the rugs shown in these pages primarily utilize wool, the shorn hair of sheep. Wool insulates against cold and repels dampness; it is the logical material to fulfill the function of a rug. Sheep were one of the first animals to be domesticated by man. Their care led early peoples into a pastoral existence. The early sheep had many hairy qualities. Domestication resulted in genetic changes, eventually turning the coat from hair into wool. In true wool a minute overlap of scales extends lengthwise on the fiber and interlocks when spun and when used in felt making. Many classifications of sheep are used in agriculture, with a variety of subdivisions. For our purposes a division between wild and domesticated sheep is useful.

Among the wild sheep of Asia are the species *Ovis karlini, ovis argali,* and *ovis poli. Ovis poli* (Kachkar or Arkhar) is over 3' high, weighs from 400 to 430 pounds, and is distinguished by enormous horns that spiral backward. It is not domesticated. *Argali,* another large species, also inhabits the mountains and plains of Central Asia. It is found in small flocks. It is agile, strong, and timid, much like domestic sheep in its habits, and can be tamed if taken young.[5] *Argali* is also found in the western mountains of North America and is known as the Rocky Mountain sheep.[6]

A breed of wild sheep found in western Asia, southern Europe, and North Africa is the moufflon (*Ovis musimon*). Somewhat smaller than the previously cited species, the male is horned and the female is not. It can be domesticated and was prized in ancient Greece.[7] The wild mouflon is still abundant in Asia. It is hunted by Qashqai tribesmen in the Zagros Mountains and by Baluchi tribesmen in eastern Iran.

Another breed, *Ovis cycloceros,* found in the warmest regions inhabited by wild sheep, has been sighted close to sea level in the hottest parts of Baluchistan. A specimen measuring 20'' at shoulder height had horns measuring 14'' around a curve.[8]

Of domestic sheep (*Ovis aries*) fat-tailed, long-tailed, and fat-rumped varieties are common. The sheep of the Bakhtiyari in Iran are tall and brown and black in color, "with great pendulous tails weighing as much as 8 pounds," as Isabella Bishop reported in 1891.[9] The tail of the broad, or fat-tailed, sheep can be enormous; weights of 30 to 40 pounds have been mentioned. It sustains the sheep during the summer drought. The fat-tailed breed is found throughout Asia and North Africa. The wool is relatively coarse and mixed with dark-colored hair. In eastern Turkey herds of mixed colors—rust, brown, black, and white—are found. As is the case with all sheep, the quality of the wool depends on pasturage and climate. The finest fleeces have been developed in Iran in Khorassan and in the district of Kerman, where much attention has been paid to the breeding of sheep for carpet wool. In the cool, dry climate of the high mountains of Asia wool is much finer and silkier than in hot, sandy districts.

Long-tailed sheep are found in parts of Afghanistan near Pakistan, in India, in parts of Arabia near the Persian Gulf and in North Africa.

Appropriately named for the accumulation of fat in the posterior loins and rump, the fat-rumped variety is found in northern Asia and Russia. It is domesticated by the nomadic Turkmen and Kalmuck people. These sheep can travel long distances, endure great hardship, and yield a plentiful supply of milk. Some fat-rumped sheep are found in North Africa. Five breeds that compose the flocks of central and northeast Arabia are named by H. R. P. Dickson in *The Arab of the Desert.* They are of a variety of colors (black with white face, all black, all brown, or white). The sheep of the Qahtan tribe are small with short, coarse wool (*habasiyah*), while the sheep from Najd and Kuwait have long, straight hair (*argiyah*).[10]

PREPARATION OF MATERIALS

Wool

Shearing

Shearing takes place once or twice a year, with the major portion usually occurring after the coldest weather is over—in Arabia this is March or April, in Peru March. The Navajos shear in April and May. Landreau says that in the Van Hakkari area of eastern Turkey the long wool of the sheep is sheared in late spring or early summer, and the short wool of the lamb is sheared in late summer or early fall.[11] The Qashga'i clip their sheep once a year. Leix says that among the Kirghiz and Turkmen the sheep are shorn twice, with winter wool amounting to 10 pounds and summer wool 3 pounds.[12] This may correspond to the Van Hakkari pattern cited: if the winter wool is actually sheared at the end of winter, then the spring and summer shearing is of lambs. As far as weight per fleece is concerned, there is great variety. Mumford cites an average weight of 5 pounds (Asia Minor, 1905),[13] but two to three times that weight is possible with certain breeds under certain conditions. In Pomona in southern California 13 pounds is the current average. Scientific methods in England, Australia, South Africa, and other wool-producing areas achieve equivalent poundage.

Washing

Washing sometimes precedes shearing. In some areas the sheep are driven into the water, washed, then sheared. Wool is usually washed after shearing, preferably in running water, often a nearby stream or river. After one washing the wool is sorted and washed again. Soft water is preferred. Hard water sometimes necessitates the use of potash, which reduces the durability of the finished product. A great deal depends on the quality of the water: a given source is often continually utilized for generations.[14]

Careful repeated washing, sometimes with soap and other alkalis (including plant materials such as the root of the maguey cactus in Mexico), removes dirt and superfluous fat, which hinders dyeing, but leaves the natural fat, lanolin, that gives the finished rug its sheen. The Qashga'i scour the wool in boiling water to which potash or carbonate of soda is added.

Certain dyes take better with some wools if they are washed in water alone. Navajo women in North America avoid using wool that is very dirty or greasy, do not wash it at all before spinning, and rely on the carding process to eliminate residue.[15] In other desert areas in which water was scarce the fleece was not washed but shaken and exposed to sunlight. In all cultures the wool is put in the sun to dry—wind, warmth, and exposure are all important. The weight of the fleece is reduced considerably by the washing and drying process.

In parts of Central and South America the finished wool product is boiled after weaving to shrink the fibers and to make the garment waterproof. In some areas (Guatemala, for example) the finished wool product is fulled, beaten by hand, or treadled by foot with hot water to thicken the fabric. In Oaxaca (Mexico) weavers in a Zapotec village wash finished tapestry-woven rugs several times after they are taken from the loom for two purposes: washing softens the rug and washing shrinks the wool, tightening the final weave.[16]

Carding

The usual tool for carding is a block with rows of vertical pins that are close together across which the carder draws the wool. Some cultures use only the fingers for carding. Navajos sometimes comb the wool with a brush of thistles.[17] A carding device observed in Asia Minor was a large bow-shaped pole strung with gut, which was suspended from a ceiling. The wool was combed by hitting the gut with a mallet. Different natural colors can be carded together for different tones and additional colors. Navajos card brown and white together to produce their grays.

Goat Hair

Goat hair, popular for its silky sheen, is used as warp in some flat-woven saddlebags and animal covers. Goats have a fine grade of hair growing next to the skin, which can be separated from the longer fleece. The coarse grade is often used for warp in the nomadic flat weaves of Central Asia. The tougher grades are used for hard-wearing selvages, and the outside weft threads wrapped in various ways to finish the edges of pile and flat-woven rugs of the Turkmen and Baluchis. Goat hair is also used to weave strips that compose tents of many nomadic peoples from southern Arabia to Baluchistan.

Camel Hair

An even better insulator than wool, the best grade of camel hair has been more highly esteemed than that of any other animal. (Camel-colored wool is often wrongly referred to as camel's hair.) Only neck, throat, and chin hair is shorn, usually once a year. The rest, perhaps 20 to 30 pounds, is plucked out when the animals shed their winter coats.[18]

Camel hair is used as both weft and warp in flat-woven rugs, but rugs woven totally of camel hair are rare. In Central Asia it is used by the Baluchis in the knotting of pile rugs, in flat-woven rugs, in the woven fabric of their tents, and in twining ropes and strings. In Turkestan the strong knee hair of the camel is used as warp.

At molting season the bactrian two-humped camels of the plateaus of Central Asia have a very thick coat and yield considerably more hair (10 pounds per year) than the camels of tropical countries. Some hair of the single-humped dromedary of North Africa and Arabia is pulled off during molting and used in addition to that clipped at shearing time.

Cameloid Hair

The domesticated cameloids of America, llamas and alpacas, are shorn every two to three years during the rainy season. Llamas yield 4 to 6 pounds of hair, and alpacas yield 11 to 15 pounds.

DYEING

"Color is the Orient's secret and its glory . . ."[19] The natural "old" dyes boast a richness and splendor that is hard to equal, certainly not in modern synthetic dyes. The enchanting colors are due to the variety of natural dye materials, the varying hues in the most carefully prepared dyes and to the aging process. Mumford speaks of the eastern habit of washing "khilims as one washes a garment . . . even where the dyes are vegetable and thoroughly fast, this process and the subsequent drying in the sun makes very strong colors take on a soothing softness." [20] The fact is that that soothing softness is the inevitable result of fading due to the strong sun.

Dyeing with natural products is an ageless art, one that can be pursued today in the same way that it was by our early ancestors; the plants and roots from which dyes are prepared are abundant in nature. In Europe in the Late Stone Age women of the Lake Villages used roots and barks of trees to make brown and other dark shades and a little plant called woad to make blue.[21] In 55 B.C. the Romans in Britain described a tribe whose members dyed their bodies with woad, and in the literature of ancient China dye workshops were noted approximately 3,000 years ago.[22] In ancient Egypt, where linen was made, and in Mesopotamia, where wool was prized and made in quantity, dyes from all over the ancient world were procured through Phoenician traders. In the New World the remains of ancient civilizations in Peru and Chile give evidence of a magnificent weaving tradition. The dye colors used in these textiles remained fast and bright even after 2,000 years.

Mordants

The link between fiber and dye, the substance that enables the dye to color the fiber, is called a mordant. Since the majority of dyes require it to make the color permanent, fibers or yarns must be impregnated with some type of mordant. In some cultures yarn is mordanted before dyeing; in others at the same time. Different mordants produce different colors from the same dyes. Substances most frequently used in mordants are the metallic salts of alum, chrome, iron, and tin. Common salt can be used. A relevant note about the use of iron as a mordant (often in the form of iron pyrite, which yields a black color) is that it hardens as well as darkens the yarn. Rugs that show more wear in black areas than in the rest of the surface have been so treated.

Other mordanting agents are acetic acid, ammonia, caustic soda, and slaked lime. Vinegar, used after dyeing as a rinse, is also a mordant. Vegetable mordants were predominant in Asia and included different species of sumac and valonia, the leaves surrounding the fruit of the Asiatic oak. In North and South America vegetable mordants include juniper ashes, lime juice, and rosemary leaves. Pomegranate rind and divi-divi (the pods of the cariaria tree) are mentioned. Tannic acid, present in sumac, oak bark, and the hard swellings on certain oak trees, called gall nuts, is an example of a dye that contains its own mordant.

A mordant from an animal source, urine, was used in North America by Navajo and Salish weavers, in South America (Peru), and in North Africa.

Dye Types

Dyes can be animal, vegetable, or mineral. When the purple of the Phoenicians became known, it was in great demand. Whole villages were occupied in dyeing purple. The dyer belonged to the highest social class. In the street he wore the sign of his trade, a piece of dyed material behind his ear, and was also known by his colored hands. Tyrian purple was an animal dye, extracted from the mucous gland of the murex shellfish, or whelk.

Nature does not provide the same diversity of color in all parts of the world. The characteristic colors of certain tribal weavings recall the landscape in which the weavers live. The somber dark reds of Turkmen rugs and the dark blues and tans of Baluchi saddlebags communicate the harshness of their physical origin, while the natural sheep colors occurring in the wool of Navajo blankets express the sun-scorched starkness of the Southwest American desert.

Reds

Among animal sources of dye is the cochineal, a worm found in cactus in North and South America that produces reds and pinks, as does the scale insect kermes, found on oak trees near the Mediterranean and an insect that punctures certain trees, leaving a resinous crust, lac. Other red dyes are derived from vegetable sources: madder, beets, ivy berries, and bloodroot are found in Europe and Asia. Lichen, a wide-ranging species that yields many colors, is found in Morocco and many other places; brazilwood and prickly pear fruit are native to the New World.

Madder, an ancient dye source found from Asia Minor to China, is the root of a shrublike plant, *Rubia tinctorum*. A fermented liquid from its flowers and the root itself produces many shades of red familiar in oriental rugs. Mumford describes the method of achieving the red "most common in Persian fabrics" as the combination of alum water, grape juice, and madder.[23] Madder and cochineal were combined to make some reds. Madder, when dried and pounded, is also a mordant. Henna, which is used as a red dye in many parts of the world, particularly for the body and hair, is not so stable. An Egyptian writer of the 11th century complained that "most dyers of red silk and other thread and materials dye with henna in their workshops instead of madder (*al-fuwwa*) and the dye appears bright but when the sun strikes on it, its color deteriorates and its brightness disappears."[24]

Blues

Blue was obtained from the leaves of the delicate indigo shrub, prized for the clarity and fastness of its color. Originally from the Orient, indigo was prevalent in the Mediterranean region in 450 B.C. when Herodotus described its use in powdered form, just as it is used today. Indigo was not originally native to carpet-making countries and was imported in large quantities. In Persia in the province of Kerman indigo plantations existed as early as the 10th century.[25] Indigo is native to Africa and was used by the ancient Benins in Nigeria (see Chapter 9). It is grown and used in the Ivory Coast, Cameroun, Ghana, Liberia, Mali, Senegal, Sierra Leone, and the Congo. In the southern part of Algeria the Taureg, a Berber people of the Sahara, wear garments of imported indigo-dyed cloth, which rubs off on their skin, leaving a residual stain. Tauregs prize the color; outsiders call them "the Blue Men."

Yellows

Weld, an annual herb native in parts of the Mediterranean region, gives yellow dye, particularly pleasing when used for wool. Fustic, a tree of the mulberry family, also a shrub of southern Europe, yields a yellow dye that can be used to produce browns and greens.

Saffron is extracted from the stigmata of the crocus, which grows throughout the mountainous area of Persia. Large saffron plantations were found in areas adjacent to those where the plant flourished and in carpet-making centers where saffron was processed into a beautiful yellow. This has been largely abandoned because of production difficulties.[26]

Safflower, an annual plant, is cultivated in Iran. The petals and buds are dried and pounded just as they were in ancient Egypt.

Turmeric, a plant native to India and China, yields a yellow important in carpet dyeing in those countries. Persian berries (*Rhamnus saxatilis*) growing in Asia Minor and on the Caspian Sea give a yellow that is also used in carpet dyeing.

In the Middle East the fruit skin of the pomegranate is dried and chopped, and an extract is prepared in boiling water. When combined with the mordant of ash or alum, yellow is formed; when combined with iron water, violet-blue results. Heartwood of the jackfruit tree was used in Thailand to make the yellow of Buddhist monks' robes. In Turkestan three plants yielded strong natural yellows: the flowers of *esparuk, tukmak,* and *maksat* (local names for *Delphinium sulphureum, Sophor japonica,* and *Safflor* or *Carthamus tinctorius*).[27]

Among other yellow-yielding plants and flowers growing in meadows, on mountainsides, and in deserts around the world are marigold, dahlia, zinnia, coreopsis, onion (skins), rabbit brush, goldenrod, Queen Anne's lace, jointweed, leaves and green fruits of the black cherry, bark of apple trees, and barberry.

13

With different dye methods and different mordants sources of yellow can produce greens, ochers, oranges, burnt oranges, rusts, roses, and browns.

Dyers

In the towns and cities where carpet weaving flourished dyers were specialists, each known for a particular hue, such as the Tyrian purple already mentioned. Secret recipes were handed down from father to son. Since the tradition was oral in many cases, some recipes were lost. It is said that many shades of unique beauty have never been reproduced in modern times in spite of innumerable experiments.

In all Moslem countries Jewish men seem to have been the principal dyers, although the craft was not confined to them alone. In each area they found dye materials and developed dye recipes unknown to others. There were, according to one source, 2,000 Jewish dyers in Thebes. Their dyes were sent to Central Asia with a caravan of Arab merchants on the second day of every month.[28] In Persia Jews were assigned postal stations by the Shah in recognition of their ability to maintain lines of communication due to their common language and peaceful reputation. In exchange they were given the duties paid for the movement of dyestuffs across the country. In this way they were able to become knowledgeable possessors of dye material as well as purveyors of dyes. There are still Jewish dyers in southern Arabia and North Africa as well as in Iran and other Asian countries.

In small villages and in nomadic encampments there is no such division of labor, and the weaver and the dyer are often the same person. Women, who are not dyers in urban workshops, collect herbs, plants, and roots from the countryside, helped by children, in a tribal environment. Older women are the logical repositories of tribal dye information.

Procedures

All dyeing requires submersion in water. Pots, cauldrons, and pits are used in different areas. The dyeing of wool requires heat. The amount of heat and water, the duration of submersion, and other factors such as rinsing with additives for fastness vary with the fabric being dyed, the dye material, and the recipe of the dyer.

For indigo dyeing the leaves are fermented before using. Here is an outline of the inherited procedure, unchanged over 1,000 years, performed by the Abokwariga, a Hausa subtribe in Nigeria.[29] A pit (2' x 8') is dug. A stone is placed in the bottom to prevent water loss, and clay is pressed around the sides to make it watertight. *Katsi,* a mordant made from white baked balls of old indigo, hair from the tannery, horse manure, and juice from soaked roots of a dafara tree, is prepared. Ripe indigo is cut, left to rot, and chopped into small pieces. Ten baskets of indigo are poured into the dye pit, which has been filled with water into which ashes have been added. After 3 to 4 days the dye is vigorously stirred with poles until it foams, then recovered for 5 more days. The dye is again stirred, and *katsi* added. The process continues until the liquid is thick. Cloth is first soaked in older inactive dye, then placed in the dye pit and left until the desired shade of blue is obtained. The cloth is then removed, washed in clear water to rinse away ashes and excess indigo, and hung to dry. Additional procedures are followed to achieve a high sheen and to remove obvious joinings.

Synthetic Dyes

Synthetic dyes, derived from coal-tar substances, are composed of various chemicals including aniline in the form of a colorless, oily liquid. Their use spread rapidly after they were first produced by an English chemist in 1850. So many badly dyed rugs were exported from the rug-producing countries that regulatory measures were in effect by the 1880s.

The objections to the use of synthetic dyes in rug making are both aesthetic—the pleasing patina of age achieved by changes in coloration of natural dyes can be lost in a weaving that utilizes synthetic dyes—and practical—aniline dyes, for example, rob the wool of some of its natural oil, making it brittle and less able to stand wear. Actually, good synthetic dyes, properly used, often have more fastness (to water, for example) than dyes from nature and are difficult to distinguish except by chemical analysis.

Wool dyer drying wool, Herat area, Afghanistan. (Photo: Adrienne Harris Pitts)

methods

Swifter than a weaver's shuttle.—Job 7:6

SPINNING

"Spinning was the occupation of the humble peasant woman when not engaged in other tasks. In Tanella the women even spun during their long walk to and from the orchard."[1]

It is often noted by observers that in rug-making cultures women are always spinning. They spin "when tending their flocks" and while riding on mules in migrations. Speaking about the Baluchis, Masson says, "On a march the females will sustain incredible labour; they will be seen without coverings to their heads and feet, arrayed in a coarse black gown, driving before them a camel, cow, or ass, laden with their miserable effects; while on their backs they carry their infant children, and as if they had not enough to do, on the road are busily engaged in twirling their hand spindles and spinning coarse threads of wool or hair."[2] "Woman's work is never done"; she spins as if she were a spider, as if the spindle were an extension of herself.

Men spin, too. In many cultures since that of ancient Egypt, where men spun and wove in textile workshops, men have been spinners and weavers, generally when textile weaving and rug making were large-scale businesses or professions. In some sub-Saharan African cultures where cotton weaving is a tradition men spin and weave. Among the Ashantis in Ghana, the Tiv in Nigeria, and in Liberia and Senegal men weave while women spin.[3] Men seem to spin as part of their profession, as paid artisans. Mumford says that "the shepherd setting forth at morning with his flock, carries wool and spindle and distaff . . . and whiles away the hours of the long day, twirling his spindle and singing to his own delectation the 'songs of Araby and tales of fair Cashmere.' "[4]

If we suppose that weaving is a further development of the plaiting process, a softer, more pliable material than the reeds and grasses used in weaving mats and baskets is required. Before warm woolen rugs were woven, man had to learn to spin yarn, as no such material was available in nature. The domestication of sheep and the process of turning wool into a material suitable for weaving brought about the invention of spinning, which is the twisting of fiber into yarn or thread.

SPINNING AND WEAVING EQUIPMENT

Distaff

A piece of carded wool is tied to a distaff, often a simple forked stick. The distaff is used in one hand, as a helpmate for the spindle, thus the use of the word "distaff" to refer to a woman. It is sometimes tucked into a belt or under the arm so that spinning can be done with the other hand.

Spindle

The most important piece of spinning equipment is a simple, ancient device, the spindle. The drop spindle is a stick pushed through a weight called a whorl. Spindle whorls found in archaeological sites are used for dating and attest to universal use of spindles since prehistory. Drop spindles, short and long, of many shapes, are used for spinning in South America from Colombia to Chile as well as in Portugal, Crete, and mainland Greece and Turkey.

The thigh spindle is used in North America by Navajos (who use a left-hand twist) and Pueblos or Hopis (who use a right-hand twist). In Central Asia and in other areas it is used by many tribes. The Kirghiz have been observed to use a thigh spindle with the whorl on the bottom, while the Turkmen have been seen with the whorl on the top.[5] In the Van area of eastern Turkey the thigh spindle is used in an upward rotation to make Z-spun yarn, downward to make S-spun yarn.

A variation on the long-staffed spindle rests the wide weighted end on the ground, on a gourd, or on a broken piece of pottery. It is used, for example, in El Djem, Tunisia. In Mexico it is used in a gourd. The principle is the same as that of a thigh spindle.

A more complex spinning device is the spinning wheel. The Asian spinning wheel, called the Ghandi wheel in India, is low, moved by the hand of the operator, who sits on the ground. This wheel is known in Korea and Afghanistan as well as in India.

Spindle and distaff used for spinning in northern Portugal, early 1900s.

Turkmen girl spinning on a handmade spinning wheel, Kabul, Afghanistan.

Other wheels are used; in Mexico spinning is sometimes done on a detached bicycle wheel, an ingenious use of the available. European spinning wheels are of the traditional type (called Saxony), with the wheel adjacent to the "mother of all," the castle wheel, which places the "mother of all" above the wheel, saving floor space,[6] and the walking wheel, a large hand-pushed wheel with a spindle shank for yarn takeup, which requires walking in a certain pattern to spin the yarn.

Looms

A loom is the apparatus used to interlace the two sets of threads required for weaving and to produce the warp tension necessary for a sturdy fabric.

Horizontal Looms

Some of the simplest looms are used by many of the tribal and village weavers described in this book; they are horizontal looms, located close to the ground. Hawley states, "Among a very large number of those tribes that are wandering in search of new pastures for their flocks and herds, it is customary to let the loom lie flat on the ground while the weaver sits on the finished parts of the rug."[7] Hubel makes clear the reason for this loom: "The simplest forms of the loom are used by the nomads, since they need to fold up their work and loom each time they move. They do sometimes use a vertical loom with a collapsible frame, but usually prefer the primitive horizontal loom without side beams."[8]

Horizontal ground looms can be four-sided or two-sided, with or without a frame and are often raised from the ground by stones. This loom is commonly used by nomadic people and is termed *charkh* and *chatmah* in Persian. In small villages in Iran four stakes are driven into the ground, and two strong beams are used to make the basic loom. Warp is strung between the two beams, and tension for weaving maintained by additional stakes that push the beams further apart. In the case of nomadic Turkmens the looms are poles that they carry with them on their moves. Turkmen of Yomud tribes in northern Iran buy their loom poles in market towns, as no trees from which suitable poles can be made are available in their region.

An observer saw looms in an eastern Turkish village that consisted of two cross-beams inserted into slots cut into large side pieces, with tension produced by tight warping[9] and looms in a nearby village with no frame, the two beams holding the warp were held by stakes in the ground.

A tripod arrangement above the loom frame, termed *sepayeh* in Persian, is used in many areas to support the harness sticks (also called heald rods or heddles) that move the warp to allow the shuttle bearing the weft through the shed (the space between warp threads that accommodates the weft).

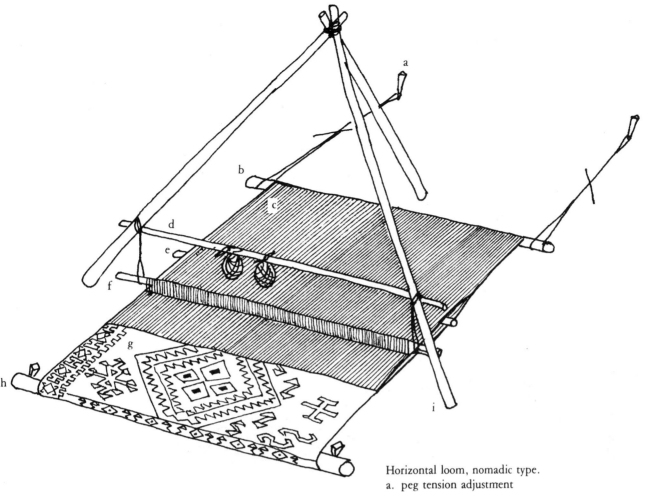

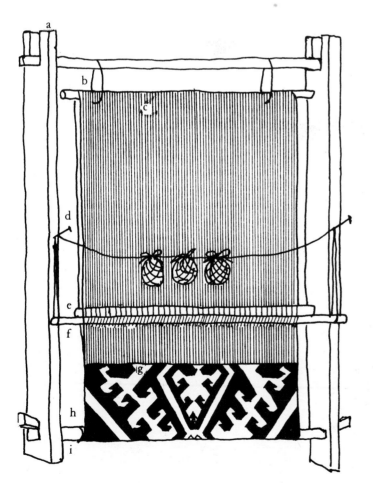

Horizontal loom, nomadic type.
a. peg tension adjustment
b. warp beam
c. warp threads
d. harness support (also holds extra yarn balls)
e. batten or weaving sword (holds one shed for half the warp threads)
f. harness stick with string heddles (holds opposite shed for half of warp not held by batten)
g. rug in progress
h. cloth beam
i. tripod support for harness

Vertical loom.
a. upright loom supports
b. warp beam
c. warp threads
d. harness support (also holds extra yarn balls)
e. batten or weaving sword—holds one shed (half the warp)
f. harness stick with string heddles—holds opposite shed (the other half of the warp)
g. rug in progress
h. tension wedges
i. cloth beam

17

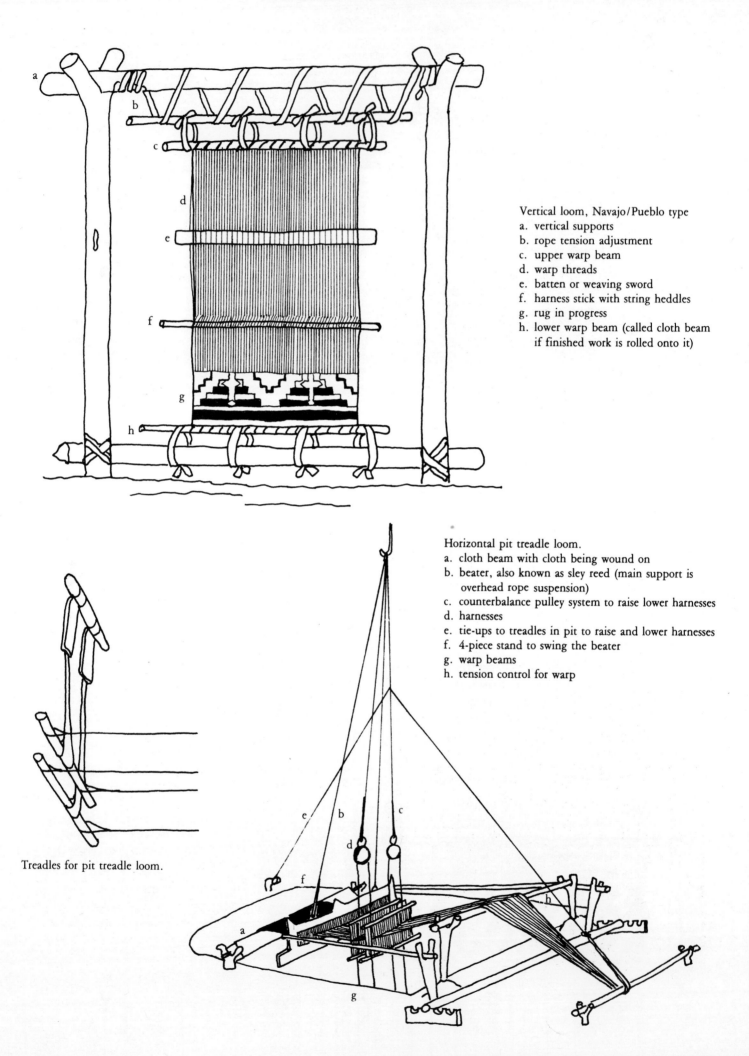

Vertical loom, Navajo/Pueblo type
a. vertical supports
b. rope tension adjustment
c. upper warp beam
d. warp threads
e. batten or weaving sword
f. harness stick with string heddles
g. rug in progress
h. lower warp beam (called cloth beam if finished work is rolled onto it)

Horizontal pit treadle loom.
a. cloth beam with cloth being wound on
b. beater, also known as sley reed (main support is overhead rope suspension)
c. counterbalance pulley system to raise lower harnesses
d. harnesses
e. tie-ups to treadles in pit to raise and lower harnesses
f. 4-piece stand to swing the beater
g. warp beams
h. tension control for warp

Treadles for pit treadle loom.

Vertical Looms

When warp is stretched between two horizontal bars attached to a framework in a vertical position, a standing version of the horizontal ground loom results. Two slender trees growing at a convenient distance from one another are often used for the posts in various parts of the world.

In North America the vertical loom is used by Navajo women weavers and Hopi men weavers. The maximum length of the finished piece is determined by the height of the loom. The weaver works from the lower part of the loom upward. Reichard states that it is common for a Navajo weaver to turn the warp upside down part way through for symmetry.[10] By adding harnesses to the simple Navajo loom more complex weaves can be produced.

Yoruba women in Nigeria weave cotton cloth (sometimes mixed with silk) on a similar loom, said to have been used since the Yoruba immigration to West Africa over 1,000 years ago. The vertical loom is placed in the home of the weaver and a small hole is dug in front to accommodate her legs when she sits in front of it on a mat.[11] Navajo women sit with their legs to one side, as do some women weavers of Asia.

In Turkey and Persia a village type of vertical loom with warp beams in slots on strong hewn vertical beams, is used for flat weaves and knotted rugs.

Another homemade loom is the warp-weighted loom. This is the Penelope loom of ancient Greece. As seen in many figured vases of the 6th to the 4th century B.C., the warp on the loom was suspended from a top beam, thread by thread, and weighted with stones or clay to provide tension. The loom frame in the Greek example was inclined, or oblique, to increase the tension of the warp. A warp-weighted loom is still used, with minor variations, by the Salish and Chilkat people in the Northwest United States and in Scandinavia.

Another vertical loom, called a Tabriz loom in Iran and also known as a Bunyan loom, has a similar structure, but the work can be longer, two times the height of the loom, because the warp is continuous and may be moved around the loom.

The roller-beam loom, called an Isparta loom in Turkey, is used in carpet-making centers and in court workshops. Warp beams turn in sockets. There is no maximum length, as unwoven warp is rolled on the top beam and unrolled as the work progresses. Tapestry looms, used for the classic pictorial tapestries of Europe, fall into this category. This same type of loom is used by Berber women throughout North Africa for knotted rugs as well as flat-woven ones. The single harness stick is attached to the wall, making it immovable (fixed).

An oblique loom with a four-sided frame leaning against a wall is used in Asia Minor and throughout South America from Peru through Bolivia and into Chile. It is the same loom as the vertical loom of the Navajos, but the uprights are not stably anchored as are those of the Navajos and thus enable the entire loom to be moved when necessary.

The backstrap loom, used to make many of the wonderful textiles of South and Middle America, is a very simple oblique or semivertical loom. Albers cites its use in Japan, Malaya, China, Burma, Tibet, Peru, Guatemala, Mexico, and "some remote regions of Asia."[12]

Mechanical Looms

Treadle looms are more complex looms worked by a lever that lifts the harnesses and opens the shed.

The pit treadle loom is a horizontal loom, called a Hindu loom with a hand-operated pulley to open the shed. The loom is set on a floor over a pit, which houses the treadles and the weaver's legs. Archaeologist Albert Le Coq observed such a loom in eastern Turkestan.

A horizontal treadle loom is also used in Africa. In Mediterranean or North Africa it is used by men in Tunisia, who make *mergoums* and other brocaded wool rugs in workshop conditions. In the rest of Africa the use of cotton is prevalent and cotton weaving for cloth has flourished in many cultures. Narrow horizontal treadle looms with warp forming an angle to the ground are used by the Ashanti in Ghana for weaving Kente cloth. Horizontal treadle looms are used in Nigeria by the Dakakari, the Edo, the Egba, the Gbari, and the Hausa.

In all these cultures it is men who operate the horizontal treadle loom. Women weavers usually use a vertical loom, which is broader than the treadle loom.

The floor loom is the village loom of Europe. In the Western Hemisphere, where it was introduced by the Spanish, it is used in Central and South America and in Chimayo, a village in New Mexico. It has a large frame and foot treadles for changing sheds. The weft can be thrown across the entire width of the shed for speed. In the Far East an intricate version is used for silk weaving.

Other Equipment

Scissors and knives are used for cutting. Weft-beating utensils for packing weft threads into place include combs made of wood or metal, often carved or figured, and battens, often called weaving swords, usually fashioned from wood. Shuttles, most of which are of wood, vary in complexity from sticks to carved "belt" shuttles and bobbins to the complex boat shuttles used on European looms.

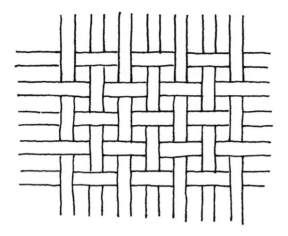

Plain weave.

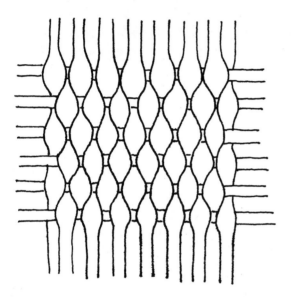

Warp-faced plain weave. Warps have been beaten tightly, causing them to fill empty spaces.

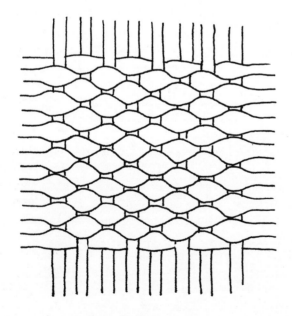

Weft-faced plain weave.

WEAVING

Plain Weave

Interlacing of warp and weft on a loom produces plain weave. Each weft unit passes first over one warp unit, then under the next, in continued alternation. Half of the warp units lie above the weft and half below.

Plain weave can be evenly balanced, warp-faced, or weft-faced, depending on the size of the thread and the spacing of the warp and weft elements. Plain weave can be monochromatic or polychromatic, with simple stripes (or blocks) of color that can be horizontal (weft-faced) or vertical (warp-faced). The ground weave of many rugs and saddlebags is plain weave. Wefts can run full length of the loom to create solid cross stripes.

Tapestry Weave

Tapestry weave is a plain weave in which the warp elements are covered by the weft yarns. The unique character of this weft-faced tapestry is the use of discontinuous weft patterning, wefts woven back and forth in defined color design areas. When two colors meet, a connection or joining may be made or there can be no connection made.

Emery explains that "the structural feature that is most significant in distinguishing between varieties of tapestry weave is to be found at the meeting point of the wefts of laterally adjacent areas."[13]

Detail of a kilim rug in slit tapestry weave.

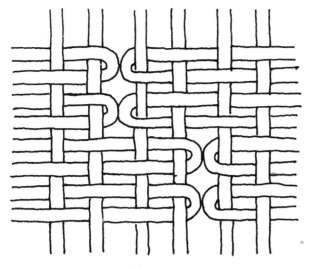

Slit weave.

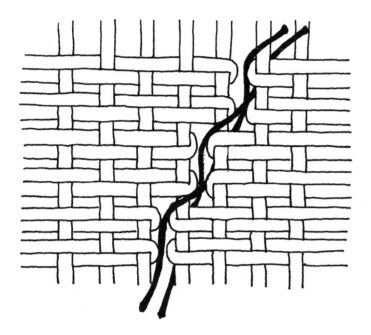

Outlining.

Dovetailing.

Slit Tapestry

When the weft turns back into its own color area in row after row without a joining, a slit between areas occurs. A large pencentage of kilims utilize this slit-weave method. If the weft turns back around a lateral progression of different warp threads, the tiny slits create a diagonal line, producing a structurally sounder fabric than if there were larger slits.

Slits that are thus created as a byproduct of tapestry weave can be used as a design element such as allowing light to pass through or to create a shadow mark.

Slits are sometimes eliminated by sewing together adjacent areas after the weaving has been removed from the loom. In some Turkish kilims a supplementary weft in contrasting color is wrapped around adjacent warps. In addition to joining together adjacent color areas this method is used for outlining around pattern figures, often throughout a rug.

Dovetailing

Dovetailing (warp sharing) is a method of joining in which wefts from adjacent areas turn back around a common warp. Mexican weavers use a dovetail joining called *pasa y abraza,* or "pass and embrace."

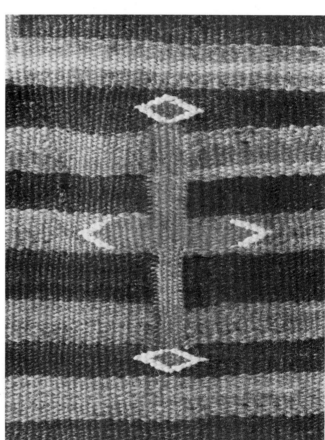

Detail of kilim with dovetailing technique.

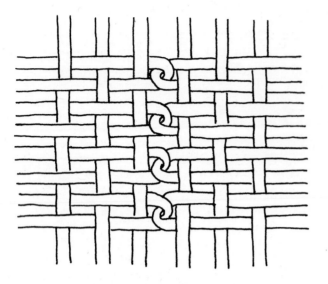

Single interlocking.

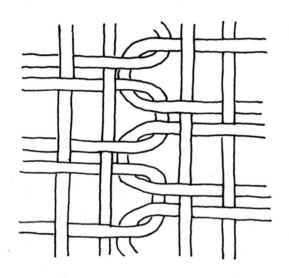

Double interlocking.

Interlocking

Interlocking

Interlocking (simple locking) is another method of joining without forming slits by linking with each other the wefts of adjacent areas. Navajo weavers use these one lock joinings.

Double interlocking occurs when wefts link once as they move in one direction in a row and again in the next row in the other direction. Double interlocking creates a ridge on the surface of the second side.

Other joinings are possible and have been used in various weaving cultures. Diagonal joinings are used as design elements in Mexican weaving. Vertical and horizontal joinings were used decoratively in the beautiful textiles of ancient Peru.

Soumak Weave

The word "Soumak" refers to a technique in which wefts are wrapped onto the warp elements in lateral progression across the work. Rows of Soumak usually alternate with one or two shots of plain weave ground wefts. This supplementary weft method is Soumak brocading. Soumak wrapping when used without ground wefts becomes the basic structure of the fabric.

The Soumak technique utilizes a formula: for example, in Caucasian Soumak rugs the wrapping sequence is consistently forward over two warp threads and back under one warp thread. Soumak can be plain, meaning that every row is wrapped in the same direction, or countered, meaning that every row reverses the direction of the wrapping. The term "Soumak" also refers to a rug made in the Soumak technique. This type of rug is associated with the Caucasus, although Soumak textiles have long been found in other areas. The Caucasian Soumak rug is countered and woven with discontinuous wefts in different pattern areas, as in tapestry. Its designs are related to those found in early knotted rugs of Asia Minor.

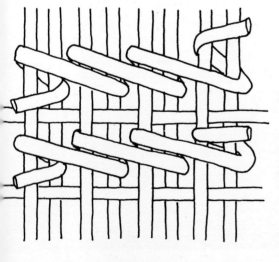

Soumak weave.

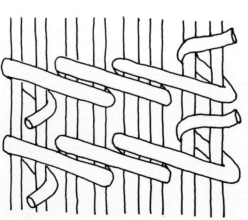

Soumak wrapping with no ground wefts.

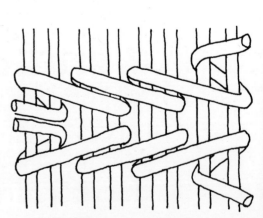

Countered soumak weave.

Brocading

The technique of introducing supplementary wefts or supplementary warps to create patterns is called brocading. Soumak is therefore a variation of brocading. In many cases of brocading the supplementary threads are left loose on the back of the weaving.

Examples of brocaded rugs from most weaving areas are shown in this volume. Included are Turkish *ciçims,* brocaded rugs of the Baluchi and the Turkmens in Central Asia, and *hambels* from Morocco.

Weft-float Weave

When supplementary wefts are worked back and forth in a specific pattern area, they are said to be discontinuous. The float produced by discontinuous supplementary wefting appears on the reverse side as groups of threads parallel to the weft, not as loose threads. The float in the technique called weft-float or skip plain weave is on the reverse side of the fabric not on the face. The word brocading is not used when supplementary wefts are continuous across the entire fabric.

Compound Weaves

A weaving in which two or more sets of warps or wefts are used is classified as a compound weave. Brocading is a compound weave. Another example of a compound weave is double cloth in which two separate layers are woven at the same time and are structurally interconnected.

Embroidery

A rug in which patterning is inserted with a needle or any needlework added by stitchery after the rug is off the loom is called an embroidered rug.

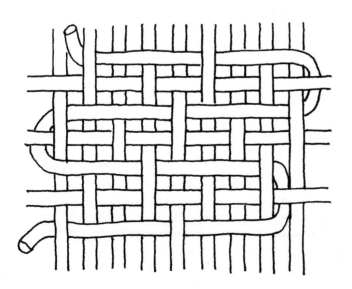

Section of brocading.

Mixed techniques

Many rugs, bags, or other pieces employ two or more techniques. Certain tribes—for example, the Bakhtiyari of Iran—weave intricate saddlebags combining tapestry weave, brocading, and knotting.

WEAVERS

Women are the primary weavers of flat-woven rugs. Among nomadic tribes as well as villagers weaving is a domestic task that falls to the woman, usually after other daily tasks are done. Men do weave—sometimes a husband and wife can be seen weaving together. Landreau, observing weavers in eastern Turkey, describes Kurdish village men as "Men, who will not normally do women's work but who often show sudden interest when a photographer is near."[14]

The same looms are often employed to make knotted and flat-woven rugs. Much of the weaving of knotted rugs is done by men in the Caucasus. Armenian men there and in other areas make knotted rugs. Where rug making is an industry, men are often the weavers. In the rug-making workshops of the Persian court, as in workshops throughout Persia, men were the weavers.

For a woman excellence in weaving has a variety of rewards, both to herself and to her community. She takes pride in fine work and competes to weave an outstanding piece. At a marriageable age, having learned her craft, she weaves dowry rugs, showing off her skill and completing the best possible pieces to take to her new home.

When urbanization took place—for instance, in Persia in the 1920s as a result of governmental pressure for tribal settlement—men went to the cities alone to seek work. By the time his family joined him, the man was the family's prime producer, and the woman no longer shared in the family's productivity, as she did in tribal life. Becoming more dependent, she faded from public view in the manner of orthodox Moslem women in cities.

In the tribes women had more visibility and more equality, both results of the nature of the work they did. As tribal girls know, their value in the marriage market increases as their weaving improves. A bride price is the price that a man must pay the father of the bride, part of the marriage custom throughout the Near and Middle East. The weaving skill of a girl is a pivotal factor in establishing her bride price.

4

turkey

No food for a woman who cannot weave a carpet.—
old Turkish proverb

HISTORY

The majority of the population are Turks in the narrow sense, which denotes the sedentary Turkic-speaking people of modern Turkey. The Turkish people are a composite of Osmanli Turks (founders of the Ottoman Empire) intermixed with Seljuk Turks, who came during an earlier migration and later converted to Islam. Wide differences of physical appearance and culture are seen among the Turks. They do speak closely related languages and share the religion of Islam.

The tent-dwelling nomadic, seminomadic, and village people of Turkey are called Yörüks. They are descended from the earliest Turkic immigrant tribes and are often called Turcomans. Their language is a dialect of Turkic.

The largest ethnic minority in Turkey is the Kurds. Other minorities are Armenians, Greeks, and Jews. An estimated 90% of the population is Turkic-speaking.

The written language, previously Arabic in lettering, was changed to the Roman alphabet in the 1920s, and place names were standardized according to the new spelling.

Turkey is the place where East meets West. The narrow strip between the Bosphorus and the Sea of Marmara where Istanbul, once called Constantinople, is situated is the bridge between Europe and Asia. European Turkey, bounded by Bulgaria and Greece, had a population in 1970 of 2,655,768 and comprises only 3% of the total territory.[1] The other 97%, which had a population in 1970 of 35,666,549, lies in Asia Minor, a large peninsula surrounded by four seas, and is called Anatolia.[2] The boundaries of Turkey were defined in 1918 at the collapse of the Ottoman Empire, and the nation became a republic in 1923 with Kemal Ataturk as its president.

In ancient times Turkey was a meeting place for oriental and occidental civilizations, connected as it was with Greece on its coasts and with Mesopotamia through the Tigris and Euphrates rivers. Asia Minor, conquered first by the Persians, then incorporated by Alexander the Great into his Empire, was under constant attack from the West during the Byzantine Empire until it fell to Arab domination. During the rapid Arab expansion in the centuries following the Hegira (622 A.D.) Turkey adopted Islam and became a central nation in the Islamic world. The Caliphates of Islam, ruling from 661 to 1258, had capitals first at Damascus, then at Baghdad.

The Seljuk Turks from Central Asia had appeared in Persia in the 10th century, adopted Islam, conquered Persia, entered Baghdad, and conquered most of Asia Minor and the Caucasus, a major cause of the Crusades. The Seljuks were in turn overrun in the 13th century by Genghiz Khan and his successors. Mongols and Turks assembled in hordes (the mixture of ethnic stocks came to be called Tartar), which dealt a final blow to the Byzantine Empire.

When that wave of conquest receded, the Osmanli Turks, a minor tribe, apparently among the last of the invaders, who functioned as guards of the Byzantine border areas for the still ruling Seljuks, forged an organization that enabled them to complete the overthrow of the Byzantine Empire and to become masters of the Seljuk Empire in Anatolia in 1359.

Anatolia, a crossroads of history, is a high plateau interspersed with mountains and valleys. The plateau naturally lends itself to the grazing and pasturing of flocks, while the valleys and mountainsides provide natural dye materials.

We do not know when the first Anatolian kilims were woven, but some evidence seems to support the existence of weaving thousands of years ago. The earliest Turkish pile carpets for which physical evidence exists were traced to central Anatolia and dated in the 13th century. Examples of these have been found in mosques, such as the Ala-ed-din Mosque in Konya, named for the Seljuk sultan of Iconium, the older name of Konya. Rugs found there are now in the Turkish Islam Museum in Istanbul.[3] These predate physical examples of knotted carpets from Persia, the Caucasus, and other rug-making areas except for the Pazyryk carpet mentioned in the Foreword.

Fragments found at Fostat (old Cairo) came from similar Anatolian rugs of the same period. When the Polos of Venice, Marco, his father, and his uncle, visited "Turkomania" in 1271, they described Anatolian carpets as "the finest in the world."[4] The Fostat fragments show that Anatolian rugs were exported to Egypt. We know that they were exported to Europe through their depiction in paintings from several countries, where they were prized for their bold designs and rich oriental colors.

Invasions and changes of dynasty affected court looms and city workshops. Whole workshops closed, and the designs produced were forgotten. Kurt Erd-mann refers to weaving areas and their designs as "a fan which opens and then closes again."[5]

The carpets found in Konya (at the Ala-ed-din Mosque) were geometric: simple rows of identical motifs framed by borders with larger motifs, with their colors and design expressing severity. Another group of carpets very different in design was depicted in European paintings of the same period. They showed double-headed eagles and other stylized birds arranged in rows in the center field, as were the nonfigurative motifs of the Konya carpets. Erdmann makes a convincing case for the origin of the stylized group of carpets as western Anatolia. That area is close to Byzantium, and the carpets could have been copied from Byzantine textiles, which exhibit such animal motifs. The carpets could easily have been exported by Venetian and Genoese merchants, who had trading posts in western Anatolia.[6]

Without tracing the design history of Turkish knotted rugs beyond this point, it seems that most flat-woven rugs, made by nomadic weavers unconnected to urban workshops and unaffected by stylistic changes, are related to the early Seljuk designs, particularly those found in Konya, and perhaps share the same origin in the steppes of Central Asia from which their ancestors had come.

Detail, Seljuk carpet, Konya, 13th century.

Ciçim weave.

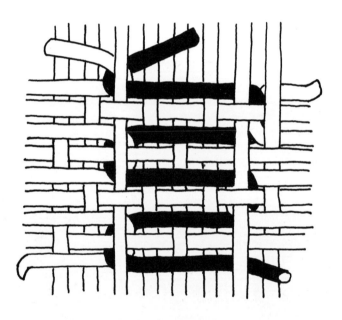

Zili weave.

CHARACTERISTICS OF TURKISH FLAT–WOVEN RUGS

Some features of Turkish flat-woven rugs are listed below.

1. The majority are not reversible (though some are). The custom was to leave weft threads hanging loose on the back, creating a right side and a wrong side.

2. The slit-tapestry weave technique is used in most kilims.

3. In many; a supplementary yarn of a contrasting or matching color wrapped around the warp outlines the pattern figures. Outlining functions as a design element and fills the spaces left open in the slit-weave technique.

4. A wide variety of brocaded rugs are found. The terms *ciçim* and *zili* are used in Turkey to describe supplementary weft technique weavings worked in certain materials and design.

5. *Ciçim (djidjim, jijeem)* refers to supplementary weft methods and to a variety of objects made by these methods. *Ciçim* work often combines spot brocading with floats across the fabric. The floats are usually worked in a set formula throughout the weaving. The word *ciçim* also describes a brocaded rug of *ciçim* weave made in strips, with as many as six strips sewn together vertically.

6. *Zili* refers to a variety of bags and rugs closely related to *ciçims*. The formula, over three warps and under one warp across the fabric creates a ribbed surface.[7]

7. The plain ground of most *ciçims* and *zilis* can be distinguished by its color, a characteristic raspberry red, dark gray, or white, depending on the area of origin. If this ground is left plain without supplementary patterning, it is called *tzoul*, which refers to a simple, sometimes striped woven fabric used for wagon covers and the backs of saddle bags.

8. Wool warp and weft are the most common fabrics in Turkish flat weaves. Some *ciçims* have a cotton ground. Some of the brocading threads in older rugs and bags were of white cotton, which heightened the design effect (cotton was whiter than the natural wool).

9. Long braided ends are frequent.

10. Designs are mainly geometric, bold, and freely drawn as are border designs. In eastern areas designs are more intricate.

Small mats are called *yastik*, a Turkish word meaning "pillow." Some are used as pillow covers, others as bags and storage sacks. These specifications describe color plate 2, which appears on page 193.

A.
Warp: wool
Weft: wool
Brocading: wool
Technique: ciçim weave
Size: .80m x .52m, .68m x .42m (shown)

B.
Warp: wool, .90m x .55m
Weft: wool, .68m x .42m (shown)
Technique: slit-tapestry weave

C.
Warp: cotton
Weft: cotton
Brocading: wool
Technique: ciçim weave
Size: .90m x .52m, .68m x .42m (shown)

D.
Warp: wool
Weft: wool
Technique: weft-faced plain-weave stripes of solid colors, alternating with brocading *(ciçim)*
Size: 1.10m x .60m, .90m x .28m (shown)

Ciçim portière or cover
Warp: two-ply wool
Weft: two-ply wool
Brocading: two-ply wool
Technique: balanced plain weave with spot brocading, woven in six bands, sewn together along selvages
Colors: tan, apricot, blue, green, orange, black; pale apricot ground
Design: geometric
Size: 3.3m x 1.6m

FORMATS OF TURKISH FLAT WEAVES

The most familiar formats of Turkish flat-woven rugs are the following.

1. The long kilim was often made in two matched parts, which were sewn together.

2. The small one-piece kilim or brocaded rug often had a prayer niche *(mihrab)*, a center panel, or a double-ended prayer niche. A rug of this format (from 3' to 6'), knotted or flat, is called a prayer rug, a *seccade,* and is suitable for *namaz* or *secde,* Muslim prayer. A *namazlik* is a *seccade* with a single *mihrab* design.

3. Long one- or two-piece kilims and brocaded rugs (3.7m x 1.3m or 3.37m x 1.2m) are called *kelle (keley)*, a designation of size in the rug trade.

4. Sacks, bags, and mats are usually approximately .45m x .80m or .352m x .61m in size.

Kilims are used throughout Turkey by village people, nomadic people, and townspeople. They are used in mosques, alongside pile rugs, and in other public places. They are the major furnishings of poor and middle-class homes, where furniture as it is known in the West is not used. In nomadic tents rugs and other covers are laid on the ground. Decorative bags store belongings and bedding, which is rolled out at night.

Some pieces are kept for special occasions. They are prized belongings that a girl takes to her marriage and keeps for her entire life. They are made by weavers in numerous villages and by tribesmen throughout the country. If the flat-woven rugs of Turkey were laid end to end, a beautiful woven girdle might encircle the earth.

ETHNIC GROUPS

The Yörüks

"Yörük" in Turkish generally refers to migrating tribes-people, although many settled peoples in Turkey still think of themselves as Yörüks. The terms "nomadic", "seminomadic", and "transhumant" have been used to refer to people who seasonally move their livestock to regions of differing climactic and acquatic conditions; all of these people can be considered nomadic until they give up migrating completely. Yörüks, descended from many tribes, some originally unrelated, have lived for centuries along the Aegean and Mediterranean coasts of Turkey and have migratory patterns (*il rah*) set centuries ago.

Like other still seminomadic people, the Yörüks have two home bases, chosen because they fulfill the need for grazing land for their flocks. One is the Yayla, a mountainous location with water and pasture where a tent-dwelling nomad can spend the summer months. In one tribe the duration of the migration to the Yayla was one month, traveling about five hours a day with stops at set watering and resting places. The route traveled by each tribe each year is a transitional one, which changes due to special circumstances. The return to the winter quarters at Kislak in the flatlands is more rapid.[8]

Girls in Turkish kilims. (Drawings by Lauren Dreiband)

The migratory schedule is based on the agricultural cycles of the villages through which the tribes pass. The Yörüks rent rights to grazing lands along their migratory route, sell pastoral products, and buy grain and other supplies from villagers. These factors in the Yörük economy affect the size of the flock that a family is able to maintain and their subsistence level. No pastures, either in winter quarters or in the Yayla, were owned by the Yörük tribes studied by Daniel Bates. Access to grazing lands was negotiated anew each season.[9]

Thomas Joyce wrote in 1911 that the Yörüks were "extremely polygamous" and that a plurality of wives was an economic necessity because so many "hands" were required to perform the many daily jobs (to a city dweller a plurality of wives would be an expensive luxury). "To enable him to pursue his callings of flockmaster, camel breeder, etc., and as he cannot afford to hire such hands, he obtains them by marrying their owners. Each wife has, however, her separate tent and her special occupation. The care of the flocks will be apportioned to two or three, each tending a certain number of the broad-tailed Karamanian sheep; a fourth looks after the camels, a fifth collects and draws water for the joint family, a sixth will make butter and cheese, while the seventh weaves on a primitive loom the brightly hued rugs, camel's hair cloth, and other fabrics for clothing and tent furniture."[10] What the writer was really saying is that a large labor pool is an economic necessity in a pastoral society. In modern Turkey polygamy is illegal, although it is practiced in areas where tribal customs are still strong.

Many Turkish women, tribal and rural, still observe the Moslem tradition of *purdah,* the custom by which adult women are veiled from public view. Many of the weavers in the following Asian and African chapters are veiled in varying degrees, from the facial mask (*yashmak*) used in Turkey to complete concealment, to the *burga* (complete face mask with slits for eyes) of Arabia and the *burka* (pleated robe with attached headpiece) of Afghanistan.

Color plate 3 (pages 194–195).

1. The woman leading the camel is the recent bride of the family son or a marriageable daughter. She is wearing her best clothing to lead the migration, as is the custom of the Yörüks.

2. At the *yayla* of the Sachikara Yörüks in the Taurus mountains near Kayseri. The open tent is covered on one side by a brocaded rug of Turkmen design influence.

3. A Yörük woman and child inside a tent, divided by a Soumak rug.

4. A Yörük woman mixing dye. The camel bag hanging in the tent is customarily kept by the son as an heirloom. (Photos: Daniel G. Bates)

The Kurds

The Kurds are one of the major tribal peoples of Turkey.[11] For centuries they struggled against Ottoman rule and dreamed of achieving nationhood in Kurdistan, an area extending through parts of Turkey, a corner of Iraq, and three Iranian provinces. Their most recent tragedy was a crushing defeat in Iraq after failing to settle the rebellion that started in 1961.

The Kurds speak their own language, Kurdish, classified as an Indo-European language related to Persian. Of two major dialects Kermanji is spoken in Turkey, the USSR, and Syria, while Sorani is spoken in Iran and Iraq. Until recently Arabic has been used for writing Kurdish; the Roman script is now more common, particularly in publications on the subject of Kurdish nationalism.

Historically the Kurds had a well-defined culture, with centers in feudal courts and urban centers under their chieftains, called Khans. They had a reputation for being fierce and for plundering. I. B. Bishop, writing about her stay in the area of Lake Van in 1891, felt that the fear of the peasants in Armenia and in Erzerum was based on a "long reign of terror perpetuated by Kurds."[12] Raiding has been considered a prerogative of tribal life, executed according to set patterns, not only among the Kurds. The Kurds, warlike or not, were self-sufficient, independent, proud, and unadaptable.

In a pattern similar to that occurring in other countries approaching industrialization the Turkish government has pressured tribal peoples to disperse and settle. The expansion of agriculture has reduced the availability of the grazing lands upon which tribal life depends. A government land-distribution policy has allocated land in an attempt to develop a broader-based society. In 1967 28,000 families were given 420,000 hectares (roughly two and a half million acres) of land. In 1972 420,000 hectares were allocated for pasture.[13] Some Yörük tribes have dispersed in great numbers. Whole tribes have been assimilated into the general population. Certain of their rug designs have disappeared as well, but weaving has continued among settled Yörüks throughout Turkey. The effect of the pressure to settle the Kurds has been traumatic, and it is claimed that Kurdish nationalism was essentially a brave last stand against the encroaching mechanization of the period.

Saph, a multiple-niche kilim prayer rug, this one, from the 18th century, with a triple prayer niche (Collection of the Victoria & Albert Museum, London)

Warp: wool
Weft: linen and silvered copper threads
Size: 1.7m x 1.23m

A *saph* is placed in the mosque with its niche facing the *gibla* wall that holds the prayer niche.[14] Its *mihrab* indicates the direction of Mecca, the Holy City of Islam. The three niches and the wide border are filled with geometricized trees; the inner and outer borders, replicates of each other, are geometricized flower heads. Prayer rugs are carried to the mosque or used at home. When the call to prayer comes from the muezzin, a Moslem spreads his prayer rug and prays with his knees at the bottom of the arch and his forehead touching the apex.

Yörük *çuval*
Warp: gray cotton
Weft: gray cotton
Brocading: wool
Technique: zili, plain-weave back; front
and back woven in one piece, sides sewn
Origin: Kozak near Bergama, western Anatolia
Size: .9m x .55m
Colors: gray, gold, pink, green, black, orange
The design consists of stacked prayer-niche-like motifs,
called "saddle tree" (*egher kast*) or "stacked in colors"
(*catmah ala*).[15]

Çuval means "sack." Since the size and format is
relatively uniform, the term is used in some areas as a
measure of volume. This *çuval* still has a residue of
straw. A similar design was described by Dr. May
Beattie as "A Turkoman design, much woven in
Anatolia."[16]

Yörük animal cover
Warp: dark brown loosely spun horse hair
Weft: dark brown wool
Brocading: wool
Size: 1.1m x 1.86m
Technique: Zili weave, rows of Soumak in
end borders
Origin: Silifke
Mediterranean Silifke is one end of the migratory route
of a group of Yörük tribes. Similar pieces are found in
Ezine. This cover exhibits the same "saddle tree"
design, horizontal bands of arches such as those found
in silk patterned fabrics from Loulan (eastern
Turkestan), which date from the 1st century B.C. to the
1st century A.D.[17]

Mosque rug
Warp: light wool, undyed
Weft: wool
Brocading: wool
Size: 3.6m x 1.47m
Technique: ciçim weave with some Soumak
detailing
Colors: dark red, dark blue, greenish blue, white
The brocaded rug shown in color plate 4 (page 196) was probably made for a mosque in northwestern Anatolia. It is customary "to arrange the comfortable and more costly thick pile rugs near the prayer arch and to use the more humble but colorful flat-weaves elsewhere." The design, again the same as in the ancient cloth fragment from Loulan, is also reminiscent of Islamic architectural detail and tilework. For certain tribes a red kilim is used to seat the visiting elder, who helps settle tribal accounts during an annual visit. "One day we'll have this

out on a red kilim," a tribesman might say to his adversary in a controversy.[18] Rugs, flat-woven and knotted,[19] are seen in mosques in cities, towns and villages throughout Turkey. "A Turkish family marks its important events—such as the birth of the first son—by a gift of a rug or a kilim to the local mosque. And the rug that covers the corpse on its journey to the grave is given to the mosque in memory of the life that has ceased. Where they have been preserved, these rugs furnish priceless documents of the weaving of the area over a period of years."[20] Contributing to the mosque is part of Islamic tradition, called "pious endowment" (*vakif*). A museum of Pious Endowment in Istanbul has collected thousands for study. (Photo of mosque: Tony Landreau)

Details from a kilim rug
Size: .95m x 1.2m, .3m x .175m (shown)
The design, consisting of rows of cross-filled rosettes connected by a trellis or lattice, is frequently used in rugs woven by Turkmen of the Ersari tribe. (One of the silk fragments found at Loulan has such a trellis-and-flowerbud design.) A similar kilim from the 18th century is in the Turk-Islam Eserleri Museum in Istanbul.[21]

Two atypical kilims are shown in color plates 5 and 6. The design of the kilim shown in color plate 5 (page 197) is reminiscent of Turkish knotted rugs of the 17th and 18th centuries, although simplified. The double-ended prayer arch, on a solid color field surrounded by a floral border, a main border with cloud bands, and an outer trefoil border all appeared in 18th-century knotted rug design. It is similar to rugs called "Transylvanian" found in churches in the Transylvanian Alps of eastern Europe, attributed to Turkey. A double-ended prayer rug of the early 17th century has a similar format and the same pale red prayer arch. Other antique knotted rugs have the same format with a white outline around the double arch. The medallion in the rug on this page is outlined by zigzags varying the length of the slits as a design element.

Warp: 2-ply light and dark wool
Weft: wool
Technique: slit tapestry, reversible
Size: 2.75m x 1.95m

The kilim shown in color plate 6 (page 197), made in the mid-20th century, shares design characteristics of 16th-century Turkish knotted rugs called medallion Ushaks. Ushak, an important weaving center, borrowed the graceful elongated medallion from Tabriz, across the Persian border, effecting a stylistic change from the earlier infinitely repeating patterns. The presence of multiple medallions, the cartouches in the medallions, and the quarter medallions bordering the center field indicate that the weaver either copied a medallion-Ushak design or followed a tradition of kilims that is not generally known.

Warp: 2-ply wool, natural with some dark
Weft: wool
Technique: slit tapestry, reversible
Size: 3.75m x 1.88m
Date: 1947

The slits between different shades of blue in the center field are used as an ornamental detail. The rug, when hung in front of a light, looks as if it were woven with silver thread.

The design of the antique 19th-century kilim rug shown in color plate 7 (page 198) antedates the use of the large center medallion.

Warp: wool
Weft: wool
Technique: slit tapestry, reversible
Size: 2.68m x 1.98m

The outer border and the inner border (called guard border) are ribbonlike designs geometricized from their origin as a running vine. The bold meander of the main border displays opposing trefoils at the ends and latch hooks at the sides.

In the 16th century Sultan Solyman the Magnificent brought artisans from Northwest Persia to Ushak. Their knotted carpets exhibited intricate, well-balanced designs. In the 19th and early 20th centuries Ushak was the largest rug-making center in Asia Minor, producing rugs that were bolder and much simpler in design than the classics. These rugs were often large and always lustrous.

Hawley, writing in 1913, mentioned the large kilims of "Oushak" and attributed them to Christian weavers who "lived permanently in the area and were not under the necessity of making pieces more convenient for carrying by their nomadic weavers."[24] Further, "the oldest pieces, formerly known as *yapraks,* distinguishable by their strong colors of red, green and blue . . . are massed to produce striking effects . . . many are too large and heavy for domestic use, but are well adapted for public halls."[25]

Detail of Ushak kilim rug
Warp: wool
Weft: 1-ply wool
Technique: slit tapestry, reversible
Colors: turkey-red ground, blue, dark brown, "Ushak" turquoise, plum, pumpkin, off-white
Size: 4.2m x 3.6m (complete rug)

The warp is the same color as the major color of the weft, red. The foundation warp and weft of some Ushak knotted rugs are the same color, which helps to establish the attribution. The outer border is a medacy, the reciprocal trefoil design associated with Turkmen rugs of the Caucasus and Persia.

Kilim rug
Warp: 2-ply natural wool
Weft: wool
Technique: slit tapestry with outlining and
brocaded details. Single faced.
Size: 4.5m x 1.1m
The hornlike scroll design resembles that found in certain knotted rugs from the Caucasus. The scrolls are thought to be representations of rams' horns, also seen in Moslem weavings from central Asia. The ram is a sacrificial animal in the Moslem religion.

Çuval (Sack)
Warp: wool
Weft: wool
Size: .9m x .6m
Brocading: wool
Technique: *zili* weave—the consistency of its formula gives the surface a three-dimensional effect. Plain weave back.
Colors: brown, orange, gold, green, white, pink
Design: This ancient pattern is directly related to Turkmen *güls*. This design motif, also frequently seen in Caucasian kilims, is very similar to the basic Uzbek Dschulchir *gül*. In this Turkish version the latch hooks face inward.[22]

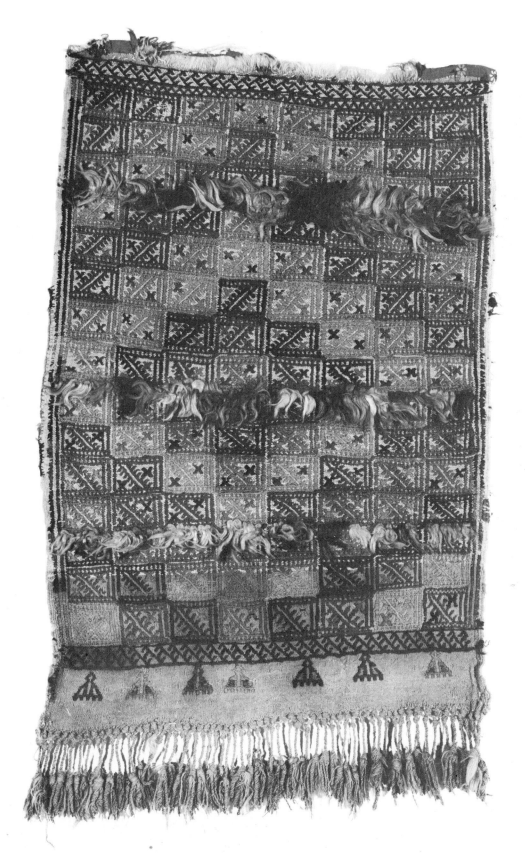

Brocaded cover
Warp: white wool
Weft: white cotton
Brocading: wool
Technique: ciçim weave with added tufts of
varied colors
Colors: pink, turquoise, blue, orange, red,
brown
Size: .98m x .65m

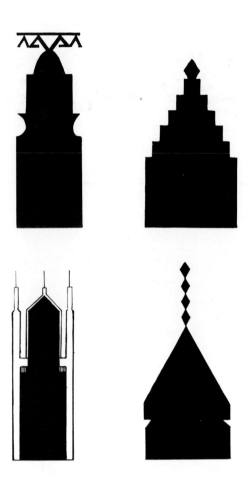

Mihrabs in Turkish flat weaves. The pointed arch, used as a structural element for the first time in the Mosque of Ibu Tulun in Cairo (870 A.D.), became an emblem of the faith. In each Moslem country the arch developed a different form in architecture, mosaic, and ornamental detail. Nowhere is the arch used in rug design as richly as it is in Turkey, as seen in these examples from Turkish kilims and brocaded rugs. (Drawings by Lauren Dreiband)

Saph multiple prayer kilim
Origin: Cukurçimen, central Anatolia
Date: late 18th century
Size: 1.7m x 1.38m
The *mihrabs* are two gray-green arches on a cream-colored field; other colors are red, yellow, pink, light blue, and gold. (Courtesy: Textile Museum, Washington, D.C.)

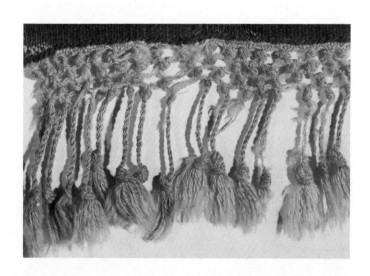

Contrast the crudely tied braiding in a recent kilim with the finely tied, fine warp braid in an older kilim. The recent weaver had less patience, less skill, and less time to spend.

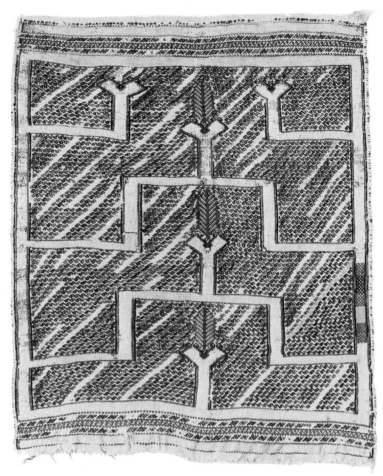

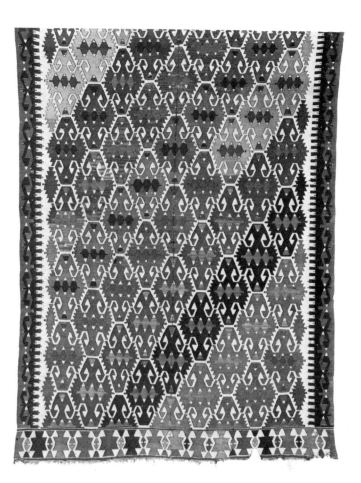

Prayer rug
Origin: Konya area, Yörük
Size: 1.6m x 1.3m
Warp: 2-ply wool
Weft: wool
Brocading: wool
Colors: blue, light blue, green, brick red, pink, salmon, yellow, dark brown
Technique: ciçim weave

The province of Konya is known for its appealing *ciçims,* usually woven on a white ground. This prayer *ciçim* with multilayered squared *mihrabs* is from neighboring Helvaci, which means "little sweet." The form of an espaliered tree with a conventionalized cypress at the top of each arch emphasizes the concept of the tree of life. Other nearby towns known for kilims are Eskill and Obruk, the latter on an old caravan route. There are hundreds of towns, villages, and encampments in Anatolia where flat weaves are made.

Kilim rug (two-thirds shown)
Warp: 2-ply wool
Weft: 1-ply wool
Technique: slit tapestry, reversible outlining throughout
Colors: dark brown, brick red, sea green, beige, blue
Size: 3.74m x 1.83m

The same design is seen in the kilim in the room view: repeated medallions in ascending order in strongly contrasting colors create an optical effect. This juxtaposition of color areas and the use of white in between for contrast are successful design features of kilim weaving.

Cappadocia, a biblical area in central Anatolia, covers ten Turkish provinces. It was occupied by the Hittites from the 16th to the 8th century B.C. The largest city, Kayseri, which lies due north of Jerusalem and Beirut, has been a center of commerce from Roman times and possesses significant architectural remains including early Ottoman mosques. Cappadocia's natural wonders, strange volcanic towers in conical form, were carved out as dwellings and chapels by a cloistered community of medieval Christians between the 5th and the 12th century A.D. There is little evidence of the stylistic influence of these cultures in the kilims from the area, though the design is distinctive.

In another village in Cappadocia a visitor saw a two-part kilim separated in the middle, allowing smoke to escape from a stove in a floor pit. A family in Cappadocia celebrates a Moslem holiday. The kilim might have been woven by one of the women. (Photo: Three Lions Inc.)

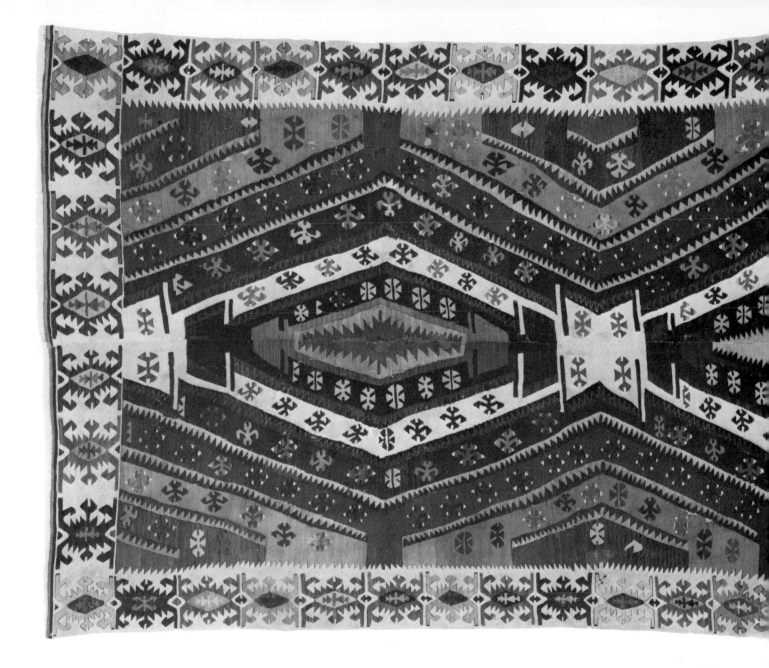

Kilim rug
Warp: 2-ply wool
Weft: 1-ply wool
Size: 4.13m x 1.65m
Technique: slit tapestry with outlining, two parts sewn together
Although both parts of two-part kilims are designed to be joined when completed, a mismatch is always possible: a slight miscalculation of length during warping, for instance, may be the cause, as may one or two additional rows in a pattern area. A perfect match such as this one shows the skill of the weaver. Similar kilims have been identified as from central Anatolia, Konya, Kirchehir, Malatya (many kilims of Malatya were woven by Armenians, who at one time made up a large part of the population), and Karabagh.

Prayer kilim
Origin: Sivas area, north-central Turkey, early 19th century
Size: 3.77m x 1.83m
Many *saphs* are made in this area. In some, such as this sample, the *mihrabs* are side by side when the rug is viewed horizontally, which means that they were woven sideways from the weaver's point of view. (Collection of Ahuan, London)

The very fine rug with a mosaiclike design shown in color plate 8 (page 199) was probably made for a mosque. Weavings with tilelike designs, often filled in with animal and bird motifs, are called *Vernehs* in the rug trade. *Vernehs* are made in the Caucasus and Turkey and are prized by collectors.
Verneh
Warp: red 2-ply wool
Weft: red 1-ply wool
Technique: ciçim weave with countered soumak detail outlining the squares
Size: 4.12m x 1.92m

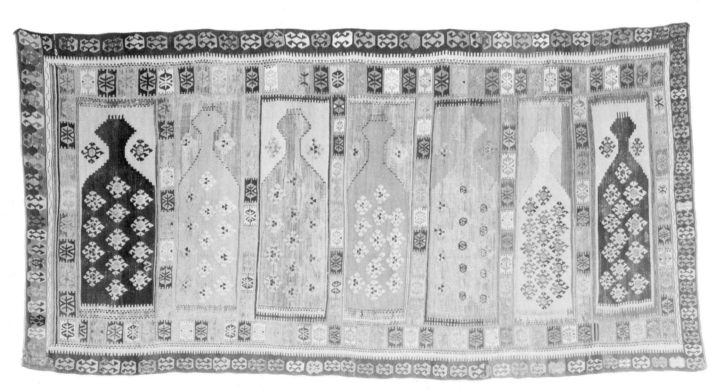

In 1973 Landreau, Beattie, and Yohe documented kilim weaving in the Van Hakkari district. They visited Kurds whose ancestors from the Hakkari tribe had invaded the region in the 13th century. Landreau found that most weaving is done in the winter, with some kilims and plain-weave bags from the Yaylas made in the summer. Kilims were produced "out of the head" of the weaver in the few designs of these Kurdish tribes. Two weavers were observed working on a Van kilim at the same time.[26] Metal-wrapped threads, common in older kilims, were found in some newer pieces, and Van weavers were observed weaving with such threads. The metal, possibly Lurex, is wrapped around a cotton core.

Kilim
Warp: wool
Weft: wool (very rich in lanolin)
Colors: tan ground, two blues, off-white
Technique: slit tapestry made in two badly matched parts, with rows of Soumak defining bands
Size: 2.1m x 1.65m
Kilims of the Lake Van (Van Gölü) area are easily identified as two-part slit weave in technique and are usually closely woven with strong wool. They are relatively short compared to their width with large geometric designs edged by latch hooks. Very few colors are used, mainly dark reds and blues. Similar light-colored kilims are made by Kurdish weavers in northern Iraq. Rugs with this design were also woven entirely in Soumak technique.

Khorjin (Khurdjin) double saddlebag
Warp: 2-ply light wool
Weft: white cotton wool
Technique: mixed—slit tapestry center panels with some outlining, woven in one continuous piece with a striped kilim back
Origin: Yörük
Size: 1.61m x .84m
Repeated use of the latch hook becomes a striking design feature in this ornamental bag.

iran

*Where lies thy carpet
There is thine home.*—Persian proverb

HISTORY

Iran, known as Persia before 1935 and still often called by that name, is set on a great plateau linked to the Anatolian plateau of Turkey on the West and to the USSR by the mountainous Caucasus in the northwest and the Caspian Sea and a section of common border on the North. On the East the plateau meets Afghanistan, while in the Southwest it abuts the Persian Gulf and in the south the Gulf of Oman.

"Now you must know that Persia is a very great country." Marco Polo's observation on the country began with those words.[1] The greatness of the Persian Empire was established in ancient times by Cyrus (6th century B.C.) and endured under his successors, the last of whom was Darius, the Achaemenidae, for 200 years. Persepolis, the Achaemenidaec capital, was of gigantic stature, built and ornamented by artisans from all over the Empire. A new art compounded of Greek, Assyrian, and native Iranian elements developed.

Ruled successfully by Alexander the Great, the Seleucids, and the Parthians, the Sassanian kings, heirs of the Achaemenidae, built a new empire that persisted while the Roman Empire faded. Under Khosru II the Sassanian court at Ctesiphon was legendary in its splendor. The arts, including textiles, flourished. An ancient carpet known as the Spring of Khosru was among the loot taken from the Sassanian kings, according to literary sources. It was designed as a garden. The materials were gold, silver, precious and semiprecious stones, and silk. It was over 200 feet long, and the design was a *firdaus,* or paradise scene, with running streams marked out by crystals, the ground in gold thread, the leaves worked in silk, and the blossoms represented by precious stones. There is no known record of its technique; it may have been brocaded.

Carpets in this tradition might have been made subsequently; we have no record of the exact manner of its weave with which to make later comparisons.

The Arab invasion toppled Ctesiphon in 642 A.D., and Persia became another tile in the Islamic mosaic. The next invasions were those of the Mongols, culminating in the horrifying sack of Baghdad in 1258 when nearly one million people were massacred:

"Waves of blood the dainty threshholds of the Palace beauties whelm

While from out my heart the life blood dyes my sleeve with hues of woe.

Fear vissitudes of Fortune; fear the Sphere's revolving change;

Who could dream that such a splendour such a fate could overthrow."—Threnody by Sadi[2]

With the Mongol victory Arabic art waned and the great art of Persia emerged, which used as its model the art of the East, particularly that of Turkestan, the cultural center at that time.

Tamerlane (Timur, the lame), the greatest Asiatic conqueror known to history, conquered Persia piece by piece in the late 14th century. Finally, with the Safavid dynasty, Persia was again ruled locally, with order and unification the result. The Safavids converted the country to the Shiite faith, a significant act in terms of culture and art, which flourished particularly under the reign of Shah Abbas (1587–1629). Shah Abbas was an administrative genius. He was responsible for abundant bridge and road building to improve communications in the Empire. When the Polo family of Venice and later travelers crossed Persia, the trip was hazardous. Roads that had been plied by traders during the flourishing Arab period had been destroyed.

During the reign of Shah Abbas carpet making became a high art. Several garden carpets of the period

have been preserved. Elaborate flat-woven silk rugs were made, as well as knotted garden designs. A 17th-century Polish king, Sigismund III, ordered carpets from Kashan; several silk tapestry-woven rugs with Polish coats of arms survive. It is thought that other kilims preserved from that period might have been made in Kashan. The predominant motifs were animals, flowering plants and leaves, and figures from the hunt, all of which closely filled the intricate fields. The silk tapestry-woven kilim with metallic threads, known as the Doisteau kilim from the name of the donor to the Louvre, is one of that group.

Silk kilim
Size: 2.49m x 1.39m
Date: 17th century
The heroic scene in the center medallion is thought by Arthur Upham Pope to be based on a story of Bahram and the Dragon in the *Shah Nameh* by Firdawsi.[3] (Collection of the Musée du Louvre, Doisteau gift)

The great period of rug making started during the reign of Shah Tahmasp (1524–1576) when the great Ardabil carpets were woven. Some courtly examples of the period still exist. These rugs represent a great achievement in technique and design. They express the Shia spirit with graceful scrolls and arabesques, which are bountiful with animals, trees, and flowers.

The last of the Safavid monarchs failed to maintain the excellence of the weaving established under Tahmasp and Abbas. When the Afghan invasion took place, the great period of carpet weaving ended. The art did not disappear, but it shrank. Not until the 19th century when the Qajar dynasty was firmly established were carpets again woven on a grand scale, and the old models were used for copying.

By the time Persian carpets found their way to the West in appreciable quantities, old rugs were becoming valuable. Merchants easily collected pieces from homes and bazaars, since the custom was and still is to keep rugs that could be converted into cash. These pieces were for home use; they had not been factory-woven but were tribal or village pieces. As demand in the West increased, the supply of old pieces decreased, new rugs were produced for export in sizes, colors, and designs that would please western taste. As a result the tribal knotted rug was used in the 1880s as a prototype for copying purposes, as tribal kilims are beginning to be used now.

THE PEOPLE OF IRAN

The majority of the people of Iran are Persian, descendants of Indo-Aryan tribes. Among settled people, there are a large number of Tajiks (Tadzniks in Russia and Afghanistan) of related origin. The tribespeople are Kurds, Shahsavan, Afshar, and Qashga'i (all Turkic); Khamseh, a confederation of five tribes including the Turkic-speaking Baharlu and Inanlu, some Arabic-speaking tribes and the Bassiri of seemingly mixed origin;[4] the Lors, including Bakhtiyari, Boyr Ahmad, Mamasani, and Kuh Gilu'i; some Baluchi tribes; some Turkmen tribes; and some Arab tribes. Settled minorities include Armenians (the largest community is in Esfahan) and Jews (they formed a majority in the Hamaden area).

The official language of Iran is Persian, now called Farsi, which is a descendant of the literary version of Middle Persian as it was used by the Sassanians. Many Arabic words were introduced after the conversion to Islam. Other languages are those of the Kurdish, Luri, Turkic, Baluchi and Arabic tribes.[5] The written language is a form of Arabic script.

The tribal people of Persia are scattered throughout the country. The largest tribes, and the most powerful, are concentrated in the Zagros Mountains, which are suited to the pastoral life. The Zagros chain has spectacular gorges through which access to the interior is made. Inside there are deep flat valleys covered with grass and vegetation for grazing.

There are old cross-routes in several places, with scattered towns along the way. The tribal movements from summer to winter quarters bring tribesmen into contact with settled peoples who live along their migratory path. This brings about a cultural interaction that can be reflected in changes in traditional weaves.

Large-scale relocations were forced upon tribal units by rulers of various periods to diminish tribal power, as punishment, or to help defend a region.

In the catalog of the Tehran Rug Society's 1975 exhibition, "Tribal Animal Covers from Iran," Wertime and Tanavoli show the cultural interaction when tribal "groups entering a new area brought their own traditions with them and both influenced and were influenced by the indigenous peoples with whom they came in contact. This is reflected in the things they wove and has made it difficult to distinguish between pieces of branches of tribal groups in different parts of the country."[6] Intermarriage, tribal dispersal, and new groupings formed by new alliances add to the diffusion; and, as seen in Turkey, whole groups of rugs can disappear when weavers disperse.

The number of tribespeople still unsettled has diminished dramatically. At the beginning of the 19th century the tribes were estimated as comprising half the population. In 1950 they constituted approximately one-fourth. In 1973 462,000 people were listed as tribal nomads in a statistical yearbook of the government.

The total population was listed as 25,789,000; the tribal grouping represents under 1.5% of the population according to the definition of tribal population as "numbers of tribes or sub-tribes that were still nomadic and continued to live in tents or in separate summer and winter quarters."[7] The count cannot be anywhere near the actual number; the Qashqa'i alone claim that many tribesmen.[8] There are numerous difficulties in taking such a census; the possibility of government reluctance to accept a high nomadic census is one factor.[9] Nonetheless, the nomadic life in modern Iran has become a minority style.

The following pieces are shown in color plate 9 (pages 200–201).

A. Salt (*Namakdân*) or condiment (*Qâshogdân*) bag
Warp: 2-strand vat-dyed brown wool
Weft: 2-strand red wool
Technique: weft-float weave, weft-wrapped guard strips, striped plain-weave back
Tribe: Kurd
Size: .53m x .41m
The narrow neck of this bag allows storage of loose or pulverized materials.

B. Spindle bag (*Gailenden*)
Warp: 2-ply natural wool
Weft: 2-ply natural wool
Technique: warp-faced complementary wrap-pattern weave
Tribe: Qashqai
Size: .38m x .25m
Very fine, intricate weave, with front and back in different patterns.

C. Reverse side of B.

D. Saddlebag (*khorjin* or *khurdjin*)
Warp: 2-ply natural light and dark wool
Weft: 2-ply natural light and dark wool
Technique: Soumak, plain weave back
Tribe: Baluchi
Size: .46m x .44m
The loops slip through the holes and interlace to hold the bag closed, a characteristic throughout the Middle East.

E. Donkey bag (*Chanteh*)
Warp: dark wool
Weft: wool
Technique: weft-float weave, floats on the reverse, also called skip plain weave
Tribe: Baluchi
Design, color, and technique are typical of Baluchi bags from Iran and Afghanistan.

Animals in Persian flat weaves. (Drawings by Lauren Dreiband)

CHARACTERISTICS OF PERSIAN FLAT WEAVES

Following are some features of Persian flat-woven rugs.

1. They are usually woven in one piece.

2. The majority are reversible (*doru, daruye,* or *druya,* two-faced in Farsi).

3. The most common technique is slit-tapestry weave. Some rugs are made in an interlocking-tapestry technique, and some in Soumak and brocading techniques.

4. A cotton warp is frequent in kilims (*gelim* in Farsi), particularly in those produced in recent decades. Most tribal weavers in Iran have always used wool for the warp because it is available. Cotton has been available in towns and cities, and most late 19th- and 20th-century kilims made by Kurdish weavers, including many Senna kilims, for example, have a cotton warp.

5. A rich array of saddlebags, storage bags, and animal trappings, in a variety of techniques, are made by the tribes; some of these pieces are prime examples of intricate weaving techniques combined with a superlative use of color and design.

FORMAT OF PERSIAN FLAT WEAVES

Common formats are listed below.

1. A common format is a medium-sized kilim (*dosar*)—1.3m x 2.46m, 1.5m x 2.4m, and 1.24m x 2.42m are typical sizes.

2. The kilim runner (*kenareh*) is common in the Veramin area and around Hamaden.

3. A larger kilim with the width approximately twice the length (*keley*) measures from 1.5m x 2.9m to 2.1m x 4.2m.

4. Luri tribespeople make rugs in an almost square format.

5. Narrow "eating rugs" are made by the Baluchi and Kurdish tribes in the East.

The pleasing design shown in color plate 10 (page 202) is similar to the center medallion of classic Tabriz knotted rugs found in Bijar. The scale indicates that this one might have been reduced in width and have originally had a trefoil border continuing on the two sides.

Kilim runner

Size: 2.6m x .65m

Origin: northwest Iran

Warp: 2-ply undyed light wool

Weft: 2-ply wool, with two threads used together

Technique: reversible slit-tapestry weave with eccentric beating; heavily bound selvages indicate a probable reduction in width

Kilim
Warp: 2-ply wool, brown and white
Weft: wool
Technique: dovetailed-tapestry weave, reversible
Colors: ground, cherry red; white, yellow, blue, green, black
Design: bold geometric border surrounds a plain color field containing a diamond medallion formed by four smaller diamonds
Origin: northwest Iran, probably Azerbaijan
Size: 2.18m x 4.68m

Brocaded rug
Warp: 2-ply hair
Weft: 1-ply wool, with two yarns used together in each shed
Brocading: 2-ply wool
Technique: Plain weave with discontinuous weft brocading; striped ground continues from selvage to selvage under the side borders; four-sided border is continuous countered Soumak brocading
Size: 3.18m x 1.5m
Origin: Azerbaijan
This rug is similar to brocaded rugs made by Kurds in northeastern Iran.

45

THE SHAHSAVANS

The Shahsavans are a Turkic tribe from the province of Azerbaijan, which joins the Russian province of the same name in the North. Until the 19th century the southern Caucasus was part of Persia, and tribal groups crossed back and forth. Azerbaijan is a plateau that offers fine grazing and still sustains the pastoral nomadism of the Shahsavans and Kurds. The weaving of the Shahsavans was little known to rug collectors until recently, and many of their bag faces and rugs have been attributed to others, particularly to weavers of the Caucasus.

The Shahsavans are a confederation of tribes originally formed by Shah Abbas in 1600 to counter the turbulent Kizilbash, who made up his forces. He invited members of all tribes to enroll as "Friends of the Shah," or *Shah Savan*. Thousands joined the tribe, and the shah was released from dependence on the Kizilbash.[11] Several of the clans were transplanted to north-central Iran near Tehran by Fath Ali Shah, a Qazar, at the beginning of the 19th century.

Animal cover
Warp: 2-ply wool
Weft: 2-ply wool
Size: 1.7m x 1.5m
Technique: Plain weave with brocading, made in four parts
Origin: 19th-century Shahsavan
Colors: red, rust, light brown, black, three blues, blue-green
The shape of this horse blanket is common to many tribes in Iran and Afghanistan. (Collection of the Museum of Art and Industry, Hamburg)

Mafrash kilim
Warp: fine 2-ply wool
Weft: wool
Size: 1.75m x 1.15m
Technique: reversible slit tapestry, seamed across center
Colors: red, rose, wine, teal blue, light blue, dark blue, white, beige, black vegetable dyes (similar to those in old Caucasian kilims)
Origin: probably northwest Iran near the Caucasian border

The first kilim shown in color plate 11 (page 202) could have been put together from two sides of a cradle or bedding bag or reduced from a long bed-roll kilim. The word *mafrash* is used in the rug trade to describe such pieces and comes from the Farsi words meaning "made into" and "rug." The second piece is similar in design and color to the first.

Saddlebag
Warp: wool
Weft: wool
Technique: slit tapestry, back and front made in one piece
Size: 1.28m x .55m
Date: 19th century

Bag face
Warp: wool
Weft: wool
Size: .65m x .57m
Technique: Allover Soumak brocading

A bag with the same two-headed bird motif, called "tuning fork," seen in this bag's border,[12] was found in a Shahsavan summer encampment. The two-headed bird or tuning fork is a rug and bag design from the Caucasus and Central Asia as well as Iran. The main border of a Yomud pile rug from Khiva also has this design.[13] The center motif is a widely used Caucasian and Armenian design relating to dragon carpets.

Bedding bag
Warp: wool
Weft: wool
Size: .92m x .49m x .4m
Technique: four sides countered Soumak
brocading, striped plain-weave bottom (made in
five parts), selvages joined by "fishbone" wrap-
ping with varied colors of yarn
Bags of this shape are used to store bedding and
household objects. They make attractive decorations
when stacked around the tent interior. (Loaned by
Khalil Zahiri)

Kilim
Warp: 2-ply wool
Weft: 2-ply wool
Size: 2.3m x 1.88m
Origin: Shahsavan, attribution uncertain (acquired in Meshkin Shah, a Shahsavan market
town)
Technique: slit tapestry, loose threads left on
back at color changes, made in two parts
The striped kilim ends terminate in heavily braided
tassels in varying colors. The center seam is embellished
by a braided stitch in varying colors: light blue, dark
blue, and black. The white field of the geometric
medallion and the field of the smaller medallion in its
center are filled with geometrically drawn *boteh* leaf
designs known as Persian pears in the West from the
designs on paisley shawls. (Loaned by Masood Haroonian)

In the rug shown in color plate 14 (page 206) the
ground is filled in according to the Soumak formula of
over six warp threads and under three. Sections of plain
ground are left exposed. The Soumak brocading could
be confused with embroidery. The rug was made in five
strips, sewn together vertically along selvages.
Rug
Warp: white cotton
Weft: white cotton
Brocading: 2-ply wool
Origin: Shahsavan
Size: 2.44m x 1.24m
Technique: mixed—warp-faced plain-weave
ground; Soumak brocading and Soumak wrapping

THE KURDS

Kurdistan is one of 23 administrative districts in modern Iran, but historically it covers a much wider area. A leader of the Dehbukri tribe explains that the Kurds of Iran think of themselves as Iranians, having been in Iran for thousands of years (they are of Iranian stock).[14] Many live together in villages; many have dispersed. Mukri Kurds have become sedentary businessmen, professional men, and farmers.

Nomadic Kurds are organized along traditional lines in a hierarchy starting with their clan chieftains (*kadkhodas*), followed by chieftains of larger groupings (*kalāntars*), and *khans*, tribal chiefs, usually a hereditary calling. According to a Danish anthropologist who studied the Kurds in 1961, they accept the age-old tribal division into two castes, the aristocracy and the "peasants," nobles and serfs.

In tribal life marriage patterns are complex and traditional, and upward social mobility is unusual. Marriage is used to further alliances deemed necessary for political or economic reasons.[15] Kurds are monogamous; women are either partly veiled or unveiled and are respected. Some tribes have been successfully ruled by women. Kara Fatima, a 19th-century chieftain, created a great sensation during the Crimean War when she and her armed followers, all women in gay tribal dresses, rode into Constantinople to answer a call to rally in defense of the European conquests.[16]

Senna (now Sanandaj) is the capital of Persian Kurdistan and the home of very fine kilims treasured by collectors who often overlook other flat-woven rugs. They are tightly woven; some of the older ones incorporate silver and other metallic threads; some are made of silk.

A Kurdish woman in the village of Lighuami weaves on a narrow loom with harnesses supported by a tripod. (Photo: Mercedes Eicholz)

The *mihrab* of the kilim shown in color plate 12 (page 203) is divided into narrow stripes with seven different ground colors. The intricate curvilinear drawing indicates skilled weaving. The flowers, buds, and stems in the spandrels are surprisingly naturalistic. The stepped outline of the *mihrab* minimizes the length of the slit at each color change strengthening the rug. (Courtesy of the Textile Museum, Washington, D.C.; loaned by Jerome A. Straka)
Prayer kilim
Warp: 4-ply light wool
Weft: 2-ply wool
Technique: slit tapestry, reversible
Size: 1.635m x 1.194m
Origin: Senna

Kilim
Warp: wool
Weft: wool
Technique: slit tapestry, reversible
Size: 1.63m x 1.08m
Origin: middle 19th century
The overall *boteh* (*mir-i botar*) design on a dark field enclosed by a four-sided cloud band and flower border is characteristic of 19th-century Senna knotted bag faces. According to Hubel Senna kilims are said to be so fine because they were used by ladies in the bath houses (*hamam*), where "they competed with each other in their modest luxuries."[17] (Collection of the Victoria & Albert Museum, London)

Kilim
Warp: cotton
Weft: wool
Size: 2.11m x 1.18m
Technique: slit tapestry, reversible
The dark-blue field is filled with the *herati* or *mahi-to-hos* (fish in pond) pattern, which is associated with knotted rugs, especially those of Faraghan, as are the extended white lozenge and smaller center lozenge. This is the most characteristic pattern of Senna kilims, which are made throughout the area as well as in the city of Senna. (Courtesy of the Museum of Fine Arts, Boston, Ross Collection)

Animal cover
Warp: wool
Weft: wool
Technique: slit tapestry
Colors: aqua, red rose, green, gold, pink, tur-
quoise
(Collection of the Museum of Fine Arts, Boston, Ross
Collection)

LURS

Six tribes of Shia Muslims speak Luri (an Iranian language group native to the districts of Kuh Gilu'i, Bakhtiyari, Luristan, and Mamassani). They are the Bakhtiyari of the Chahar Lang (once powerful, now mainly sedentary), the Bakhtiyari of the Haft Lang, the Lurs, the Kuh Gilu'i, the Mamassani, and the Boyr Ahmads.

Among the products of Iranian civilization in the Bronze Age was "admirable" pottery and fine metal ornaments (the Luristan bronzes).[18] The English archaeologist Sir Aurel Stein excavated caves throughout the area in the 1930s, entered remote areas, and mapped out the roads and landmarks. Some of the ornamentation on the pottery he found is identical to designs found in certain kilims of Iran and Afghanistan.[19]

The warlike reputation of the Luri tribes is based on feuding and raiding, two indisputable aspects of their tribal history. Strife and bloodshed have always been caused in part by the constant struggle of succession. In the *Journal* of the Royal Central Asian Society a visitor among the Boyr Ahmad traced the family trees of their ruling Khans back for more than a hundred years and found that, of all the large related families, not more than six potential heirs had died a natural death.[20]

As far as raiding is concerned, it is considered a prerogative of tribal life; raids are made by bands of up to several hundred men, on foot, covering as many as 40 miles a day over rough mountain trails. "They are acknowledged, alike by friend and foe, to be the bravest, toughest and [most] ruthless fighters in Southern Persia. The qualities, added to their untrustworthiness and inaccessibility, have made them the terror of their neighbors."[21] The fierce independence of all the Luri tribes long kept them outside central control.

The Bakhtiyari chieftains in this century are customarily European-educated and are active on behalf of their tribespeople. They were among the leaders of the 1906 revolution, which won a constitution for the people of Iran, and they helped form the constitutional government that followed.

The Luri tribes, like the other tribes of Iran, have been under government pressure to settle. Some groups who were forced to settle in climates unhospitable to their flocks suffered great losses. For example, some Boyr Ahmad were settled in the warm zone (garmshir), where it was too hot for the flocks during the summer; some were required to settle in the cold highlands, where it was too cold for the flocks during the winter. Disease and starvation resulted.[22]

When Sir Aural Stein was excavating in Luri territory, he was interested in how the Lurs were able to disguise their traditional habits from administrators present to enforce ensettlement. At Sar-kashi Stein found that huts built by official order were completely deserted. Their black woven tents and other prized possessions had all been burned under compulsion or safely hidden away in the mountains, but the Lors saved the reed-woven screens used inside the tents and were now occupying them, although not in comfort.[23] When the first shah abdicated, the Luri tribes returned to their migratory patterns, as did other tribal people throughout Iran.

This migratory pattern works well for the Lurs. The terrain, marked as it is by physical diversity, provides what they need for their pastoral nomadism. Availability of water and grazing land determines tribal movements, and the cycle of that movement guards the health of their animals. "Flocks live in lowlands, brilliantly green in spring. As weeks pass the flocks gradually work north, month by month, until they rest. . . . Thus they have fresh grass five months a year and this luxurious diet makes them fertile enough to drop lambs twice a year."[24]

When the Bakhtiyari (totaling between 300,000 and 500,000 people and millions of animals) cross the Zagros Mountains from their winter encampment (*kislak*) to their summer territory (*ailak*), they are undertaking a dramatic journey. A film, *People of the Wind,* traces the migration of the Babadi subtribe from the first river that they cross, along their ascent, through the 10,000-foot "pass of the women" where the strong wind can blow a person off the cliff, through a 12,000-foot waterfall, across the deep, dangerous Bazuft river to the 15,000-foot peak of Zardeh Kuch, where they struggle across the snow-clad cliffs down into the summer quarters. This journey has been described as the most hazardous test of human endurance still undertaken, year after year, by an entire people.[25]

The tribes travel one by one or in groups, according to a carefully coordinated plan. In 1891 Mrs. Bishop traveled with the Pulawand subtribe, composed of 1,000 families. During the migration they slept in the open. Upon arrival they spread out and encamped; a group of 70 tents was set up in two hours. Each tent contained a household of eight to ten persons, since the Bakhtiyari were polygamous. The *khan* had sixteen wives.[26]

G. Reza Fazel studied the Boyr Ahmad and analyzed the status of women and the dynamics of tribal politics. In the patrilineal tribal societies of the Middle East male visibility dramatizes female invisibility. Fazel shows in what ways the women of the Boyr Ahmad have and exercise power. As mother a woman can play an important role in influencing leadership succession; as communicator with the other women of the tribe she can contribute to tribal decisions; as producer of household possessions (rugs, for example) she exercises economic power. Women of the elite are in a position to exercise considerably more power than women of the lower class. This is logical in view of tribal organization and the method of tribal succession, fraught as it is with potential violence.[27]

Color plate 13 (pages 204–205) shows activities of the Boyr Ahmad tribe. (Photos: G. R. Fazel)

A. At the end of the harvest men fill sacks (*khur*) with grain.

B. Women weave tent cloth from black goat hair. The metal combs are beaters for tightening the weft. The Boyr Ahmad and most nomadic tribespeople in Iran use two- or three-sided black tents.

C. Two women weave a rug while a young bride visits. The tripod is used for churning butter. The buildings in the background are the winter quarters of this pastoral-agricultural tribe.

Kilim
Warp: cotton
Weft: wool
Size: 3.98m x 1.34m
Origin: probably Kurdish
Technique: reversible slit weave
Colors: dark blue (major field), beige, gold, red, white, brown
Very geometrized *boteh* with enclosed crosses fill the field. The four-sided outer border design is the reciprocal trefoil. The sawtooth guard strips are a frequent kilim feature. The cotton warp is common in Kurdish kilims.

Salt-bag face and back
Warp: wool
Weft: 2-ply light wool
Brocading: wool, goat hair, white cotton
Technique: Soumak
Size: .5m x .42m x .35m
Origin: Bakhtiyari or Luri
In the Boyr Ahmad region such a bag is used to transport and hold in place a container of cooking oil.[28]

Saddlebag (open)
Warp: 2-ply cotton
Weft: white cotton wool
Size: 1.275m x 1.035m
Technique: mixed—top section Soumak; mid-section symmetrical knotting; bottom section plain-weave stripes, brocaded detail

The use of three techniques in saddlebags is a characteristic Bakhtiyari feature, as is the Soumak brocading on a white cotton ground.

Ru-kursi
Warp: wool
Weft: wool
Technique: double interlocked tapestry weave, Soumak detail in border
Size: 1.1m x 1.06m
Origin: Luri

Ru-kursi are communal lap robes used as covers over the embers of a brazier to confine the heat while members of a family sit on sides of the square. The design, usually executed on a camel color field, is a central cruciform, or "eye-of-life," shape. The double interlocking technique forms a ridge on the back of the weaving, common in Luri weaving but uncommon in other areas.

Kilim
Warp: very fine wool
Weft: very fine wool
Technique: double interlocked tapestry weave,
plain-weave striped aprons turned under
Origin: Bakhtiyari
Size: 1.15m x 1.05m
This rug might be from Shushtar, the winter territory of
the Bakhtiyari. It is called a *shushtari* (clothes-bundle
wrapper) because it is used for taking clothes to the
public bath. (Collection George and Valerie Justin)

THE QASHQA'I

The Qashqa'i are the largest group in Fars, a district known for its nomadic rugs. One of the most powerful and richest tribes of Iran, they played an important political role in the 19th century. The Qashqa'i, like their Luri neighbors, suffered under the forced settlement policy of Riza Shah Pahlevi; the Il Khan (Sawlat-al-Dawle), their principal chief, was imprisoned along with chieftains of other tribes. The famed horse breeders of the Darreshuri *taifeh* or subtribe, for example, lost nearly all their horses when the ban on migration forced them to spend the winter months in the high mountains.

The normal migratory pattern of the Amaleh *taifeh* of the Qashqa'i takes them from their winter quarters close to the Persian Gulf (oil reserves are part of their land's resources), past Shiraz,[29] to their summer grounds in the Kuh-i-dina Range, southwest of Esfahan, the longest annual migration of any Persian tribe.[30]

In the winter encampment the men and boys tend the flocks, hunt for game and birds in the surrounding hills, and concern themselves with tribal politics. The ever-changing tribal alignments and relationships and the decisions about migratory routes and dates are some of the matters that occupy a great deal of time.

The Qashqa'i are monogamous. Each tent houses one integral family. The family tent is part of a *beyleh*, a group of tents that works together as a cooperative. Women perform the domestic tasks; baking *nan*—thin sheets of bread—milking the goats, making yogurt and cheese, spinning whenever their hands are free, and weaving rugs for their own tents on their horizontal ground loom. The goat-hair panels for their black tents are woven on a similar but narrower loom (which resembles the looms of their mountain neighbors, the Boyr Ahmad).

When the time comes for the spring migration, the looms are moved with whatever weaving is on them. On arrival at the summer encampment the weaver continues the work. Many kilims have seemingly erratic color changes: a medallion of one border section, for example, may show a new color not consistent with the rest of the design, the result of running out of the original yarn color. Qashqa'i kilims, like Qashqa'i knotted rugs, are usually double-wefted (two strands used per shed). Pile rugs are tied with the Turkish knot (a balanced knot), although most rug weavers throughout Iran use the asymmetric Persian knot.

The Qashqa'i have a proud bearing and adorn themselves dramatically. Travelers to Shiraz, the capital and market center of Fars province, comment on their sweeping walk and commanding presence. They are said to be the finest weavers in Fars; their pile rugs are woven of lustrous wool, as are their kilims, which are strong and dramatic, proper reflections of the Qashqa'i spirit.

The design shown in color plate 15 (page 206)—boxes with serrated edges separated by flower heads—is considered typical for a Qashqa'i kilim. The Luri use a similar style.

Kilim
Warp: 2-strand light and dark wool
Weft: wool and cotton (white area) double-wefted
Size: 1.95m x 1.55m
Technique: slit tapestry with rows of weft-float brocading on its aprons
(Collection: George and Valerie Justin)

In *The Lord of the Mountain* Marie-Thérèse Ullens de Schooten describes her travels with the Qashqa'i. She was invited by the *khan* to observe the migration to summer quarters. Respect is shown to honored guests according to tribal tradition, and guest tents and a large tent called a reception tent are fitted lavishly. "The more modest and humble tents are made of goat's hair. All have as sole furniture, rugs and carpets that vary in quality and design. There are three principal kinds: Kali, the beautiful carpets woven on looms; pileless rugs known as Gelim, and the gaily colored checkered blankets decorated with tufts of wool called Jajim. The other tribes of Fars also make jajims with tartan-like patterns."[31] The following rugs are shown in color plate 16 (page 207).

A. *Jijim* (*jajim*)
Warp: wool
Weft: wool
Size: 1.1m x 3.55m
Technique: warp-faced even twill weave, heavily tasseled

In this tartanlike pattern the direction of the continuous diagonals formed by the twill weave is reversed on the other side.

B. Kilim
Warp: wool
Weft: wool
Size: 2.15m x 1.55m
Technique: double interlocked tapestry weave with brocaded guard strips

The diagonal rows of isolated diamonds, each holding a hooked figure, and the outer of two main borders distinguish this design from similar Luri styles. The inner border is typically Bakhtiyari.

C. Kilim
Warp: 2-ply light and dark wool
Weft: 1-ply wool, double-wefted
Technique: slit tapestry
Size: 2.52m x 1.57m

Selvages consist of two strands twisted to form a cord. The diamonds are linked in this dynamic Qashqa'i example.

Kilim
Warp: wool
Weft: 2-ply wool
Technique: slit tapestry, tightly woven to
minimize slits, weft-float brocaded guard strips
Size: 3m x 1.55m
Colors: white, orange, red, light blue, turquoise,
teal blue, green, dark blue, black
The diamond-shaped medallions with cruciform centers
are enclosed by successively larger medallions until the
field is filled. The outermost diamonds are incomplete
in a characteristic and daring kilim design. (Loaned by
Marood Haroonian)

Bag
Warp: wool
Weft: wool
Technique: compound weave, one-weft double-
cloth, tufted details, squarebraided warps end in
tassels
Colors: dark blue, off-white, undyed tan
Size: .35m x .41m

Khorjin (double saddlebag)
Warp: wool and white cotton
Weft: 2-ply wool
Technique: mixed, warp-faced complementary warp-pattern weave, twined rows at ends, tufted details, all one piece
Size: 1.03m x .53m
Origin: Qashqa'i

The design, in dark blue and white with shots of orange and yellow, is striking in its starkness. The two sides of the bag have separate sets of loops, here shown in the locked position.

Kilim
Warp: goat hair and wool
Weft: wool
Size: 1.18m x .93m
Technique: dovetailed tapestry
Origin: Varamin area

The empty dark-brown field is surrounded by zigzag motifs in a dramatic juxtaposition of colors (yellow, claret, and mauve). The zigzag, or lightning motif, is similar to designs on potsherds found in Luristan. Robert Haas (Director of Arts, UCLA Extension), when asked if there was a possible comparison, commented: "We have always said that the nature of the simple nomad loom dictates pattern. Here is a case which might contradict that theory. The pattern might have been copied out of long tribal tradition, in this case, a pottery-making tradition."

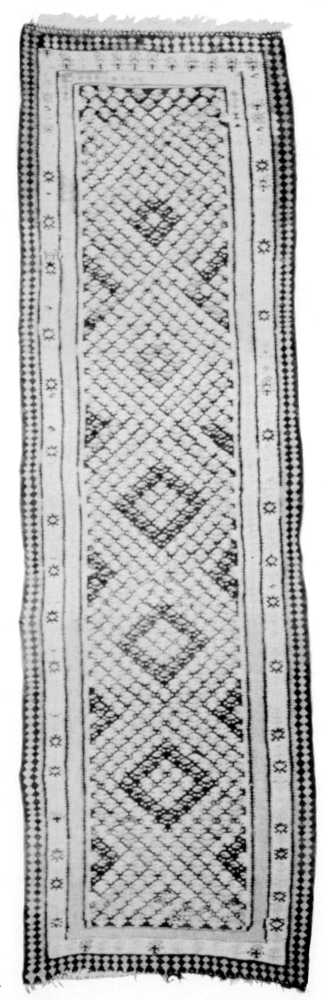

A. Kilim runner
Warp: white cotton
Weft: undyed tan, pink, blue, and gray wool, double-wefted
Size: 1.13m x 3.68m
Technique: reversible slit tapestry with eccentric beating
One small figure of a cat is woven into the border.

B. Kilim runner
Warp: white cotton
Weft: brown, blue, yellow, rose, and tan wool, double-wefted
Size: 2.65m x 1.04m
Technique: reversible slit tapestry with eccentric weft beating to achieve curvilinear forms

C. Kilim runner
Warp: white cotton
Weft: brown, dark blue, camel, red, and yellow wool
Technique: slit tapestry, reversible
Size: 5.34m x 1.02m

The first two of these runners were found in Varamin. They are probably made by Pazeki (predominantly Kurdish) tribespeople who settled in Varamin and Khar, near Tehran. A piece similar to the runner shown in B was identified as Kharaghan in origin.[32] The third runner, Kurdish in origin, has the camel-color ground typical of rugs from the Hamaden area. Some of its pile runners are made with natural camel hair.[33]

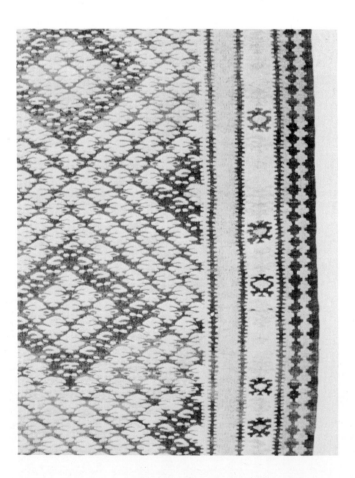

A

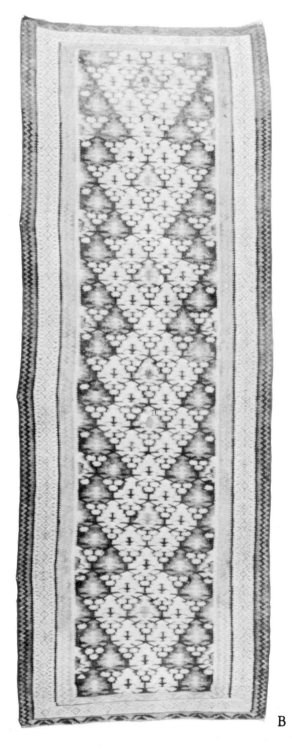

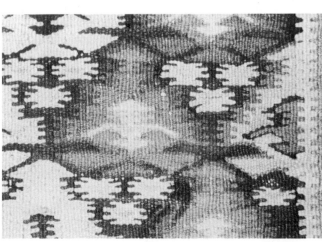

B

C

61

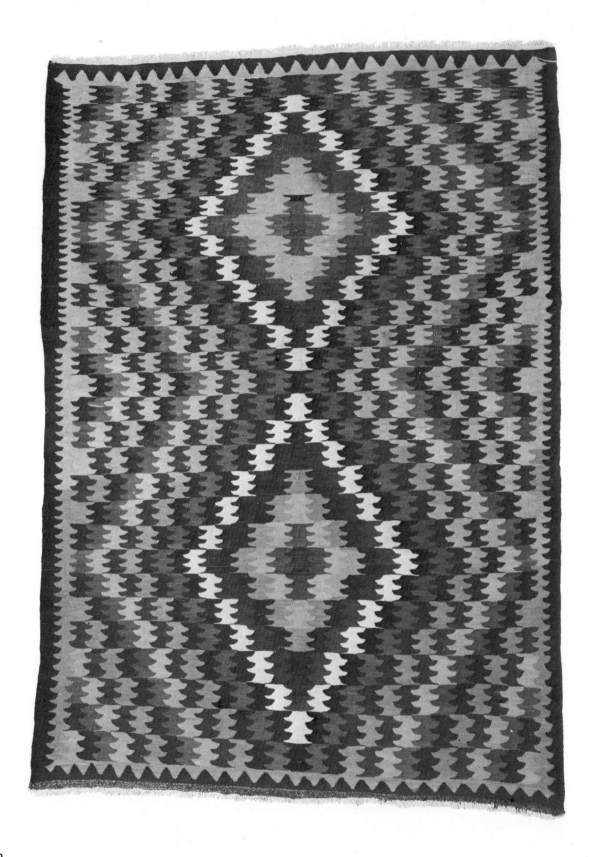

Kilim
Warp: cotton
Weft: wool
Technique: dovetailed-tapestry weave, reversible
Size: 2.15m x 1.55m
This rug was bought in Zarand, north of Kerman. The
dazzler effect is known locally as the Shiraz design and
is similar to some from Fars. The brown warp, the dove-
tailing (rather than slit tapestry), and the deeper colors,
which include a rich apricot, are all typical of Garmsar.

THE BALUCHI

The Baluchi, in contrast to the tribes already discussed, do not have set summer and winter quarters, except for a minority that winters on the coast of the Persian Gulf and the Arabian Sea.[34] Baluchis occupy ("wander in") the largest desert areas and some low mountainous areas in eastern Iran and western Afghanistan.[35]

Khorjin (double saddlebag)
Warp: wool
Weft: very dark blue, tan, ivory, and brown wool
Technique: continuous weft-float weave, Soumak detailing, plain-weave back
Size: 1.32m x .55m
Origin: Khorassan
The folded ribbon motif fills contrasting dark and light stripes. Tightly woven saddlebags of the Baluchi are made in various shapes. This bag is used across the pack animal. Donkeys are kept by semisedentary Baluchis, horses by rich Baluchis.

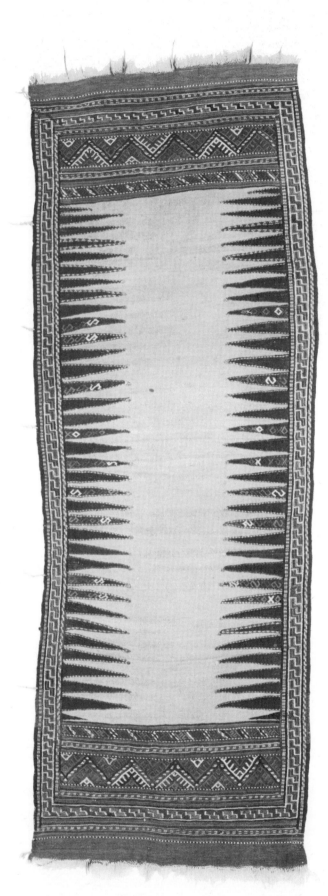

Bag face
Warp: wool
Weft: wool
Size: .98m x .64m
Technique: soumak
Origin: Kuchan area, northeastern Iran
This design of boxes, each enclosing a hooked figure of contrasting color, is reputedly woven for or by dervishes. The side borders hold the "running-dog" figure also seen in Caucasian Soumak rugs. These pieces are woven by Kurds transplanted from Kurdistan in the 17th century by Shah Abbas to serve as a buffer against rebellious Uzbekis.

Sofreh
Warp: wool
Weft: wool
Technique: mixed, tapestry-woven field, Soumak end panels and borders
Colors: camel, black, red, gold, dark greenish blue
Size: 1.82m x .65m
Origin: Kurdish (similar pieces are made by Baluchis)
The design is similar to that of a backgammon board or the board of a Middle Eastern game called *tabala*. The plain center defined by serrated sides indicates that this is a *sofreh*, a rug on which food is laid for honored guests. Diners sit around the rug on the ground or floor.

THE TURKMEN

The majority of the Turkmen people, settled and nomadic, ring the Kara Kum (the Great Desert) in areas that are now part of the USSR, Afghanistan, and Iran. They are a Turkic Mongol people renowned for their horsemanship, caravan raiding, and slave trading as well as for their fine rug weaving. The westernmost tribe is the Yomud, which occupies the Gurgan Plain east of the Caspian Sea; their homeland stretches into adjacent Turkmen S.S.R. It is divided into two groups: the *charwa* are pastoral, the *chomir* are agricultural.

Joval
Warp: wool
Weft: wool
Size: .78m x 1.19m
Brocading: wool and white cotton
Technique: plain weave with Soumak brocading, plain-weave back
Colors: dark red, lighter red, dark blue, ivory
Four rows of four Turkmen motifs called *güls* outlined in white are opposed by hooked *güls* with a darker outline, creating a three-dimensional feeling.

The Yomuds pictured in color plates 17–18 (pages 208–209) migrate from their dry season camp to find water and suitable pastures during the winter and spring wet season. (Additional Turkmen weaving material appears in Chapters 6 and 7.) The *yurt*, the portable domicile used by Turkic tribes throughout Central Asia, is a circular wooden latticework structure, usually covered with white felt, which is soon darkened by the smoke of cooking fires. The warp that the weaver is stretching extends through and out of the opening of the *yurt*. The weaver inside the *yurt* works at the narrow loom used to make a tent band (*qolong*), which goes around the *tarim* (latticework) and is visible in the interior. On the *tarim* behind her hangs a tent bag (*choval, joval*), used for transporting belongings during migration as well as in the *yurt*. (Photos: William G. Irons)

afghanistan

بایت برابر کلت دراز کن

Your footstep should equal your gullum (kilim).—Afghani proverb

HISTORY

The high plateaus of Asia run from East to West. This permits a pattern of movement conducive to migration; there are no great changes of climate with which to deal. There are a few gateways through which trade and migration routes have passed, bringing to the West silks, spices, and most of the languages of Europe. On the eastern borders of Afghanistan there are now three routes through the Khyber Pass (one of which is the railroad built by the British in the 1930s), but well into the 20th century only the ancient caravan trail existed. Where that trail crosses the modern highway markers—pictures of horses, camels, or herds of sheep—are used instead of written directions, since many of the tribal people have no written language.

In the north where Afghanistan borders on three provinces of the USSR passes through the Pamirs had been made by the Chinese as early as the 2nd century A.D. In the 7th century the Chinese used the southern Pamirs for Buddhist missions. At the Wakhan Corridor the modern nation of Afghanistan arches like a tongue into China. This route, moving eastward, was traveled by the Polo family (Marco, his father, and his uncle) in 1272.

Only the western crossing, where Afghanistan shares borders with Iran, is open, flat land. Even this route was sparsely traveled. Réclus, writing in 1885, found no evidence that districts lying at a distance from major routes had been explored and believed that the direct route from Herat to Kabul had not been traversed by any European.[1] The extraordinary traveler Arminius Vambéry had explored Afghanistan in the 1860s, much

"I can point out with pleasure that in certain parts of Central Asia I was the first European traveller . . . what made my book of travels popular was . . . the dangers in which I found myself."[2] Vanberry and his "Tartar" traveling companion wear *chalats* (also known as *chapans*), robes of distinction in Turkestan.

of the time disguised as a dervish, always as a Hajji (a member of the faithful who has made the pilgrimage, or *haj*, to Mecca).

The Afghanistan of today (18,796,000 population as of the 1974 census) has been formed by a turbulent past, a long episode of which was the bloody struggle between Russia and Britain for Central Asia, which started with the first Afghan war in 1838 and ended when its independence was recognized in 1919. The countryside is a reminder of the constant need for fortification. Built to survive random raids by tribal rivals and the onslaught of organized hordes, the architectural landscape in the East is composed of a series of fortresses, a high, square mud wall with a mud tower, a lookout with room for a rifleman. Inside is a courtyard with small domiciles and oddly constructed dugouts, making the area inaccessible from the outside.

PEOPLE

The people of Afghanistan include the Pathans, Pashtuns, Afghans, Nuristani, Tadzhiks, Hazaras, Baluchis, Turkmen, Uzbekis, and Aimaks. Languages are Pushtun, Persian (Dari Farsi, an ancient Persian that predates the Persian spoken in modern Iran), and the tribal dialects. Uzbekis and Turkmen are Turkic-speaking; Baluchis speak an Iranian tongue. The written language is an Arabic script. Almost all the inhabitants are Moslem. The large majority are Sunni (including Turkmen, Tadjik, and Uzbekis).

The difficult terrain, half almost barren desert, half mountains, is host to a climate of extremes—dry, hot summers and long snowbound winters. Afghanistan, a badly watered country although close to the sea, has developed a system of intricate underground aqueducts (*khariz*). The lack of water, the sudden transitions from cold to very hot, and earth so saline that it needs constant flushing create an impoverished terrain that is hard to change. Many Afghanis farm and graze livestock in towns and villages. The relationship between

nomads and settled village people has always been strained, although the two groups account for the largest part of the country's population. In 1968 the nomadic population was estimated at 2.5 million, or almost 15%, and that is probably low, as nomads, like sheep, are hard to count because they are mobile.[3]

The Pushtun, all of whom are referred to as Kuchis tribesmen, are of two main groups. The Durani (once called Ardali) have winter campgrounds (*kishlak*) in the plain of Kandahar and the Hilmend Valley and summer campgrounds (*ailak*) in the hills near Farah. The Ghilza'i (also called Mattai) are numerous in eastern Afghanistan. Some mix with Duranis in the Kandahar area. The Ghilza'i claim a Tartar origin, and they were the chief fighters against the British, defeating them at the Khyber Pass in 1842.

Most of these tribes are seminomadic with summer and winter grounds at either end of set migratory routes. Each clan (*khal*) has a chief, usually chosen by birth. Each tribal group is governed by a *khan*. A gathering of elders (*jirga*) serves in an advisory capacity. The people live in black goat-hair tents. Some Ghilza'i build brush huts in winter and abandon them in spring.

Hazaras are of Mongol stock and are Shiite Moslems. They control the highlands in the northwest between Kabul and Herat. Most are sedentary, living in villages. Their use of the same slopes as the nomads for grazing their flocks caused a long struggle in the 19th century. Tadzhiks are Persian-speaking townspeople who control much of the country's political power. They are descended from neighboring Russian Tadzhiks inter-

Kuchi nomads in southwest Afghanistan. The camel carries their belongings, their black goat-hair tent (*khaima*), and tent poles. The young woman wears a black dress decorated with silver coins.

A Turkmen girl with traditional headdress (*borik*) covered in red and decorated with silver ornaments (Photo c. 1880).

A modern Turkmen girl with the traditional headdress. (Photo: A. Hamid)

mixed with Turkmen, Uzbekis, and Arabs. Aimaks are a Mongo-Turkic subtribe of the Kipchaks, who live in *yurts* (*urdu*) in their summer quarters where they are pastoralists and in permanent mud houses in the winter where they are agriculturalists.

During the building of the Trans-Siberian railway by the Russians at the turn of the century Turkmen knotted rugs came into fashion in Russia and were brought out of western Turkestan in large numbers. Flat-woven pieces were sent to Russia by rail as well as picked up in the market towns of Tashkent, Samarkand, Bokhara, Beshir, Merv, and Ashkabad, through which the railway passed. Andrei Bogolubov, a military governor of the Russian Transcaspian Provinces, documented the origin and characteristics of a group of Turkmen rugs and in 1908 published his authoritative two-volume work. He mentions an annual production in that area of 1,000 *palass* [4] (a Turkic word meaning textile or rug used to designate a variety of flat-woven rugs). Ulrich Schurmann lists ten groups of rug-knotting Turkmen tribes whose work can be separately identified. [5]

CHARACTERISTICS OF AFGHANISTANI FLAT-WOVEN RUGS

Following are some features of flat-woven rugs:

1. They are sturdy, large pieces for floor (tent) use, made in one or more of several techniques:
   a. tapestry-woven reversible kilims, usually in an interlocking technique, called *ghelim*, *ghilim*, or *gullum*
   b. rugs of weft-float weave with plain weave and brocading
   c. continuous weft-float weave used to make bags and rugs
   d. warp-faced and weft-faced bands of various widths, some joined to make tent rugs. Some tent rugs are woven in double cloth
2. Warp and weft are almost always made of wool.
3. Designs are geometric and repetitive.

FORMAT OF AFGHANISTANI FLAT WEAVES

These formats are common for flat weaves.

1. Many large, wide pieces are woven. *Labijar* kilims measure as large as 4.2m x 9.1m.[6]

2. Many large tent bags—*joval* (*choval*)—and shallower tent bags (*torbeh*) are made in addition to other bag shapes.

The main elements of traditional Turkmen knotted-rug design, appearing in every example, are the major and minor *güls*, the Turkmen motifs. They probably originated in *tamghas*, tribal signs from ancient times used to identify tribes and their belongings and to name them in their shamanistic religion. The *gül* functioned in the same way as a coat of arms: anyone seeing it woven on the saddlebags and animal trappings could identify the tribe. The *gül* was "honoured like a flag, which lived and died as the fortunes of the tribes rose and fell."[7]

c

d

a

e

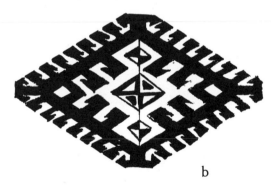

b

f

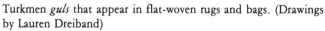

Turkmen *guls* that appear in flat-woven rugs and bags. (Drawings by Lauren Dreiband)

a. Yomud *dyrnak gül*
b. Yomud *dyrnak gül*
c. Tekke minor *gül*
d. Yomud minor *gül*
e. Kisilajak minor *gül*
f. Ersari Beschi *gül*

Torba
Warp: wool
Weft: wool
Brocading: wool and silk (green, gold)
Size: .82m x 1.04m
Technique: weft-float weave with brocaded
details, fringe added
Colors: dark red, black, green, gold
Origin: Ersari Yomut, or Saryk, Turkmen
The light areas, two shades of gold, are continuations of
the *gül,* creating background and relief, an example of
dramatic design skill.

70

Joval
Warp: wool
Weft: wool
Brocading: wool
Size: 1.21m x .63m
Technique: tapestry weave, weft-float weave
borders
Colors: dark red, light red, dark blue, white
Origin: Yomut, Turkmen

Tent bands
Warp: white cotton, handspun
Weft: white cotton, handspun
Brocading: dark wine and black wool
Size: 1.25m x 12.1m
Technique: weft-float brocading

In addition to the *qolong* (see Chapter 5) other tent bands made in different sizes to perform different functions are hung inside. Some showing a bridal procession were made for use in a bridal tent. Their function is a decorative one, made by Turkmen and Uzbek people from "an innate wish to have beautiful things in their life."[9] Recent pieces have been made commercially.

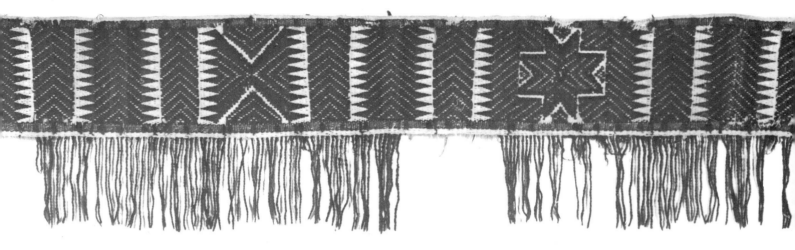

B.
Warp: white cotton, handspun
Weft: white cotton, handspun
Knotting: wool
Size: .51m x 6.15m
Technique: warp-faced plain ground, pattern
knotted with a symmetrical knot
Origin: Turkmen
Qolong are made on a narrow loom such as the one be-
ing warped by the Turkmen woman outside the *yurt*
(see Chapter 5).

Tent rugs
Warp: 2-ply wool and cotton
Weft: 2-ply wool
Size: 3.43m x 1.9m
Technique: warp-faced complementary warp-float weave
Colors: white, dark red, dark blue. golden yellow (from asparuk)
Origin: possibly Gilza'i
Tent rugs are made in narrow widths that are sewn at the selvages.

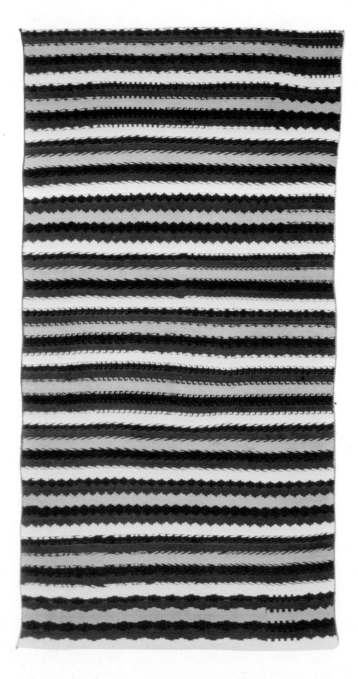

Warp: wool
Weft: wool
Technique: warp-faced warp-float weave
Size: 3.6m x 2.4m
Colors: white, red, blue, green, yellow
Tent rugs are woven on the same loom as are tent bands. A variety of narrow bands used to lash things together in the *yurt* and on the pack animals are tablet-woven, not made on a loom.

A Turkmen mother and daughter weaving a rug. A tent rug hangs behind them.

74

LABIJAR

In Labijar (which means "little river") large one-piece kilims are made. Their design consists of rows of solid-color boxes of three or more colors, with matched colors ascending diagonally. Inside each box is a figure, some of which have long forgotten meanings, others of which are still living symbols.

The symbol in the boxes of the top kilim in color plate 19 (page 210) means hunting and prosperity. The S-shape in the bottom kilim represents light and energy. The first two rugs were probably made by the Ersari Turkmen. The bottom one was made by settled Uzbeks or Aimaks. Tribal origin of the weavers is hard to ascertain[10] now that the design is woven by several groups.

A. Kilim
Warp: 2-ply wool
Weft: wool and cotton double-wefted
Size: 3.7m x 2.4m
Technique: dovetailed tapestry with continuous weft-float weave in the end rows and hair wrapped selvages

B. Kilim
Warp: dark and light wool and hair
Weft: double-wefted wool
Size: 3.77m x 1.95m
Technique: dovetailed tapestry

C. Kilim
Warp: 2-ply dark and light wool and hair
Weft: wool, double-wefted
Size: 4.12m x 2m
Technique: slit tapestry with rows of weft-brocaded detailing

One might venture to speculate on the design origin of these boxes with zoomorphic content. Sir Percy Sykes makes the point that the design of Turkmen (knotted) carpets is based on the *Bazubandi*, the metal box containing a portion of the Koran, the holy book of Islam.[11] Perhaps the boxes in Labijar kilims once related to the *Bazubandi* as well.

The brocaded rugs with a dark-red background and continuing diagonal patterning with the tribal *gül* shown in color plate 20 (page 211) are among the classics. Early oriental rug writers Mumford (1900) and Hawley (1913) class them as Merv kilims, made in the desert near the old capital of Merv. They are made by many of the Turkmen tribes. "It appears that all the tribes (i.e., Turkmen tribes) made this type of brocaded carpet, but a very thorough familiarity with these pieces and special study is required before any attempt can be made to match them up with the other tribal weavings."[8]

Brocaded rug
Warp: light and dark wool
Weft: wool
Brocading: white cotton, other colors wool

Size: 4.2m x 2.05m
Technique: weft-float brocading on plain weave ground, weft-float weave borders
Colors: dark red, dark blue, medium bluish green, white
Origin: Yomut, Turkmen

MAIMANA

Maimana is a town in which big, colorful kilims are marketed. They are made in Maimana and the neighboring areas by Turkmen, Uzbek and Hazara people. Some are made in Ankhoy, a town near the Russian Uzbekistan border. The designs are large, bold connected diamonds or long lightning-stroke patterns enclose large diamond medallions. These kilims have minimal or no side borders. Older pieces were made with natural dyes; now American, German, and English dyes are used.

Kilim
Warp: 2-ply hair
Weft: wool, double-wefted
Size: 3.72m x 2.1m
Technique: reversible slit tapestry
The slits are inconspicuous because of the closeness of the weave. There is Soumak detail on two sides.

A

B

A. *Khorjin* (double saddlebag)
Warp: wool
Weft: wool
Brocading: wool and cotton
Size: 1.6m x .67m
Technique: continuous weft-float weave, weft-float brocading, Soumak detailing and plain-weave back
Origin: Larghabi, near Herat

B. Bag
Warp: wool
Weft: wool
Brocading: wool
Technique: continuous weft float weave with braided fringe and macramé-knotted sides
Origin: Larghabi
Size: .75m x 1.16m

C. *Khorjin* (camel bag)
Warp: wool
Weft: wool
Size: 1.87m x .85m
Technique: dovetailed tapestry weave, striped plain-weave back, made in one piece with tassels added
This striking design makes effective use of a motif widely seen in Yomud weaving.

C

THE BALUCHI

Baluchi knotted rugs are easily identifiable. One frequent example is a small prayer rug with a camel-hair field and a geometricized tree of life in the center. Another distinctive design is a scattering of small starlike figures, often in white, in a center field. When Baluchi rugs were first seen in America, they were called constellation rugs because the stars followed the location of well-known constellations in the night sky.

Baluchi flat-woven rugs are different in design from knotted rugs. Some flat-woven pieces are made by tribes that make no knotted rugs. An interesting observation was made by Richard Kassow on reports from early 19th-century travelers among the Baluchis: "Certainly the mention of rugs (a subject seldom dwelt upon by travellers in Baluchistan) diminishes whenever the desert makes its appearance, to be replaced by occasional notices of flat-woven textiles and felts."[12]

Following are some characteristics of Baluchi flat weaves.

1. Camel wool is used by certain tribes for the weft, thus making a camel-color rug.

2. Goat hair is used for the selvages or sides.

3. There is a limited range of color, based on the colors available in the landscape. Dark blue (indigo), dark red (madder), black (wild pistachio), yellows and oranges (onion), and natural sheep wool and goat hair are common colors.

4. Many tassels and beads are used to decorate saddle- and other bags.

5. Common designs on bag faces are rows of small diamonds and other infinitely repeated figures. Zigzags (lightning strokes) are used on patterned ends.

6. Bags and rugs are heavily woven (as if to insulate the contents against the relentless wind, the whirling dust, the burning heat of the plains in summer, and the freezing plateaus that make up the extreme climate of Baluchistan).

Sofreh
Warp: 2-ply hair (light) and wool (dark)
Weft: wool
Size: 1.42m x .65m
Technique: dovetailed tapestry weave, brocaded sides, tufted details
Origin: Baluchi

In Afghanistan a *sofreh* is called *distar khan*, meaning "hand of the khan." The traditional hospitality of the khan to invited guests extended as far as the *sofreh* was long.

Rug
Warp: 2-ply goat hair
Weft: double-wefted wool
Size: 2.15m x 1.33m
Technique: mixed—bands of interlocked
tapestry weave and bands of weft-float weave,
Soumak and tufted detail, made in two parts
Colors: dark blue, brown, ivory, dark red,
orange and green (tufts)
Origin: Baluchi

Salt bag
Warp: hair
Weft: wool—very dark blue, brick red, purple, saffron, natural dark and light tones
Brocading: wool
Technique: continuous weft-float weave, six stripes of Soumak detailing, striped plain-weave back
Origin: Baluchi
Size: .53m x .43m

Kilim runner
Warp: 2-ply wool
Weft: dark brown horsehair, white cotton, wool
Colors: brown, blue, black, red, white
Technique: slit tapestry, wrapped tassels, double-wefted
Origin: probably Arabian tribe
Size: 4.7m x .9m

Afghani *durrie*. (Loaned by Khalil Zahiri)

DURRIES

Durries, flat-woven rugs made with cotton warp and weft, are commonly identified with India but are also made in Afghanistan and in other parts of Asia. They were made by weavers in their own households and in prisons with convict labor. *Durries* are now a good-sized industry, providing new and traditional designs for export. *Durries* are called *satrangi* in Afghanistan because of the frequently used design motif of elongated side triangles, which resemble those on a *tabala* (*satrang*) board.

A Turkmen dealer in the Kabul rug bazaar holds up an Afghani *durrie.*

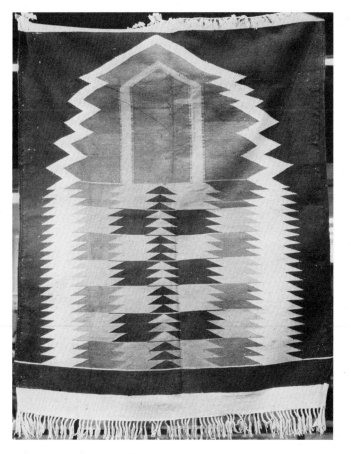

Prayer *durrie*
Warp: cotton
Weft: cotton
Technique: dovetailed tapestry weave
Colors: ground, dark green; pink, yellow, light green
Origin: Afghanistan
Size: 1.57m x 1.22m

ussr

To a good sheep, good pasture.—Ukrainian proverb

The Union of Soviet Socialist Republics, the world's largest conglomerate, covers one-sixth of the earth's surface. It sprawls across Asia, reaching to the seas on its entire northern and eastern borders and covering more than one-third the territory of Asia. In the South, moving from East to West, it shares common borders with China, Afghanistan, Iran, and Turkey. In the West it extends into Europe, bordering Poland and Rumania, reaching the Baltic Sea, and extending North to border Finland.

This vast country has been evolving into its present shape for 500 years. Its population of 241,720,134 (1970) contains more than 100 ethnic peoples, organized into 15 republics, of which some are subdivided into Autonomous Soviet Socialist Republics, some into Regions (*oblasts*), and some into Territories (*krays*).

The weaving peoples among the Soviets inhabit western Turkestan, the Caucasus, and Eastern Europe. Most of what was once Turkestan is now in the U.S.S.R. What was known as Turkestan extended from the eastern shore of the Caspian Sea to the easternmost reaches of the Tarim Basin, now in Sinkiang Province, China. The occupation of this area by Russia in 1881 was followed by the creation of the political divisions that reduced Turkestan to one of five republics: Turkestan, Uzbekistan, Tadjikistan, Kazakistan, and Kirgizistan. The Turkmen share ancestors with the Mongols to the East and with the Turanians to the North. The easternmost of the Soviet Turkestan Republics is remote Kirgizistan.

THE KIRGIZ

One of the most nomadic of the tribes encountered in this volume are the Kirgiz. They were at one time the most numerous tribe as well, estimated at 3 million in the 1880s.[1] In many respects they follow the same pattern as did their Mongol ancestors in inner Asia. In a 16th-century drawing by a Moghul artist one can see a soldier of the Moghul emperor wearing the same conical felt hat that the Kirgiz tribesman shown here wears.

Like their neighbors, the Turkmen, the Kirgiz rely on their horses, the animal par excellence of the steppes. Another prized animal of the Kirgiz is the double-humped Bactrian camel, which is powerful and tall, averaging more than 6' at the hump and weighing as much as half a ton. The humps may hold 200 pounds of fat, used by the camel when other food is not available. As the fat is used, the humps shrink, sometimes almost completely. The thick undercoat of wooly hair protects the Bactrian camel in the extreme cold and is used by the Kirgiz for weaving. A Persian proverb says, "The camel eats useless weeds, carries heavy burdens, and does no one harm."

Although the Kirgiz produce flat-woven and knotted rugs, they have been known primarily as felt makers. The earliest felt rugs known to man have been found in this area. Along with the knotted rugs found in the *kurgans* (burial tombs) at Pazyryk in the Altai Mountains (5th century B.C.) were felted rugs.[2] Those felts and others found in northern Mongolia and eastern Turkestan show vestiges of a tradition of finely designed and beautifully colored pieces made for a nomadic aristocracy. Fine felts with more complex designs than recent examples were widely used in central and western Asia in courts as well as in nomadic dwellings.[3] (Some nomadic dwellings were courts, and the Khan of Khiva, for example, had a sumptuously appointed *yurt* in the inner courtyard of his palace.) In the same group of tombs at Pazyryk were found the bodies of horses used in funeral processions, which wore richly decorated saddles and trappings. Elaborate felt saddle covers were found, as well as covers decorated with fine embroidered Chinese silk, showing that the highly civilized nomads from this Scythian-related culture were in touch with China in the East (as they were with Persia in the West). Felts had ceremonial uses as well as utilitarian and decorative. Purple or scarlet felt draped the funeral pyre of a friend of Alexander the Great in 324 B.C.; blue felt covered the minarets of the mosques of Tabriz when the city mourned the death of a Genghisid ruler; and white felt was used for a variety of purposes, usually to denote honor or respect.[4]

Felt made of unspun wool makes a relatively light and flexible material, not difficult to transport on a beast of burden. It is the major textile of the Kirgiz. The conversion of loose wool into felt is accomplished by beating the spread-out wool into a flat mass, then saturating it with hot water and rolling it (the Kirgiz roll it in a straw mat), usually moving it around while applying some pressure. The yaks of the Kirgiz drag the rolled felt back and forward for this purpose.[5] The patterning elements are added by cutting and laying cut

patterns out on the finished felt, then stamping and pressing them in until they fuse with the background. Some are decorated by sewing on the cutout designs.

Much of the felt is made from undyed wool, in colors natural to the sheep of the region. White felt is prized; it is used for the covering of the bridal *yurt* (or *alajak*), which later turns dark, as well as for the tent of honored guests. White tents are usually a sign of richness; poorer tents are darkened by the cooking fires or initially made from darker wool.

The designs of the felted rugs (*koshma* in Russian, *namat* in Turkic) among the Kirgiz and the other tribal peoples of the five Russian provinces that constitute Turkestan vary from tribe to tribe and are based on traditional motifs; those of western Turkestan are geometric, while those of eastern Turkestan are undulating, formed in ribbonlike lines.

In addition to the use of felt, a fine material for insulation, for the *yurt* and the *namats*, it is used for saddlebags, animal covers, tent ornaments, and articles of clothing, including ornamental felt stockings called *paypaq*. The importance of felt for the nomads of this area is shown by the Chinese rubric "the land of felt."[6]

The very simple designs of this felt rug and one

A Kirgiz family in front of their felt *yurt*. They wear *chalats* made from silk ikat, an intricate resist-dyed fabric. (Photo c. 1880)

shown on page 150, one from western and the other from eastern Turkestan, show a deterioration from ancient examples. These are used as saddle covers and tent rugs. Bogolyubov (Governor of Russian Turkestan at the end of the 19th century) estimated an annual output of 60,000 *koshmas* from the entire Transcaspian area.[7] The Kirgiz, although Sunni Moslems, retain shamanistic beliefs. It is thought that the use of certain symbols served a ritual purpose, to pay honor to a god or to ward off sickness.

KAZAKHSTAN

The Kazakhs are a Turkic-speaking Moslem people whose nomadic ancestors settled in this region in the 13th and 14th centuries. They were formerly called the Kirgiz by the Russians, who had a phonetic conflict with the word "cossack." The original name was restored, and in 1925 their state was named Kazakh.

Kazakhstan is an arid steppe. The Kizil Kum desert was traditionally a land of pastoral nomads, who are now sedentary. Alfred Hudson studied the Kazakh social structure of the mid 19th century just before the Russian conquest of Central Asia.[8] At that time the Kazakhs lived in *yurts*, as do many of their descendants today. Their tents, called *kibitkas* in Russian, were grouped in fives or tens, called an *Yj*. Several hundred *kibitkas* made an *aul*, the functioning community, sometimes equaling the whole encampment. Population was calculated by multiplying the number of *kibitkas* (*yurts*) by the number of people comprising one family (usually 5). Kazakh life was organized into summer (*çaz*) pasturing on open ranges, which were reached in a May to June migration, followed by autumn (*kyz*) shearing of sheep (*kyzem*), harvesting (for those who were agriculturalists), and winter preparation. Winter was a season of comparative relaxation after the busy fall. The pattern of the past was to graze herds in the open throughout the winter. At the time of Hudson's study tribesmen were storing up supplies and building shelter for the animals against the weather.

The word that designates Kazakh tribal organization, *orda* ("horde"), is used to describe the groupings during the time of Genghis Khan and Tamerlane. The Kazakhs were originally separated into three *ordas*, which apparently became mixed with Kirgiz in the East, with the Uzebekis, a reform movement under Uzbek Khan, in the center, and with the Turkmens in the West.

The status of women in Kazakh society and to some degree in Turkic-Mongol nomadic society in general depended largely on her place in the family. The senior wife generally dominated the household. Each wife had her own *yurt* and brought up her children more or less separately when possible. All children of a father referred to all the wives as mother (*cece*). After infancy boys were brought up by the father, girls by the mother, and the usual division of labor set in. The girls learned to do all the usual domestic tasks and to spin, weave, and make felt.

The Kazakhs lived in felt *yurts*. In summer the felt was removed, leaving the openwork reed matting, a very suitable way of dealing with the elements. Inside the *yurt* the ground was covered with felt rugs, decorative felts, and some woven hangings. On the women's side of the *yurt* were kept the domestic utensils. On the men's side were kept saddles, animal gear, hunting equipment, and weapons. A similar division of belongings occurs in the tents of most nomadic peoples.[9]

Bag face
Warp: wool
Weft: wool
Brocading: wool
Size: .46m x .69m
Technique: brocaded with heavy fringes and added long tablet-woven ties
Colors: dark red (field), gold, white, black

A very graphic effect is created by the dark outlining around the four medallions, a common design technique of these weavers. Neither the design in the border nor the white outlined design that occurs four times in the center field is a classic *gül*. In previous times a tribal weaver would never weave a *gül* or motif of another tribe. In recent times cultural diffusion and commercialism has brought about many hybrid designs. Bags and flat-woven rugs done in the same design, color, and technique are known in the bazaars of Central Asia as *kazakh*.

UZBEKISTAN

Western Turkestan was the western part of the empire founded by the Turks in the sixth century, and, like most of Central Asia, it had been Turkic-dominated until the arrival of the Russians. The Uzbeks were not one of the original Turkmen tribes. The first Uzbeks were the followers of Uzbek Khan, a 14th-century leader. People of many tribal origins, like Uzbek Khan, were willing to abandon pre–Islamic shamanistic beliefs and to embrace Islam. After the conquest of the area by Islam Turkestan was a political and cultural center of the Mohammedan world. Under Timur (Tamerlane), whose capital was Samarkand, artists and craftsmen were brought to the area from all over the world. Its buildings are covered with colored tiles that reflect light; the large blue domes and minarets of its mosques are visible from a distance above its walls. The old saying, "While Mecca is the heart, Samarkand is the head of Islam," shows how important was the cultural influence of Samarkand in the Moslem empire.

Bokhara, famous as a center of learning (Mohammed is said to have said, "Elsewhere the light descends from above; in Bokhara it radiates upwards"), was also renowned for its bazaars. Many of the knotted rugs of Central Asia that became so popular in the West after the Russian penetration of the area were found in Bokhara and wrongly attributed to that city; they were actually made in various places by nomadic Turkmen from subtribes including Yomud, Salor, Tekke, and Ersari. Bokhara and the other cities of western Turkestan are completely dependent on irrigation from the four rivers that water that rich area. The Amu Daria, one of those rivers, has changed its course more than once, leaving entire cities and towns in the Kara Kum desert in ruins.

Khiva, the third famous city of what is now Soviet Uzbekistan, was known as one of the chief slave markets in Asia. The Turkmen, specialists in raiding towns and caravans for slaves, sold their gangs of captives here. The feared Turkmen had stopped killing most captives taken in raids, except for the aged and infirm, after having discovered their value as slaves. Being Sunni Moslems, their raids on villages and caravans of Shiite Persians were considered a religious pilgrimage against the heretic. The Turkmen did not usually kidnap or kill "Sons of David"—Christians and Jews—or members of other Sunni groups. After the Russian penetration, however, many Russians were enslaved, as they were prized as laborers. They were primarily sold to the khan of Khiva and other dignitaries; many rose to the highest positions in the state. The Russian Governor General proclaimed the abolition of slavery after a bloody slave rebellion by Russian slaves in 1873.

Before the arrival of the Russians in western Turkestan the political supremacy in the settled areas belonged to the Uzbekis. Of Turkic stock, their language, called Jagatai or Uigur, is one of the most polished of the Turkic tongues. The Manghit Uzbeks, part of the Khanate of Bokhara, claim to be the oldest and most noble.

A great number of Uzbeks were settled, though some were nomadic. Many live in northern Afghanistan, particularly in the area of Maimana, where they long maintained independence from Bokhara, Persia, and Afghanistan. Many of the rugs shown in Chapter 6 were made by Uzbeks.

The population of Uzbekistan, in addition to Uzbeks, consists of a large number of Tajiks and some Iranians, Turkmen, and Sarts, the name given to members of the mixed settled population. Lindahl maintains that a large part of the population of present-day Uzbekistan is Arab: "Many Arabs who, from the 8th century onwards emigrated to Central Asia, have adopted the way of life and language of the Uzbeks and Tadiks but they still retain traits of an independent culture in their kilim patterns."[10] Other sources do not refer to settled people as Arab, assuming that, unless they are whole tribes, they have been absorbed.

Uzbeks are known to weave with very fine wool. "Uzbek Tartars have the finest wool of any people for they feed their sheep with great care and generally undercover, protecting them even when exposed as we do our horses."[11] With centuries of care sheep with long, silky fleeces have evolved, the cold dry climate of the plateau providing a healthy habitat.

Dowry rug
Warp: 2-ply wool
Weft: double-wefted wool
Brocading: wool
Size: 2.03m x 1.14m
Technique: plain-weave ground, Soumak detail, weft-float weave
Colors: white (background), red, blue, yellow
Origin: Uzbek
The repeating figure is the ram's horn, a classic Turkmen motif. Such a dowry rug is used to divide the *yurt* during wedding ceremonies.[12] It separates the bride and groom's section for a set period, always more than a year. Before and after marriage there is a carefully regulated tribal code governing the relationship between bride and groom among Turkmen as well as Uzbeks.

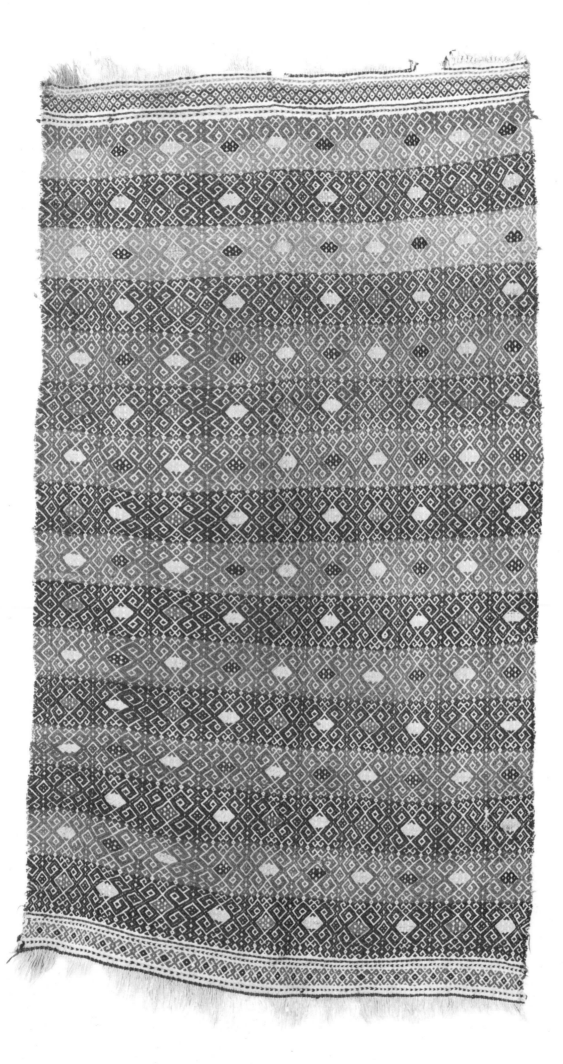

Embroidered rug

Warp: unplied wool, some hair carded in, two threads treated as one

Weft: same as warp

Embroidery: very fine 2-ply wool

Size: 3.5m x 1.36m

Technique: balanced plain-weave ground, five or more different embroidery stitches

Colors: deep red, white, off-white, yellow, salmon, dark blue

Design elements from several Turkmen tribes are apparent in this rug. The rhomboid, divided into four parts, is the Uzbeki *gül* known as *kalkan,* which is similar to the Salor *gül.* Made in a quiltlike manner, each rhomboid is separately attached, as is each star in the end borders and the sections of the side border. Around each rhomboid is a series of small birds' feet, a Tekke design element. The group of dots in the *güls'* centers is used by Yomud tribes. The stars in the end borders are eight-pointed Stars of Solomon, representative of the totemic origin of this ancient design. There is some question as to the traditional method of constructing these pieces. A recent observer saw one being assembled in an Uzbeki home by several women. It is possible that they were woven in long, narrow strips, which were cut and later sewn together.[13]

A. Complete rug
B. One *gül*
C. Back of one medallion

A

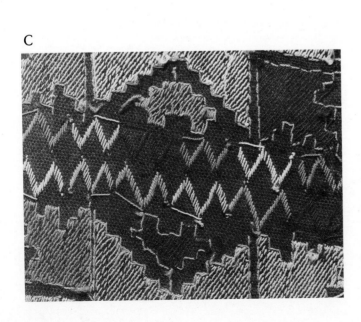

C

B

88

Sofreh
Warp: 2-ply hair
Weft: wool
Technique: double interlocked tapestry, double-wefted
Color: natural brown (background), red, green, blue, yellow, white
Size: 6.9m x 66m
Origin: probably Uzbek
The plain field is covered with four isolated geometric cruciform motifs, similar to the "eye of god" in Mexican folk art and used in many cultures since Sumerian times. The generosity of the owner of this *sofreh* cannot be questioned, since its length permits the serving of a large number of honored guests.
A. Half view
B. Quarter view

A

B

TURKMEN SSR

Salor, Tekke, Saryk, Karakalpak, Yomud, Ogurjali, Chaudor, Ersari, and Kizyl Arak are the tribes of the Turkmen. No oasis in this region or in all of ancient Turkestan is without its periods of dominance by various Turkmen tribes, although the area was so difficult to inhabit that it was never hospitable even to the Turkmen, thus reinforcing the Turkmen's nomadic proclivity. The case against settlement—why build a city when it will be ruins and sand in a thousand years?—was reinforced again and again by history: Merv is an example.

As mentioned in Chapter 5, the Turkmen were nomadic, marauding, and fierce, and it was dangerous to travel in Turkmen country. A proverb stated, "You will never reach Mecca, I fear: for you are on the road to Turkestan." An 1822 best-seller referred to as the earliest authentic description of the Turkmen by a westerner tells the true story of a young soldier disguised as a Yomud who made his way to Khiva and returned to Moscow to write about it.[14] Others had not been so lucky.

The weavings of the Turkmen include the valued knotted rugs and bags (*khorjin, jolar, joval,* for example) fine brocaded rugs and bags of many sizes and shapes, a variety of functional and decorative bands and rugs for the *yurt* (*kaponuk,* the door surround, and *engsi,* used as a tent door, are distinctive Turkmen weavings), and many unique trappings (the *osmulduk,* a five-sided tasseled saddle piece, is a collector's favorite). A complete set of trappings was made for the wedding procession. The richness of the weaving reflects the skill of Turkmen women and the proud tradition of the tribes.

The Turkmen who did not cross the neighboring borders of Iran and Afghanistan at the Soviet takeover lead almost totally different lives today. Many are engaged in raising cotton and breeding sheep for Astrakhan lamb fur. As early as 1899 the Ministry of State Properties invited Tekkes to teach rug making to Russians. Rug weaving is still supported by the central government.

The capital of Turkmen SSR, Ashkhabad, is a center of production for Turkmen knotted rugs in modern versions of traditional designs: "Thus, for instance, in one carpet cotton-heads and corn-cobs were incorporated into the medallions; in another silhouette of planes, tanks, and battleships were transformed to resemble *güls.*"[15] Traditional flat-woven pieces, including *jovals* and *torbehs,* are still being exported. Some are old; some might have been recently produced in workshop conditions.

Brocaded rug
Warp: natural wool
Weft: red wool
Brocading: white cotton; wool
Technique: interlocked tapestry weave, weft-float weave
Colors: white, brick red, dark blue
Size: 2.2m x .96m
Origin: Yomud

Another classic type of flat-woven rugs, these were known as Bokhara kilims because they were found in the bazaars of Bokhara. The design elements are also found in other Turkmen and Uzbeki kilims, tent bands, and bags, but added drama derives from this format. The side borders seem hardly able to contain the dynamic design. (Loaned by Ali MacGraw)

THE CAUCASUS

The Caucasian mountain system perplexes geographers and observers alike. It rises like a barrier at the eastern end of the Black Sea, as if separated from Asia, but was thought by some people to be part of the mountain range of Central Asia and the great Asian plains. On modern maps it is part of Europe. As evidenced by myth, the Greeks sought their origins in the Caucasus, also directing the Argonaut expedition there in search of the Golden Fleece.

This land was supposed to be inhabited by the purest representatives of the race, and the term "Caucasian" is officially used in the United States as the synonym for White, Aryan, or Indo-European stock. Eliseé Réclus theorizes as to how this use of the word derived: "A sort of superstition, perhaps associated with the Promethean myth (it was to a rock in the Caucasus that Deucalion, the son of Prometheus, who peopled Greece, was bound) formerly induced savants to apply the term 'Caucasian' to all the fair European and Asiatic races, thus testifying to the instinctive reverence with which the nations have ever regarded these mountains forming the barrier between two worlds."[16] Actually, whole areas of the Caucasus are populated by Turkic and Mongol peoples. The Caucasus is a broken, mountainous region divided by hundreds of ravines. The Great Caucasus stretches from the northeast shore of the Black Sea in a south and easterly direction to the Caspian Sea. The Lesser Caucasus is parallel and the southern slopes, which turn towards Asia, face the sun and have always been the most densely populated areas. The southern region was called the Transcaucasia by Europeans.

In the northeast were found Nogai Turks, nomadic people descended from the previous masters of the Crimea, the Mongols. "Like their poor neighbours the Stavropol and Astrakhan Kalmuks, they dwell in felt tents, and when removing to fresh pastures they place their children in the panniers carried by the camels on whose hump the women are perched and in this order the caravan crosses the desert wastes. Thus are the familiar scenes of Central Asia repeated on the western shores of the Caspian, though this Asiatic region is being gradually contracted, according as the Mongoloid populations are being driven back by the Russians."[17]

Further south on the Caspian, Derbent was a great trading center. In the last quarter of the 18th century, when some Russians and Englishmen ventured into the Caucasus, Jon Bell wrote in his *Travels from St. Petersburg in Russia to Various Parts of Asia* that in Derbent "they have great store of cattle, particularly of sheep, which produce the finest wool I have seen in any part. Whether the famous Golden Fleece was the product of these parts or not I shall leave others to determine."[18] Bell also had a backstairs view of the interior of a mosque in Derbent, where he was surprised to find that the floor was laid with mats and carpets in place of the pews to which he was accustomed in western churches.

Most rug production seems to have taken place in the south and on the southeast, bordering the Caspian Sea perhaps as a consequence of climatic conditions.[19] This part of the Caucasus politically encompasses the Soviet Republics of Georgia, Dagestan, Armenia, and Azerbaijan. Russian occupation was well established by the early 1800s. Many of the Caucasian provinces had previously been under Persian rule from the time of Shah Abbas, and some southwestern areas had been Turkish.

The close relationships between the people occupying these border areas make rug attribution difficult. Some of the rugs shown in Chapters 4 and 5 are border pieces and should be examined along with the rugs on the following pages, with which they share some common features and some part of a common past.

The ethnography of the Caucasus is very complex; anthropologists report as many as 350 tribes, speaking 150 different languages. Of the people of the Caucasus, the most prolific rug weavers are settled Azeri Turks and Kurds, Armenians, and nomadic peoples of the Mughan area and the East.

According to oriental mythologies the Caucasus (*Kak-kaf* or *Kaf-dagh* in Turkic) was a section of "the chain that girdles the world." If the rugs of the Caucasus contribute one link in that chain, the chain is made stronger and more beautiful by their presence. The knotted rugs of the Caucasus are prized by collectors; like those vigorous knotted rugs, the kilims and soumaks of the Caucasus are treasures of a fine weaving tradition. Some characteristics of Caucasian flat weaves are as follows.

1. Kilims are made in one piece in medium sizes (4½' x 9', 5' x 10', 5' x 9½' are typical), with the length almost double the width.

2. Warp and weft are wool.

3. Technique is reversible slit-tapestry weave.

4. Designs are bold and simple. Horizontal rows of geometric medallions, sometimes alternating with bands of solid color or rows of diagonal medallions, make up the pattern of one type.

5. Kilims are without borders or have one narrow border surrounding the field.

6. Colors from natural dye materials are clear, cool and pleasing, such as a characteristic blue-green.[20]

7. Some animal covers and many saddlebags were made in Soumak weave. Their designs often consist of repeated, conventionalized animal forms.

8. Soumaks are made in traditional designs and techniques. Most typical are one-piece Soumak rugs of medium (4′ x 6½′, 5′ x 7′) and large (8′ x 10′, 8′ x 11′, 9′ x 12′) size.

9. The most common Soumak design is that of three or four octagonal medallions centered on a field filled with striking asymmetrical shapes, surrounded by geometricized floral borders.

10. Warps of Soumaks and kilims terminate in the finely braided ends.

Kilim (color plate 21, page 212)
Warp: 2-ply wool, dark and light yarn
Weft: double-wefted wool
Technique: slit-tapestry weave
Origin: northeastern Caucasus
Size: 3m x 1.5m

The Caucasian kilim design referred to as *palas* is shown in color plate 22 (page 212). The term may derive from the French *paillasse*, referring to a straw mattress or woven mat, which may have been mistakenly interpreted as "pileless" and used to denote rugs without pile, such as kilims and other flat weaves.
Kilim
Warp: 2-ply wool, light and dark yarn
Weft: double-wefted wool
Technique: plain-weave stripes, slit tapestry, Soumak detail
Size: 2.7m x 1.47m
Origin: southern Caucasus

Kilim
Warp: wool
Weft: wool
Technique: slit-tapestry weave
Colors: indigo (field), gold, brick red, ivory, rust, red, medium blue, olive green, brown
Origin: Caucasus, possibly Daghestan or Kuba
Size: 3.35m x 1.87m

This is a typical Caucasian kilim known in the rug trade as Kuba although the exact origin is not determined. The design is termed animal pelt, turtle, or, conservatively, palmette. The tiny figures at the edge of the field are squeezed in as if the weaver was compelled to include them. (Loaned by Sotheby Parke Bernet, Los Angeles)

Kilim

Warp: 2-ply wool, dark and light yarn
Weft: double-wefted wool
Technique: slit-tapestry weave, warp ends knotted to form 1'' of webbing
Colors: dark brown, dark blue, teal blue, red, yellow, white
Origin: southern Caucasus

This is a typical kilim of the southern Caucasus known in the rug trade as Shirvan although the exact origin is not determined. A borderless rug with rows of hexagons and triangles.

Kilim

Warp: light and dark wool
Weft: wool
Technique: slit-tapestry weave
Colors: dark blue, light blue, off-white, yellowish white, pink, rose, brown
Size: 2.88m x 1.32m

This looks like a typical kilim from the southern Caucasus but has a four-sided border characteristic of Persian kilims. The vine-patterned stripes between the rows of medallions are also found in Persian kilims. This might be a border piece from either Iran or the Caucasus.

Soumaks

Flat-woven rugs in the Soumak and countered-Soumak technique (see Chapter 3) are grouped together as Caucasian Soumaks. They have intricate designs that are in part related to the designs of certain Anatolian and Caucasian knotted rugs and in part entirely unique. They are distinct from any other flat-woven pieces.

The origins of the term "Soumak" have been discussed at length by many writers and collectors. Soumak rugs had been called "Kashmirs" from a farfetched association with Kashmir shawls—the only similarity is that loose threads are left on the back of both. In the case of Soumaks the threads left by the discontinuous-weft colors are usually not cut but left to lie flat on the back of the rug.

The designs are fascinating to study, filled with powerful elements that seem a part of a forgotten language. In the patterns of Caucasian Soumaks (and designs of certain Caucasian knotted rugs) one wants to find lost symbols. Many people with varied views have set out to decipher them. Chances are that continuing cultural diffusion and the interrelationships of weaving peoples have made their marks on Caucasian Soumaks; there is not one code waiting to be broken. Although a recurring motif in Caucasian Soumaks is a rocketlike figure on what could be a launching pad (Page 96 and Color Plate 23), the reader should stay earthbound in his interpretation!

Charles Grant Ellis analyzed a 15th- or 16th-century Soumak rug by tracing its history, describing its technique, and comparing it to other Soumak woven and knotted rugs, including some shown in European paintings. In isolating the design elements he refers to rugs from Spain, Turkey, Persia, Egypt, China, Central Asia, and the Caucasus, relating design elements, details, borders, and general style: "The compilation of so many examples has seemed useful in order to properly emphasize the comparative universality of usage of the various design ideas and details which go to make up the patterning of our Soumak carpet. . . . what group of rug designs can more properly be termed international than this?"[21]

Soumak rug
Warp: 2-ply white wool
Weft: single-ply wool
Technique: Soumak (countered?), 1 weft between rows
Colors: dark brown, dark blue, blue, rose, pink, yellow-tan
Size: 3m x 1.76m
Date: 16th century
(Loaned by the Textile Museum, Washington, D.C.)

Soumak rug
Warp: light, lustrous 3-ply wool
Weft: 2-ply wool
Size: 3.15m x 2.15m
Technique: countered soumak
Date: late 19th century
The brick-red field of the rug shown in color plate 23 (page 213) is filled with lozenges with dark blue arm-like extensions, forming geometric outlines of stacked squares in houselike shapes. This design is similar to one found in Kuba dragon rugs. The outer and inner borders show the running-dog motif, sometimes identified as Georgian in origin. Georgia, in the south-central Caucasus, was not known as a weaving area, although Tiflis, its capital, had a large Armenian population that might have produced some rugs with a similar design.

The field of the rug shown in color plate 24A (page 214) is filled with geometricized flowers. The drawing of the running-dog motif in the outer border is typical. The inner border contains meandering rosettes. The design is similar to certain knotted rugs from the eastern Caucasus. (Loaned by Marilyn Noel)
A. Soumak rug
Warp: wool
Weft: wool
Technique: countered Soumak
Size: 2.52m x .925m

The lustrous tones of the fine wools composing the rug shown in color plate 24B, C (page 214) have softened with age. The barber-pole stripes (1'' and 1½'' wide) are drawn to meet as chevrons in the center. The stripes hold S-shaped motifs, zigzags, sitting dogs, horses, a long-legged bird, and a creature that looks like a dragon from a children's book. The diagonal stripes and soft colors are typical of knotted rugs from Gendje, where this one was possibly made. (Loaned by Marilyn Noel)
B, C. Soumak rug
Warp: wool
Weft: wool
Technique: countered Soumak
Size: 1.32m x .652m

Soumak rug
Warp: 2-ply wool
Weft: single-ply wool
Technique: countered Soumak with braided warp ends
Size: 2.87m x 1.67m
Origin: probably Kuba Seichur
Date: late 19th century
The brick-red field holds four and a half intricate lozenges, each with a cruciform shape containing conventionalized flowers. The center flower also appears in Shirvan knotted rugs. Connected latch hooks forming triangular shapes fill the rest of the field, surrounded by a reciprocal trefoil border on the inside of the center-field edge. The design is called a sunburst pattern. The S-shaped motif in the three borders is seen in Seichur knotted rugs. (Loaned by Victor Dermerdjian)

Soumak rug
Warp: light wool
Weft: wool
Technique: countered Soumak with characteristic knotted-warp fringe
Size: 2m x 1.46m
Colors: black, dark blue, medium blue, light blue, white, yellow, pink, brick red, green
Date: 19th century

The three center medallions contain a bordered octagon, which in turn contains a geometric figure with a geometric red flower inside a rosette. Around the sides of the brick-red field are shapes resembling rockets on launching pads. The field has six additional octagons and is edged by a reciprocal inside border. The main border (yellow) contains alternating octagons and boxes with geometric figures. On either side is a small border of birdlike patterns. The outer border is done in the running-dog pattern. The colors were obtained from vegetable and mineral dyes—the black from iron pyrite, which can eat away the wool, thus many rugs show wear in the black areas first. (Loaned by Julia Winston)

Silés

Silé (*sileh*) is used in the rug trade to describe a rug woven in the Soumak technique in designs that "show in extreme stylization, the dragons [of dragon rugs] themselves."[22] The large S-shaped forms contain more of the same. In the openings are hourglass figures. The design usually adheres rigidly to the model. Most examples have two bird or dragon heads attached to each large S. They are made in two pieces, each with eight large forms, making a total of sixteen.

Silé

A. Quarter view
B. Detail
Warp: 2-ply wool
Weft: wool
Brocading: wool
Technique: countered soumak
Size: 2.7m x .95m
Colors: brick-red (ground), white, black, brown, indigo blue, teal blue-green, light blue, orange, yellow

This *silé* conforms to the design except that the bird or dragon heads have been geometricized into boxes with an appendage, which looks like a dragon's tongue. The blue-green typical of the Caucasus, a rich, soft tone, is obtained by mixing indigo blue with a yellow derived from pomegranate skins. (Loaned by Albert Ouzounian)

A

B

Verneh

Brocaded covers with bird and animal designs, made in the Caucasus, are called *Vernehs* in the rug trade. They are similar to Turkish examples. Among rug writers and travelers only one has named Verneh as their place of origin: "Verneh, near Shusha, has produced [woven] rugs with stylized animals and birds within square fields, or animals and small ornamental devices arranged in diagonal stripes."[23]

Verneh cover
Warp: wool
Weft: wool
Technique: brocading with Soumak details, made in two parts
Size: 2.34m x 1.88m
Colors: red (field), midnight blue (border)
Very regular rows of one-humped camels fill the field and borders, which also include two baby camels. The square border motif is one often found in flat-woven Anatolian pieces. (Courtesy of Sotheby Park Bernet, New York)

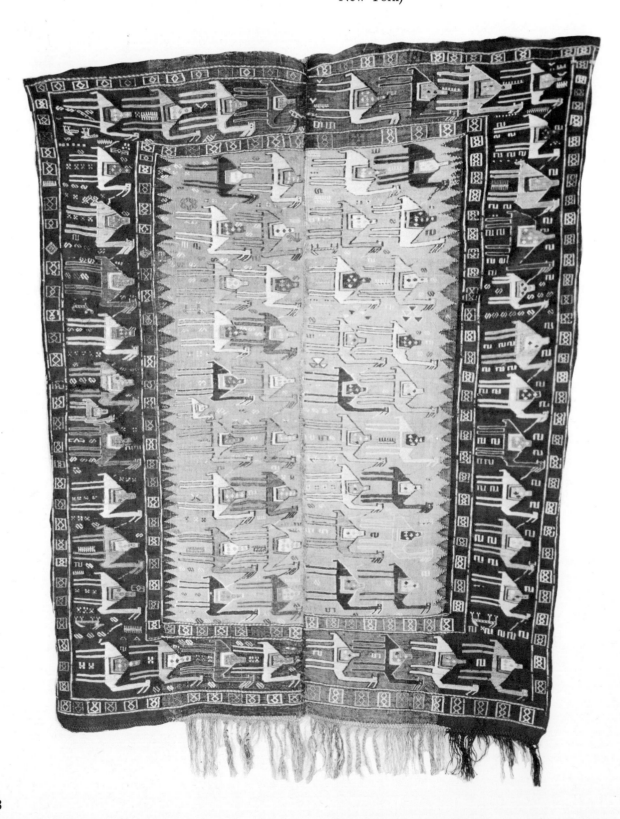

Verneh (half)
Warp: 2-ply wool
Weft: dark wool
Brocading: 2-ply wool
Technique: countered soumak with long warp fringes
Size: .961m x 1.85m
Colors: white, beige, pale green, salmon, pale orange, deep orange, brown, black
S-shapes and other small figures are organized in narrow diagonal stripes.

Bag face
Warp: wool
Weft: wool
Technique: Soumak, selvages wrapped in yarns of different colors
Colors: white, off-white, yellow, rose, greenish blue, dark-blue border
Size: .59m x .51m

Small S-shaped figures fill diagonal stripes in the center field, a Caucasian design element found particularly in Chichi knotted rugs. The border, with its eight-pointed star, the star of Solomon, used widely in Central Asia and the Caucasus, is also characteristic of the flat weaves found in the Mughan steppe, which parallels the Caucasian areas of Karabagh and Talish.

THE UKRAINE

Ukraine SSR is north of the Caucasus and comprises the westernmost part of the Soviet Union. Ukrainians are the second largest ethnic group in the U.S.S.R. (Russians are the largest). The Moldavians, another weaving people with close cultural ties to the Romanians, are a large minority in the South and occupy Bessarabia, an old province that does not appear on modern maps.

The catalog of the State Museum of Ethnography at Lviv (Lvov) states that rug weaving is one of the oldest branches of Ukrainian folk art: "Rugs and throws were used to adorn walls, to cover beds, tables, chairs, stools, chests, floors, and sleighs. They were an indispensible part of any dowry and were used for certain funeral rites."[24]

Rug making was a peasant art. Rugs were made by women living in settled villages and towns and in the countryside to embellish their interiors. The materials used are the same as those used by tribal nomads; most wool was handspun from the fleece of flocks shepherded nearby. The resulting rugs are close cousins to the kilim of the Qashqai, or Kurdish weaver, except in Bessarabia, where designs change considerably although techniques remain the same.

Kilim
Warp: cotton
Weft: wool
Size: 3.51m x 2.6m
Technique: reversible interlocked tapestry weave, very finely woven
Colors: natural (off-white), black, blue, ocher, brown, orange
The alternation of color creates a tweedlike effect that is characteristic of the kilim weaving of this area. (Loaned by Khalil Zahiri)

Kilim
Warp: animal hair
Weft: wool
Technique: interlocked tapestry
Colors: black (ground), green, yellow, rose, red
Size: 3.49m x 1.39m
Origin: Bessarabia
Geometricized roses are placed on the field in an order typical of this area. The light border is in a green color that also appears in the design. There is an obvious difference between the geometric features of the previous kilim and that of this rug, in which the distinct Bessarabian design of angular flowers, particularly roses, predominates.

Kilim (partial view)
Warp: wool
Weft: wool
Technique: tapestry weave
Size: 3.6m x 1.2m (entire rug)
Origin: Bessarabia
Date: 19th century
Bouquets of geometricized roses and branches as well as two figures of women with their hands on their hips appear in this design. (Courtesy of Victoria & Albert Museum, London)

101

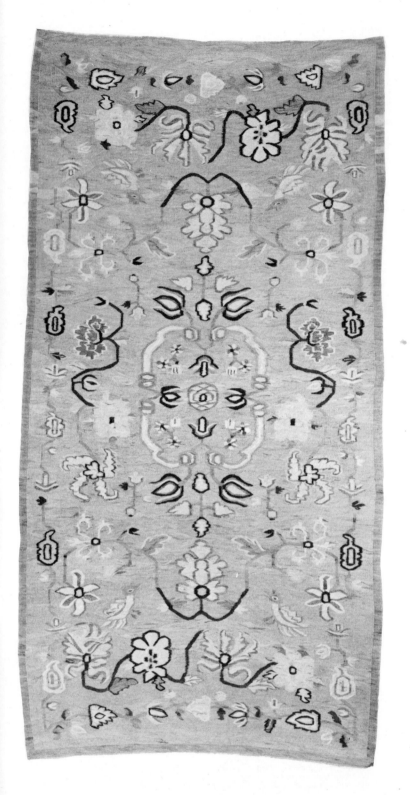

Kilim
Warp: 2-ply cotton
Weft: 1-ply wool
Technique: dovetailed tapestry weave with eccentric beating
Colors: grayish blue, lemon yellow, tan, white, pink, teal blue
Size: 3.23m x 1.65m
Date: 19th century
Origin: Bessarabian
The arrangement of the flowers, their sinuous contours, and the subtlety of the colors make this an elegant weaving, which could have been made for the floor of a nobleman's residence. (Private collection)

europe

It is better to spin with Penelope than to sing with Helen.—Greek proverb

From the Ukraine we continue into Eastern Europe and the Balkans. For the purpose of simplification the weaving-producing countries of Eastern Europe, the Balkan Pennisula, and the Greek archipelago are grouped together. They include the European part of Turkey, Bulgaria, Greece, Yugoslavia, Romania, Albania, and Poland, as they are known today. In the ebb and flow of history these countries have grown and contracted, their boundaries changing often as conquerors have tried to absorb them.

Within these areas beautiful flat-woven rugs have been made in towns and villages as part of a rich folk-art tradition. Material and technique are close to those used in previous chapters. Village weavers make tapestry-woven (usually reversible) rugs, as did the nomadic tribesmen and settled people of Turkey, Persia, Afghanistan, Turkestan, and the Caucasus. The similarities between some of the Asian and European designs are striking.

While many kilims from this area are geometric in design, some are floral and others are pictorial. Some pieces combine intricate fields of curved motifs with simple geometric borders. An important kilim group, characterized by graceful curving figures balanced in well-proportioned rugs with several borders, comes from southern Bulgaria, southern Romania, and the eastern part of Turkey. A large part of the geographical area corresponds to the ancient kingdom of Thrace.[1]

The weavers of this area achieve rich pictorial effects from curvilinear designs not usually associated with kilim weaving: "Their kilims contain some interesting and important features, disproving once and for all the argument repeated ad nauseum about the design limitations of tapestry-woven kilims. Unlike pile rugs, kilims supposedly restrict the weavers' freedom of ex-

pression to simple designs, avoiding, from necessity, curvilinear form. The Thracian weavers, however, display an astonishing mastery of their medium. By twisting and binding their warps and wefts they achieve any curve they wish and at the same time avoid bulging and unevenness in the finished product."[2]

A large area of Eastern Europe had been part of the Ottoman Empire and had been influenced by the Turks for centuries, but the biography of the region reveals a striking separation of individual group identity. Literary sources and museum records in some of these countries seem to indicate some rug weaving prior to the Turkish influence. During the Turkish occupation rugs were woven for use by the Turks; prayer rugs, for example, were made by Christian weavers for Moslems from the Turkish army.

Serbian woman at her loom, c. 1900.

CHARACTERISTICS OF EASTERN EUROPEAN FLAT-WOVEN RUGS

Some features of Eastern European flat-woven rugs are listed below.

1. Slit-tapestry weave is a common technique.

2. Outlining is frequent.

3. Outlining and eccentric beating in combination create the curvilinear patterns of the Oltenian kilims from Romania and of pieces from the area that once was Thrace.

4. Rugs of certain areas are made in two or three pieces and joined along the selvages.

5. One-piece kilims, some very large, are made in Bulgaria.

6. Small and medium one-piece kilims, often in an almost square format, are made in the areas of Oltenia, Pirot, and Sarkoy.

7. A long, narrow one-piece weaving for wall use is a common format in Romania.

8. Older pieces were woven with a woolen warp. Hemp and flax were used for the warp in Romania and other areas. Cotton is used in the 20th century.

9. Coloration is unique to each area and can be a guide in attribution. A strong red ground is favored in many Eastern European weavings. The mating of red with other colors can indicate origin. The use of peacock blue indicates that a piece is not of Romanian origin.

10. Designs are geometric and simple in some areas; figurative, curvilinear, and complex in other areas; emblematic or heraldic in others. Flora, fauna, and human figures, varying from area to area, are abundant.

ROMANIA

Eastern European national borders differ from ethnological ones, since Bessarabia and Romania are linked historically. Folk-art and rug books cite Bessarabian rugs as Romanian or vice versa. In the present volume the Bessarabians are included in the previous chapter because this area is now part of Soviet Russia.

Romania exhibits a unity of race and language; the majority of the country is comprised of Romanian-speaking (a Latin tongue) Wallachians and Moldavians. The areas or provinces that have traditionally produced weavings are Oltenia, Moldavia, Montenia (originally Wallachia), Banat, Hateg, Arad, Bucovina and Maramures. The Saxon areas of Transylvania produce embroideries and other handiwork but few weavings.

The nation was feudal until the 19th century, with most of the land belonging to a few hundred families. Those families, known as Boyars, lived rich and often cultivated lives; they acquired art and ornaments from Western Europe and from the East. Knotted oriental rugs from Turkey and Persia were frequently used in their palaces. It is thought that the designs of those rugs influenced the peasant weavers of Romania; the use of wide borders in Oltenian flat weaves is an example.

The beginning of kilim weaving in Romania is hard to ascertain. A Romanian writer expressed the opinion that the floral and pictorial kilims with curvilinear figures date back to the 18th century, while simpler tapestry-woven pieces "have always been made in Roumania."[3] The earliest known existing piece is a 1789 flat-woven rug in the Folk Art Museum.[4] Among hundreds of examples from all the provinces are five other dated pieces, all from the 19th century. Rug scholars agree that the finest work was produced between the last half of the 18th century and the end of the 19th century.

The Socialist Republic of Romania has supported the Museum of Folk Art in Bucharest and has toured a flat-woven rug exhibition internationally.[5]

Rugs were used to ornament the house, particularly the village farmer's house. They covered walls, beams, benches, and tables in a traditional arrangement that differed from area to area. They were rarely used to cover the floor. Rugs were part of the wedding tradition, and those that were to be part of a daughter's dowry had a prominent place in the best room, the room where guests were received. Rugs were part of the burial procedure (the body was laid on a rug), and some of the rugs belonging to the deceased were given away as gifts.[6]

In the homes of the Boyars rugs were used on the floor. Some of the finest kilims were made to order in workshops on Boyars' land or in monasteries. The peasant weavers were given designs to execute that differed from the geometric designs used in their own rugs. Their elegance provides a contrast with the simplicity of those seen in peasant interiors, and they can be considered "high-style" pieces, although their materials, technique, and origin are identical.

Romanian interiors.
a. main or reception room, Oltenia, 1875
b. main room, Buzau, Wallachia
These rooms contain *scoarte* (flat-woven rugs), *laicere* (long, narrow weavings hung horizontally behind benches), *cerge* (coverlets), *perini* (embroidered pillow covers used as decoration), and *stergar de culme* (decorative towels hung over the house beam).

A

B

105

Scoarța (tapestry-woven rug)
Origin: region of Oltenia

Scoarța
Warp: cotton
Weft: wool
Technique: tapestry weave with decoratively knotted warp fringe
Origin: Oltenia, 1920s
Size: 3.28 x 1.95m
The field is filled with flowers, corn, mushrooms, birds, butterflies, insects, and small geometric motifs. The serrated edge is surrounded by an unusual broken border of lozenge forms. (Collection of the Victoria & Albert Museum, London)

Scoarta (tapestry-woven rug)
Origin: Muntenia (Wallachia), 19th century

Scoarța
Warp: wool
Weft: wool
Technique: tapestry weave
Origin: region of Oltenia, 19th century
Size: 2.52m x 1.65m
Colors: blue, purple, orange, pink, red, cream
(field); red, purple, orange, beige, brown,
cream (main border); cream, green, orange, pur-
ple (inner guard)
The field and the large outer border are filled with
birdlike forms and flowers. The inner border contains a
graceful leaf and vine motif. (Collection of the Victoria
& Albert Museum, London)

Scoarța
Warp: 1-ply, finely braided fine cotton
Weft: wool
Technique: slit tapestry weave, with finely
braided warp ends
Colors: beige, pale yellow, pastel blue, brown
(border)
Origin: Oltenia, c. 1900
Size: 2.93m x 1.96m
The design of geometric motifs on an open field is
similar to that found in kilims from Montenia (south-
east Romania). Rows of brown outline and border all
areas, yielding a dramatic yet subtle effect. (Private col-
lection)

Scoarţa
Warp: cotton
Weft: wool
Technique: mixed—dovetailed tapestry weave,
slit tapestry weave (around borders and floral
sprays), outlining, double-wefted outlining,
discontinuous brocading
Size: 2.34m x 1.58m
Origin: Tirgu Jiu, region of Oltenia
Colors: brown (field); white, red, blue (borders);
5 greens, pink, melon, mustard, 3 grays, teal
blue, medium blue
The field is filled with geometrical and conventionalized floral sprays, lilies of the valley, ears of wheat,
mushrooms, and birds. Color changes in the weft give a
tweed effect. The relief effect in the ears of wheat is the
result of closely beaten double wefted yarn. (Loaned by
D. and J. Mitescu family)

Scoarţa (details)
Origin: Muntania, originally Wallachia
These details show two techniques, dovetailed tapestry
weave and slit tapestry weave. (Collection of the
Muzeul de arta populara, Bucharest)

BULGARIA

The origin of the Bulgarians and their conversion into Slavs are considered remarkable ethnological phenomena. In Byzantine times they ravaged the plains of Thrace and had soon settled in and adopted the Serbian language.

Kilims were made for village use as part of the craft output of the country. Réclus noted that each village on the northern slope of the Balkan Peninsula between Pirot and Tirnova was known for a particular product. Pirot was known as a center for kilims. In the 1880s the great annual fairs attracted merchants from the entire Ottoman empire. As many as 100,000 strangers came to Livno for its fair.[7] Pirot, near the Bulgarian–Yugoslavian border, is now part of Yugoslavia. The kilims of the area, known as Pirot kilims, are easily distinguished by their coloring: a characteristic dark blue, rich green, and deep red combined with white.

In color plate 25 (page 215) geometric medallions in two rows of the red field are surrounded by a black inner border filled with stylized roses and an outer red border with geometric figures. The curvilinear forms are created by eccentric weft beating. The color red is widely used in European peasant art. The preference for this color apparently derives from the belief that it kept away demons. Door and window frames were painted red for this reason. It is also interesting to note that the Russians sometimes use the word *krasnayt* to indicate both "pretty" and "red."

Kilim
Warp: 2-ply homespun wool, 7 warps per inch
Weft: 1-ply homespun wool, 30 wefts per inch
Technique: reversible slit and dovetailed tapestry weave with eccentric weft beating
Origin: Bulgaria
Size: 2.98m x 2.49m
Colors: red, green, yellow, peacock blue, black

According to David Black and Clive Loveless, the owners of the rug shown in color plate 26 (page 215): "This particular piece was probably made in the very west of Anatolia in the region of the Bosphorus and the only example of this type we know. It is certainly the most beautiful Kilim Saph we have ever seen. [N.B. Photographed before restoration.]"
Saph kilim
Size: 4.5m x 1.85m
Date: c. 1800

Kilim
Warp: wool
Weft: wool
Technique: slit tapestry weave
Size: 1.57m x .925m
Colors: red (ground), cream, white, yellow, several shades of blue
Origin: Pirot, 19th century
Conventional treelike forms in vertical rows contain niche-shaped compartments, which in turn contain trees with blossoms. The nichelike compartments suggest that it was woven to be a prayer. (Collection of the Victoria & Albert Museum, London)

Kilim
Warp: 2-ply white wool
Weft: 1-ply wool
Technique: very fine slit tapestry weave
Size: 1.88m x 1.8m
Colors: navy blue (field), white, gold, red
(cochineal), teal blue

The square blue field is filled with uniform tipped crosses. The wide border is divided into boxes, each containing a motif that is also common in Central Asia. Simple and striking design, combined with the fine weaving and lovely wool, make this an exceptional piece. It was probably made as a dowry rug. In all parts of the weaving world a woman's best rugs are made to show her skill in the marriage market and to become part of her dowry. In some areas they are called *kiz* kilims (*kiz* is "girl" in Turkish).

Kilim
Warp: 2-strand wool
Weft: 1-strand wool
Technique: reversible slit tapestry weave
Colors: 2 browns, black, white, wine, deep
pink, reddish pink, pumpkin, 3 greens
Size: 3.6m x 2.95m
Origin: Balkan, called Sarkoy in the rug trade

GREECE

In spite of invasions and periods of widespread intermixture with other races the Greek people have not broken with their culture or their language. Their weaving is related to the Slavic counterparts examined in this chapter, although their looms, whether in mainland towns or island hamlets, have produced work that is identifiably Greek, with marked local characteristics.

The Turkish influence on Greek weaving is particularly obvious in the case of embroidered rugs and furnishing fabrics. These beautiful pieces are plain-woven and finished with needle and thread after removal from the loom.

Often in rural and isolated areas sheep are sheared, wool is dyed, and textiles are woven in the same household. Handspinning and handweaving are widely practiced and form an integral part of the social system. In some villages every woman weaves, and rugs, covers, and decorations are made by the women of each family; the word *horiatiko* refers to all fabrics made at home. These handwoven pieces are an important part of every girl's dowry, and their display is part of a Greek wedding.

Looms are often set up outdoors in the summer and moved inside in the winter months. As in other countries where woman's work is never done, no shepherdess or goatherdess goes without spindle and distaff. Matthews discusses a town in the Peloponnisos where one kilim pattern could be traced back at least 200 years. A 12-year-old demonstrated her knowledge of the same difficult pattern, proof that the tradition is being preserved.[8] In Metsovon, a remote village in the Pindhos Mountains, a baronial home has been turned into a folk museum. In peasant homes living rooms were designed around the fireplace; a rug covered the chimney breast; woven pillows were used for seating; and hangings covered the walls, creating a warmth of color and design.

In all probability Greek weaving could be traced back to prehistoric times. Greek mythology gives a detailed account of a weaving contest between the goddess Athena and Arachne, an acclaimed weaver.

> Straight to their Posts appointed both repair,
> And fix their threaded looms with equal care;
> And round the solid Beam the Web is ty'd
> While parting Canes the hollow warps divide,
> Through which nimble flight the Shuttles play
> And for the woof prepare a ready way;
> The woof and warp unite, press'd by the toothy Slay.
> Thus both their mantles buttoned to their breast,
> Their skillful fingers play with loving haste.
> And work with pleasure while they cheat the Eye
> With glowing purple of the Tyrian dye
> Or justly intermixing shades with light
> Their colourings insensibly unite

The outcome was contested (Arachne was the apparent winner), and Athena beat Arachne with the weaver's batten and turned her into a spider.[9]

The history of weaving in Greece has not been continuously documented, though some tapestry fragments survive. In any case Greece has always been a weaving culture; woven fabrics held a place of honor in ancient Greece, as is evidenced by the abundant vocabulary concerning spinning and weaving looms and fabrics. A great deal of visual information about Greek weaving can be obtained from ancient vase paintings and sculptures. Every house in ancient Greece contained a loom and weaving materials, on which were made clothing, household accessories, rugs and tapestries, all overseen by the mistress of the house.

Interior of a house in northern Greece.

Cover
Warp: cotton
Weft: cotton
Embroidery: cotton, silk, and metallic thread
Technique: plain weave, embroidered with several stitches in many pieces and sewn together, with added fringe
Size: 1.37m x .91m
Origin: Greek Islands
Colors: several blues, white, gold, 2 greens, 2 reds, purple
This type of work can be found in pillows, towels, curtains, bed covers, scarves, shawls, socks, and other articles of clothing and furnishings. (Collection of H. McCoy Jones)

YUGOSLAVIA

Tapestry-woven rugs have long been made here by peasants and villagers. The northern area around Pirot (see p. 109) is a center of kilim weaving and marketing. The government supports kilim weaving as a workshop and home industry.

Kilim
Warp: wool
Weft: wool
Technique: slit tapestry weave, made in two parts
Size: 3.87m x 1.85m
Origin: Yugoslavia
This design is copied exactly from a Caucasian *silé* rug (see Chapter 7). (Collection of the Textile Museum, Washington, D.C.)

Wall rug (section)
Warp: wool
Weft: wool
Technique: brocade
Color: yellow, purple, blue, orange, brick red, pink, brown
Origin: Crete, 19th century
Size: unmeasured
Similar weavings are used as donkey saddle blankets. (Collection of Iraklion Folk Museum, Crete)

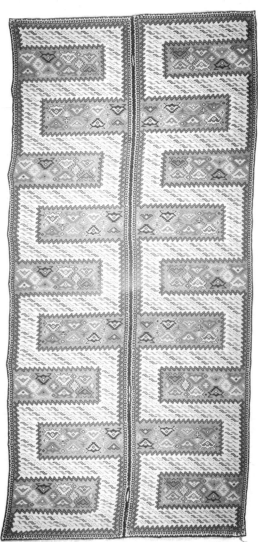

ALBANIA

A national poet described an Albanian bride who was "sold like a slave bound to work for her husband to the 'ever-active shuttle' " while the head of the family was compared to the "majestic ram marching at the head of the flock."[10] The poet who used these metaphors must have lived in a country that produced folk weaving. The February 1931 issue of *National Geographic* shows some Albanian flat-woven rugs.[11] They cannot be reproduced here because of copyright laws. Two examples, a square dark blue, apple green, and red kilim and a large red kilim are both similar to Pirot designs.

HUNGARY

Flat-woven rugs similar in technique and motif to certain Romanian, Bulgarian, and Yugoslavian examples have been produced in Hungary. "The penetration of oriental elements into Hungarian folk art is mainly due to the 150 years of Turkish conquest over the majority of Hungary's territory. It is for that matter a clue to the affinity between motifs used on carpets by Hungarians and other peoples (Roumanian, Bulgarian, Yugoslavian), since Turkish influence has been similarly strong in these countries."[12]

POLAND

"The Pole loves his kilim whether antique or ultramodern. He uses it as a rug on his inlaid floor, he spreads it over a bed or couch . . . the kilim comes out of a land which is both hyphen and highway between East and West . . . The kilim resembles both the Turkish rug and something far removed."[13]

The peasant woman who wove the traditional kilim extolled in this quotation, depending on the area in which she lived, may have had such diverse influences as Italian Renaissance design, Persian rug design of the Shah Abbas period, or Flemish and French tapestry, so filled was the fountain that watered Polish folk art throughout the centuries.

In 1925, seven years after the Treaty of Versailles gave Poland political liberty, an important exhibit of Polish folk art was presented in Paris. Europe and America applauded, and since that time Polish kilims have been marketed commercially in the West. The government has supported the industry of modern kilim weaving, although most of the work is not based on traditional models; some weavers use the traditional designs in their own way.

Kilim (color plate 27, page 216)
Warp: wool
Weft: wool
Technique: reversible slit tapestry weave, with selvages loosely wrapped in varying colors of weft yarn
Size: 1.41m x 2.32m
Origin: possibly Polish

Kilim
Warp: flax
Weft: wool
Technique: slit tapestry weave with warp ends turned under
Size: 1.98m x 1.28m
Colors: red (field); black, white, blue; dark brown, white, blue, red (border)
Origin: Panesova, southern Hungary
A simple geometric medallion in the center field is surrounded by four flowerpots, the top two woven bottom up to create the symmetry of an oriental carpet. In the large outer border are stitched geometricized flowers. There are obvious similarities to Polish, Bessarabian, and Ukrainian rugs. (Collection of the Victoria & Albert Museum, London)

SCANDINAVIA

Weaving and embroidery were important parts of Scandinavian folk art and, "like the sagas and folklore, were handed down from mother to daughter, for many generations."[14]

Sweden, Norway, and Denmark once shared a common language, the dialects of which became separate tongues. Finland had a very different language. The Finnish people also have a different ethnic makeup, due to repeated invasion by Weeksans Hungarian nomad tribes.

The rugs, both flat-woven and rya (meaning "shaggy"), made in a knotting technique, were made by peasants as covers for the bed, the sleigh, and the horse or as part of the dowry or trousseau. In Finland, as in Eastern Europe, rug weaving was esteemed by the nobility, and girls of noble families as well as peasant women wove rugs.

In Sweden horizontal and vertical looms were used to weave wall covers and throws, called *rollakan*, and tapestries with European and heraldic themes. The double interlocked joining used there for tapestry weaving is still known as Swedish tapestry throughout the world. In Norway, a rich variety of flat weaving was done (in addition to rya weaving). In northern Norway a traditional woolen blanket called a *grene* was made by settled Lappish-speaking people for migrating nomadic Lapps, who used them for coverlets in their tents and as rugs in their sledges; when they became old, they were used to cover the tents.

One flat-weave technique used continually from early times was double weaving (*flensvenad*), in which two sets of warp and weft threads were woven simultaneously but joined only at the edges of an area. Human and animal figures, often in heraldic style, were combined with geometric motifs in pieces that were hung horizontally around the room and used for animal covers.

Tapestry weave was used to make the *aakloe,* weavings that served as coverlets, pillows, and rugs. They were true kilims, geometric designs made on the horizontal loom. The richest period was the 18th century, and the southwestern areas produced the largest number of pieces. Other areas produced *aakloe* with different design characteristics. Some used conventionalized flowers similar to the Bessarabian designs (see Chapter 7). Brocaded rugs (*krokbragd, skilbragd*) were traditionally made in Norway and in Sweden.[15]

Aakloe
Warp: flax
Weft: wool
Technique: reversible double interlocking tapestry weave, also called square weave
Colors: white, yellow, red, black
Size: 1.5m x 1.2m
Origin: Norway, probably southwest, 17th or 18th century
Serrated lozenges, each with a cross, fill the field, which has no side borders. The end borders have ribbonlike patterns. In some early pieces rows of interlocking tapestry alternated with rows of slit tapestry to provide more design flexibility. (Collection of the Victoria & Albert Museum, London)

Girl in southern Norway, c. 1910.

GREAT BRITAIN

Most English handmade rugs were made for the country gentry. The technique, needlework, reached an artistic peak in the 18th century. Ireland has a parallel history. Wool was plentiful. Flocks of sheep were raised throughout the countryside, and by the 16th century wool and woven cloth were major exports.

The mistresses and daughters of isolated country houses made intricate needlework rugs from stenciled canvases, which were brightly colored, usually in garden patterns. These became the prototypes for the English rug, which was soon to be widely made by machine, and by the 18th century rug manufacturing developed into a large industry.

FRANCE

French flat-weave or tapestry rugs are called Aubusson, no matter where they were woven, just as pile or knotted rugs are known as savonnerie. The history of the Aubusson rug is identified with the history of tapestry, and the technique is the same.

Tapestry weaving was begun in the town of Aubusson, 200 miles south of Paris, in the 8th century by Moors who had settled there when their invasion of France failed. They built looms and taught the French residents how to weave. These rugs, called *tapis sarasinois,* were apparently tapestry weave. Weavers at Aubusson say that the art has never died since that time.[16]

In the 13th century renowned artists from Flanders moved to Aubusson. The tapestries and rugs subsequently produced were associated with the court. The kings of France sponsored all the arts, which were perfected for their pleasure.

The Aubusson is made on both a vertical (*haute-lisse*) and a horizontal (*basse-lisse*) loom, with the reverse side of the weaving facing the weaver. The outline of the design is traced in ink on the warp.

ITALY

In surveying European flat weaves this chapter has looked at some influences on their designs. In Eastern Europe it was suggested that the multibordered kilims of Oltenia were influenced by the oriental knotted rugs found in the homes of the aristocracy. The kilims of neighboring Muntenia, a more insular area, were more simply designed, consisting of plain and geometric bands. Similar designs have appeared in tribal pieces from all the countries covered in other chapters as well as in folk rugs from Scandinavian and Balkan countries.

In Sicily, off the southern tip of Italy's mainland, the peasant women of Erice and Petralia weave similar banded and geometric rugs. In Altamura (province of Apulia) and Isnello, an isolated Sicilian village, designs are even simpler, presumably deriving from a long and continuing tradition. In the flat-woven rugs of other Italian areas echoes of medieval and Renaissance art can be discerned. The designs of Sardinia and Abruzzo

Aubusson rug (Photograph: Musée Historique des Tissus, Lyon)

generally contain plant and animal motifs and mythological animals such as the griffin, the unicorn, the siren, the centaur, and the dragon. This bestiary, a strong design theme of medieval Europe, was put together from motifs originating in Sassanian times.[17]

Italy is a country identified with elegant fabrics, and it has a rich textile history. By the 10th century a complete silk industry existed, organized into five carefully controlled guilds. Silk production was a secret affair, as it has been throughout history, and the sale of silk was carefully regulated. Foreigners were not allowed to buy the highest-quality clothes, and the Bishop of Cremonia, for one, was arrested for smuggling. The designs of those precious silks influenced architectural ornament and furniture.

SPAIN

After the Islamic invasion in 711 arts and architecture flourished, as did silk weaving and pottery, particularly in the southern province of Andalucia. Records indicate that the palaces in the city of Cordoba were filled with the richest carpets in the world. By the 11th century carpet weaving was the chief industry of the city of Cienca.

Spanish examples are among the oldest knotted rugs in existence. Their design shows a strong influence of oriental rugs and Coptic weaving, both known in Spain, but they also exhibit marked characteristics of their own. The knotting technique used in early Spanish carpets differed from that of other areas in that the knot was tied to alternate single warp threads.

Heraldry became an important design element in the 15th and 16th centuries; long, narrow rugs displaying coats of arms were uniquely Spanish. The 15th century also brought the downfall of the Moors (the name given to the desert Arabs who intermarried with indigenous North African people after their conversion to Islam and who subsequently conquered and settled in Spain). In the upheaval of the Inquisition that followed the Moors (along with the Jews) were expelled from Spain, taking their craftspeople with them. Some famous Moorish carpet weavers were given asylum by the court but were expelled a century later, and a downward trend in rug knotting resulted.

The Moorish population of Granada had made looped woven wool rugs in the district of Alpujarra. After their expulsion Spanish peasants continued to make Alpujarra rugs, using the same designs. They were originally made as covers for the marriage bed and as carriage covers. Larger rugs were made later by sewing together two or three pieces woven on the narrow loom. Long knotted fringes were added. Designs were predominantly from nature: large birds on a tree of life, vases, grapes and vines, rearing lions, and pomegranates, a Moorish motif introduced into oriental rugs as well.

Flat-woven rugs were also made in Spain, and they too showed a Moorish influence. The island of Majorca, south of the mainland in the Mediterranean, is noted for a unique weave called *tela de lengua* ("cloth of tongue pattern"). This flat weave, which has been used for centuries, mainly as a bed cover, relies on a tie-dyed warp and a solid weft (both usually blue and white) to achieve a spotted effect.

Alformbra de artesania Popular Mallorquina
("Rug of Popular Art")
Warp: wool
Weft: wool
Size: 1.58m x 1.58m
Colors: cinnamon (ground), blue, white
Date: late 18th or early 19th century
Technique: horizontal loom, 3 parts sewn together
This design is traditional. (Photograph: Provincial Textile Museum of Barcelona)

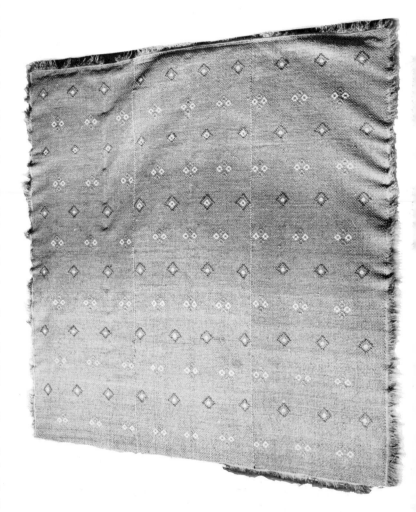

africa

Wool is white, the color of good omen.—Moorish proverb

NORTH AFRICA

North Africa consists of three geographically united countries—Morocco, Algeria, and Tunisia—whose northern coasts lie on the Mediterranean Sea. Throughout history they were more or less homogeneous provinces of the Carthaginian, Roman, Byzantine, and Arab empires, the last of which tried to unite all of North Africa. Only in the 12th century was such an effort successful when a dynasty of the Almohads, a Berber tribe from the Atlas Mountains of Morocco, ruled the entire area. Later the Turks, the Spanish, the Italians, and the French invaded. In the 16th century Moors who had been expelled from Spain and Turkish corsairs launched a large-scale attack in support of the local rulers. They preyed upon shipping, attacked coastal towns, and took booty and slaves. From that time these countries have sometimes been called the Barbary States. (Libya, located between Tunisia and Egypt, then called Tripolitania, was included in the Barbary States.) There is a distinct resemblance among the cultures and the peoples of the three countries, although each has developed its own style. The influence of the various foreign invaders pervades the arts in particular areas, giving Tunisia, which is close to Italy, peculiarities of style different from Morocco, which was so culturally linked to the Moors of southern Spain. France, which occupied Algeria early in the 19th century, has had a strong influence on all three coun-

tries, and French is widely spoken. The Arabic word for North Africa is *Maghrib,* meaning "west." It is often used to name the area.

The peoples of the Maghrib include Berbers, Arabs, Haratin, and Jews. The Berbers are the descendants of the original inhabitants. From early history they were divided into three tribes (Mamoudas, Sanhayas, and Zenatas), but many hundreds of tribes are now scattered throughout North Africa.[1] In Morocco alone over 200 Berber tribes speak separate dialects. Only the Tauregs, with a number of tribal confederations in the Sahara, still write a Berber language derived from the ancient Libyan script.

The conquering Bedouins from Arabia intermarried with Berbers in the 11th century. The majority of North Africans are an amalgam of these early groups.

The Haratin are people from the Harat area of the Sahara in southern Algeria and the southern half of the Sahara (where they are known as Chouchan or Dauada). They are oasis dwellers, descendants from black Africans who migrated north. They are Moslems who speak the Arabic and Berber dialects of their neighbors.

The Jews are a large minority in the Maghrib who have settled in North Africa for many centuries. Their presence in the oasis of the Sahara was recorded in medieval times. They were said to have migrated to the area in the 6th century B.C. and to have won over many Berber converts.[2]

CHARACTERISTICS OF THE FLAT-WOVEN RUGS OF NORTH AFRICA

The following characteristics may be noted in North African flat-woven rugs.

1. Flat-woven rugs with bands of knotting are found in Morocco.

2. Mixed-technique and compound-weave rugs featuring float weaves usually in narrow-banded patterns, with cotton threads left long on the reverse side, are found in Morocco.

3. Long tapestry-woven kilims and blankets, usually reversible, come from Tunisia.

4. Brocaded blankets of different styles and techniques are found in Algeria and Tunisia.

5. Designs are traditional, rigidly prescribed by tribal custom. Geometric symbols predominate.

6. Some pictorial designs exist—in the vivid Gafsa (Tunisia) blankets and rugs, for example.

7. Warp and weft were traditionally of handspun wool.

8. Cotton is used for brocading and in the contemporary period for warping.

Morocco

The distance from Spain to Morocco is only nine miles across the Strait of Gibraltar. The Moors came from Morocco, ruled Spain, and returned to Morocco; at a later date the Spaniards ruled Morocco. Morocco became an independent constitutional monarchy in 1956 after having been divided between France and Spain in the early 1900s.

Three inland ranges of the Atlas Mountains separate the low, fertile plateau near the Atlantic Coast from the sub-Sahara desert in the East. Most of the weaving peoples live in these mountain ranges. Some weaving is done on the plateaus as well, and at least one coastal town (Salé) is a center for brocaded rugs. A rug industry producing knotted rugs in designs different from tribal rugs is centered in Rabat.

Towns along the Atlantic Coast and in the North are famed for other handicrafts: the carved chests of the Rif range and Tétouan; the mosaic tiles, called *zellidjs*, inlaid in portals of mosques, fountains, and courtyards; and pottery, designs of which are traditional from village to village.

Most of the population of Morocco (15,700,000 in 1970) is Moslem, but there is a large Jewish minority. The language of commerce is Moroccan Arabic. (The language of the Koran is classical Arabic.) The many Berber dialects are used in Berber areas. Tamazight is one of the Berber tongues of the Atlas region. Spanish and French are widely spoken.

Bright bands of color alternate with bands exhibiting geometric and moundlike forms in color plate 28 (page 217). They are frequent in North African flat weaves and evoke desert scenes. Each traditional Moroccan rug design has a name and is always rendered exactly, although each weaving is a unique combination of these elements. Reading from the bottom of this *handeira*, the third brocaded strip is known as El-mnâyr.[3] The length of the blanket is decided by the number of sleepers to be covered.

Blanket or cover (*handeira* in Arabic)
Warp: fine wool
Weft: wool
Brocading: wool
Technique: plain-weave and brocade stripes
Origin: High Atlas Mountains
Size: 2.78m x 1.57m

The center band of the rug shown in color plate 29 (page 217) is knotted in a style, unique to Morocco.[4] The knot is a Turkish knot.[5] In this example three rows of plain weave are left between knotted rows, which are not visible because the pile is left long. Such mixed-technique rugs and completely knotted rugs are known as *Chichaoua,* the name of the town in the plains east of Marrakesh in which they are marketed. They are made in villages at the feet of the High Atlas Mountains by Ouled Besseba tribes, Bedouin Arabs mixed with Berbers. The rounded mound shapes often give a psychedelic effect. The rugs of these tribes differ from Berber pieces, particularly those from the Middle Atlas region, which exhibit repeating geometric designs. "The Chichaoua weave their carpets in flaming colors . . . the very colors of the [Atlas] range under the withering sun."[6]

Chichaoua
Warp: 2-ply dark goat hair
Weft: single-ply wool
Technique: mixed, weft-face plain-weave stripes and slit tapestry bands with eccentric beating, knotted center band
Size: 3.73m x 1.5m

Donkey or mule feed bag
Weft: wool
Warp: 2-ply dark and light hair
Brocading: wool
Technique: mixed, diamond twill with bands of weft-float weaves, also called skip plain weave[7], wefts cut and tied to make fringe at selvages
Colors: dark brown, white
Origin: High Atlas, Siroua
Size: 7.35m x .48m

Runner
Warp: single-ply wool
Weft: single-ply wool
Brocading: wool and machine-spun cotton (white)
Technique: compound weave—warp-faced warp-float weave with knotted details in every row
Colors: indigo blue, cochineal red, bright red, orange, pink, green, yellow, white
Origin: Berber, Middle Atlas Mountains, Zaian
Size: 6.2m x .89m
In this technique, perhaps unique among the Berbers of the Maghrib, lengths of cotton inserted during the weaving are held in place by the skip plain weave. The cotton shows as long loops on the back; this is classified as a two-faced textile, as are other Berber weavings of this technique. 'We are precipitated by the violent graphic design toward the center. The center is not only a point of meditation but both the end and beginning of an always recreating composition.'[8]

Brocaded rug
Warp: wool
Weft: wool
Supplementary weft: cotton
Technique: weft-float weave with four-sided plain-weave border
Colors: red, black, white
Origin: Salé
Size: 2.4m x 1.5m

Rows of geometric lozenges are bordered by rows of varying lozenge motifs. The technique and design are similar to those of the Mergoums of Tunisia. Salé, a small town on the Atlantic Coast at the mouth of the Bou Regreg River founded in the 10th century, is also a center of mat making. All through North Africa attractive woven mats cover floors of mosques, floors, and banquettes of public places, sometimes extending up the walls.

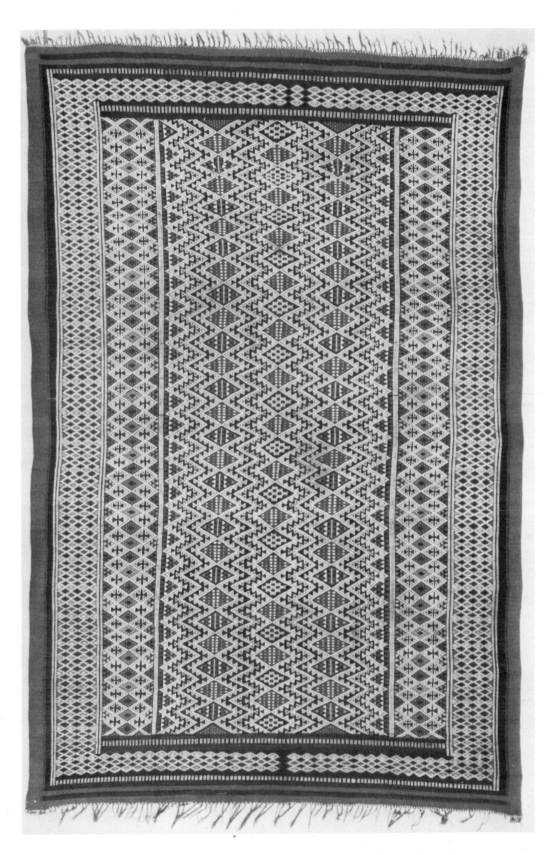

A

B

Blanket (*tamizart* in Ait Mgild dialect, *tahddun* in Zemmour dialect), outside (A) and inside (B)
Warp: single-ply wool
Weft: single-ply wool
Brocading: double-wefted wool
Technique: weft-float weave bands overlaying rows of Turkish knots, long ends left on back, two braided ties
Colors: white, brown, red, yellow, blue
Origin: Berber, Middle Atlas
Size: 2.14m x .78m

The design in every narrow band is different in some way, creating an infinity pattern. It is attributed to the Beni Ourain tribe. When this blanket is worn by a Berber woman, the loose ends show on the outside. The intricate motifs differ from village to village and from tribe to tribe; each band and each symbol have a meaning.

Glaoua
Warp: wool and hair
Weft: wool
Pile: wool
Technique: weft-faced plain-weave bands alternating with bands with knotted detail, knotted center band, bands of weft-float weave
Colors: white, brownish black, pale green, yellow
Size: 1.82m x 1.42m
Origin: High Atlas Mountains

These weavings were called *glaoua* by merchants in the *souks* (bazaars) at Marrakesh where they were sold because they came from territories under the rule of the Pasha of Marrakesh, El Glaoui.

Rug
Warp: 2-ply dark wool
Weft: single-ply wool
Brocading: 2-ply loosely spun wool
Technique: mixed—weft-face plain weave, continuous bands of weft-float weave, bands of dovetailed tapestry weave with some slits, knotted and Soumak details
Colors: undyed white, undyed brownish black, blue, pale orange, yellow, green (vegetable dyes)
Size: 3.3m x 1.38m
Origin: Ouauzguit or Sektana area.

Bag face(?)
Origin: Ouauzguit area, High Atlas, 19th century
Size: 1.47m x .75m
This rug was not available for technical analysis. (Collection of the Victoria & Albert Museum, London)

Fodor's Morocco refers to the king's horses on parade in Rabat, each a different color and each with a blanket or *hanbel* (*hambel*) woven from brilliantly dyed wools.[9] The word is sometimes used to refer to all Moroccan flat-woven rugs and covers. *Hambel* is used here to refer to mixed-technique rug-blankets from the Middle Atlas in two basic color combinations: reds, blacks, whites, and yellows; and oranges, greens, blacks, and whites. The *hambels* shown in color plate 30 (page 218) are representative. (A) is from Zemmour, where finely woven *hambels* are widely made. (B) and (C) were probably made by the Beni Mgild, as much of the brocading is in green, a color known to be used by them.

A. *Hambel*
Warp: single-ply wool
Weft: single-ply wool
Brocading: wool
Size: 3.16m x 1.5m
Technique: plain weave with bands of float weave (skip plain weave)

B. *Hambel*
Warp: single-ply blue wool
Weft: single-ply wool
Brocading: single-ply wool

Size: 2.7m x 1.68m
Technique: warp-float weave, selvages bound in horse hair

C. *Hambel*
Warp: single-ply blue wool
Weft: single-ply wool
Brocading: cotton (white)
Technique: weft-float weave: These three hambels have threads left in long loops on back

Cushion (*lusada* in Berber, *ousada* in Arabic)
Warp: 2-ply black wool
Weft: single- and 2-ply (black) wool
Technique: weft-float weave (skip plain weave)
Colors: orange, yellow, brick red, black, white
Origin: Berber, Zemmour
Size: 63m x 35m

The center band is in a reciprocal chevron design surrounded by three bands of differing sizes, all with similar trellised diamond motifs and with diamond borders in floral shapes. The back exhibits continuous plain-weave and brocaded stripes, which are folded and sewn together with braid at the selvages in herringbone stitch.

The Tauregs of the Sahara (from the Sanhajas branch of the Berbers) are nomads known as the Veiled Men of the Desert. (Men wear a *lithan*, or veil.) They are also called Blue Men, as they often wear dark blue clothing from which indigo dyes rub off onto their skins. The Tauregs make saddlebags and cushions from hides, which are tooled and painted. They use large, flat-woven woolen rugs to line their tents and to divide the women's quarters from the rest of the space. These tent rugs are bought from weavers along the Niger Bend.

Algeria

Algeria (population 14,770,000) is bounded by Morocco (west), Tunisia and Libya (east), and Mali and Nigeria (south). Its northern border lies entirely on the Mediterranean. Its plains and valleys provide the best land route from east to west across North Africa.

The Kabyle country in the Northeast is the home of Berbers, often blond-haired as are those of the Rif of northern Morocco, who separated into many individual tribes, often hostile to one another. They have been renowned for their skill in pottery since ancient times. Kabyle women are also weavers, making clothing (the *burnous* of the men and the *haik* of the women) and flat-woven blankets and rugs.

Weaving is the main occupation of the southern women, who are mostly from nomadic tribes. Laghouat is a trading center for their products.[10] Also known as centers for flat-woven rugs were Algiers, Biskra and Batna (Berber), Chellala, El Oued (near Tunisia), Kalaa, and the area of the Msabites, known for bright flat-woven rugs similar to those of the Moroccan Berbers.[11]

A study of the textiles of Djebel Amour emphasizes the rigid traditions governing weaving.[12] The Berbers of the area (who call themselves Imazighen) use five colors in their traditional patterns: red, green, orange, dark indigo blue, and white as a border. They resist aniline dyes in order to preserve their classic color combinations. A weaving removed from the loom is often dipped in hot water before washing in order to shrink the wool to a finer weave. (The people of Middle America use the same procedure.) The purpose of washing and beating with a baton (called a *khabbat*) is to soften the wool. Dyers and purveyors of dyes in Algeria are Jewish men, as is common throughout North Africa.

Algerian flat-woven rugs include these types. No examples were available for publication, but similarities to Berber and Arab rugs from Tunisia and Morocco are apparent.

Flidj are made on a narrow loom similar to that used by Kurdish weavers in northwest Iran (see page 49). *Flidj* is a tent fabric woven of goat hair and used by nomadic peoples of North Africa and Arabia. (An Arabian example is shown on page 139).

Getif are sleeping clothes for use on the ground. They generally measure 15' to 20' by 6' to 10'.

Imatt are saddlebags.

Tellis are large grain sacks.

Hembel (a variety of *hambel*) are used to separate the men's and the women's parts of the tent (called the *tag* in Djebel Amour).

Dokhali are large white and red stripe patterns on a plain ground, resembling the *handeira* of Morocco (see color plate 28 on page 217).

Ousada are pillows.

Tunisia

Tunisia (population 5,137,000 in 1970) is bounded by Libya on the east and southeast and by Algeria on the west and southwest. Its northern boundary is the Mediterranean coast. An independent country since 1954, it had been a French protectorate almost continuously from 1881 until 1946, with some interruptions during European power struggles. During World War II it was a battleground between the French and the Italians.

Tunisia was settled by the Phoenicians and later ruled by Carthage. Its capital, Tunis, is on the site of Carthage, the home base of the Carthaginians from the 6th century B.C. It was part of the Roman Empire and later occupied by Vandals, Byzantines, and Arabs.

The Berber population was converted to Islam, and Arab power and culture were reinforced by a second wave of conquest in the 11th century. Tunisia, traditionally called Ifriqiyah (an Arabic form of the Roman name Africa), attained its greatest power under the Hafsid (Berber) dynasty (1228–1374). In the 16th century Spain made inroads against its coastal cities; the Turks later conquered the entire country. Under its Turkish governors Tunisia achieved some measure of independence. Its population is almost entirely Arabic-speaking. In 1966 there were 30,000 Jews, 30,000 French, and 25,000 Italians.

Kilim
Warp: 4-ply wool
Weft: single-ply wool
Technique: double interlocking tapestry, a single shot of color appears in the joined color area
Colors: terracotta, light gray, light blue, light green, pink, yellow, dark gray, red
Origin: Tunisia, possibly Kairouan, "the doorway to the desert"
Size: 3.6m x 1.87m

Kilim
Warp: single-ply wool
Weft: single-ply wool
Technique: plain-weave, weft-float weave, double-interlocking-tapestry stripes
Colors: terracotta, dark brown, mustard, apricot, pale green, rose, white
Origin: purchased in Morocco and attributed to High Atlas Berbers by dealer but more likely area of Kairouan, Tunisia. The dyes are similar to those in the previous kilim
Size: 3.37m x 1.17m

The forms and shapes in these desert rugs evoke the Tunisian landscape. It is interesting to note that the French painter Paul Klee included similar forms and shapes after his trip to Tunisia in 1914: "He evokes clumps of grass and bushes amid the geometric shapes. Sometimes it is a city, sometimes a group of camels that emerges from the pattern of little squares.[13] After visiting Kairouan Klee said of his experience with color in that city: "I don't have to pursue it. It will possess me always. I know it. This is the meaning of this happy hour: Color and I are one. I am a painter."[14]

The pieces shown in color plates 31 and 32 (page 219) are used as rugs and as camel blankets. Strong bands of bright, solid colors are interspersed with bands of typically North African geometric designs, stepped diamonds, zigzag forms, and serrated chevrons. A dramatic use of white is a design feature of Tunisian desert rugs.

Desert rug
Warp: single-ply wool
Weft: single-ply wool
Technique: dovetailed tapestry weave, continuous warp, some lazy lines
Origin: oasis area of Tozeur
Size: 3.6m x 1.87m

Desert rug
Warp: 2-ply wool
Weft: single-ply wool
Technique: interlocking tapestry
Colors: red (field), pink (center), white, yellow, pale orange, salmon, 2 greens, brown, black
Origin: Sidi-Bou-Sid in the Sâhel
Size: 1.8m x 3m
The field holds a large serrated diamond, in the center of which is a white mosque with a bird on its minaret, palm trees in front, and a crescent moon above. The color changes of the zigzag motif in the main border create an optical effect (of motion).

Ferrâsîya
Warp: wool
Weft: wool
Technique: interlocking tapestry weave and eccentric beating, creating curvilinear forms
Origin: Gafsa, c. 1850–1900
Size: 2.35m x 2.15m

Geometric, animal, and human figures adorn this gay example of Tunisian folk art. Organized into stripes and compartments, the figures record the day-to-day observations of the women who make them. They depict the arches of buildings, nomadic tents (*bît*), snakes, lines of fish seen in irrigation canals, camel caravans (*jmel*), soldiers standing at attention, and sentry boxes at the fortified palace nearby. The human forms are shown frontally, the animals in profile. Gafsa, an oasis in southwest Tunisia on the site of a former Roman city (Capsa), is located midway between the date-growing and the grain-growing regions, a crossroads of North-South and East-West caravan routes. It is famous for these tapestries, which have been woven by the women of the area for several centuries. Much sought after by the citizens of Tunis (Moslems and Jews) and the other chief cities of Tunisia, they have long been a major article of trade with the other parts of Maghrib.[15] The *ferrâsîya*, also called *battanîya*, has a square format. (Collection of the Victoria & Albert Museum, London)

Fras (one end)
Warp: wool
Weft: wool
Technique: interlocking tapestry weave
Colors: red, white, green, black—traditional in Gafsa weaving
Size: 1.75m x 1.2m (part shown)
A camel caravan marches across the field. In boxes located under the camel, called houses, are arrows, diamonds with crosses, and other geometric figures. The diagonal rows, each consisting of three triangles, are Arabic motifs. The upper row is derived from a row of fish. *Fras* (also called *hûli*) are Gafsa blankets. They are 16' to 32' long, and plain centers are woven with these panels at either end.

Redeyev (brocaded rug)
Warp: brown and white wool
Weft: wool
Brocading: wool
Selvages: black hair
Technique: weft-faced plain weave with tightly woven skip plain weave bands, geometric side borders of slit tapestry weave
Colors: red, black, white, yellow-orange, green, brick red
Origin: Redeyev (near the Algerian border southwest of Gafsa)
Size: 2.6m x 1.34m
The field is divided into rectangular motifs that hold serrated diamond motifs. Rows of deer brocaded in contrasting colors make up the end borders. (Loaned by Joanna Crawford)

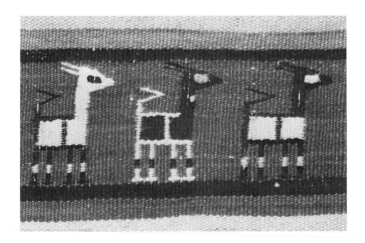

Brocaded rug
Warp: single-ply wool
Weft: single-ply wool
Technique: skip plain weave
Colors: white (ground), black, red, turquoise, orange, gray, yellow
Size: 1.35m x 2.7m
Origin: Matmâta, a southern mountain village
The overall design shows typical diamond figures. The largest end border is a fishlike brocaded figure composed of a diamond and two triangles, also typical.

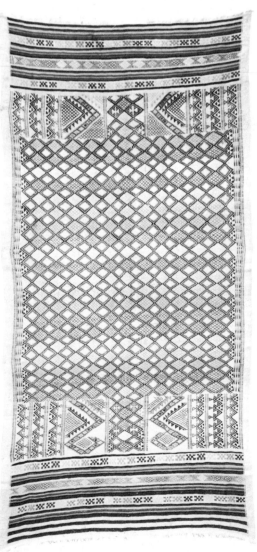

Brocaded rug
Warp: wool
Weft: wool
Technique: Plain weave with spot brocading
Colors: white, pinkish red, dark bluish black
Size: 2.25m x 1.6m
Origin: Oudref, an oasis area

Outlined boxes of small overall diamonds alternate with solid-color boxes, each with five serrated lozenges. The surrounding four-sided border contains rows of typical diamond figures. The colors are derived from madder and indigo; other vegetable dyes used in the area are pomegranate peels, saffron, henna, oak bark, and nut shells. The town of Oudref is celebrated for the quality and originality of its textiles: "In each brown-earth dwelling one or more looms are to be found in a room, courtyard, portico, or entrance corridor. The women work at them without let up in all seasons, carding, spinning, weaving from sunrise to sunset."[16] (Loaned by Ali MacGraw)

Berber blanket (*moucht'iya*)
Warp: single-ply wool
Weft: single-ply wool and cotton
Technique: plain weave with skip plain weave stripes
Colors: white (cotton), natural brownish black (wool), madder red, ocher (created by the dye discharge of the red ground)
Size: 2.6m x 1.2m
Origin: the Sahel, Djebeniana

The procedure of making the *moucht'iya* and the ritual surrounding it are very elaborate. It seems to embody as much folk belief and to be as important in the local cultural scheme as any weaving encountered in previous chapters. The *moucht'iya* is a blanket made by girls and women of eastern Tunisia (a tradition apparently deriving from Tripolitania). There are obligatory colors and patterns. The background is dyed, and some resist areas are processed after the weaving is complete and off the loom. The weaver places date pits or chick peas on the weaving and ties them into little packages. The natural-colored weaving is then immersed in a dyepot filled with cochineal (*garance*), which has been mordanted with alum and tartar, and left for the appropriate amount of time. It emerges as a red blanket with ocher discharge spots. These *taches ocrées* are considered to protect the maker: "Dieu seul fait les ouevres parfaites"["Only god can make something perfect"], says one of the weavers.[17] This sentiment is found in most weaving cultures. This particular blanket is made by the Methellith, a tribe descended from the Solayno Berbers, who emigrated from Egypt ten centuries ago. Even with 1,000 years of "Arabization" they still retain their old beliefs and customs. (Loaned by Ali MacGraw)

During the spinning, dyeing, and weaving of the *moucht'iya* (also *mustiya* or *mendi*) invocations in the form of poetic chants are made to God and the Prophet, to the sheep from which the wool was sheared, and to other weavers. Of the chants collected from weavers at El Djem (a neighboring town of Djebeniana in the Sâhel also inhabited by descendants of Berbers) three kinds of couplets were the most frequent. Their themes were rivalry among weavers, the ease and swiftness of the work, and the beauty of the tools. Here is an example of a couplet on the second theme:

Yâ mensjî, yâ zîn, yâ akheff el-amel
Akheff men er-richa ala dh'aher ej-jmel.[18]

O my beautiful loom, whose works are lighter than a feather on the back of a camel.

SUB–SAHARAN AFRICA

In sub-Saharan Africa most textiles are made from vegetable fibers. Wool is used on the Niger Bend in Mali and Nigeria, in the western Sudan, and in South Africa. Of the vegetable fibers used some are plaited and netted; one, barkcloth, is made by beating the inner bark of certain bushes; others are unspun fibers such as those from the raffia palm, which are woven; of spun fibers mainly cotton is used.[19] Cotton is grown in many areas. The weaving and dyeing of cotton cloth for the varied designs and garments of people inhabiting over thirty nations would warrant several volumes.

In the areas where wool is woven—by the Niafunke in Mali, for example—narrow bands are sewn together into larger cloths in the same manner in which cotton cloth is made across the continent. Weavings are separated into women's weaves and men's weaves depending on the sex of the weaver. Men weave on a horizontal treadle loom, which produces narrow strips of any length. They are weavers by trade and their products are made for sale. Women weave on a wider vertical loom, which produces cloths that are often as large as 4' x 6' or 5' x 6' and are used as wraparound family garments.[20]

Wedding blanket (one-quarter)
Warp: cotton
Weft: brocading wool
Colors: white, dark blue, brick red, ocher
Technique: tapestry weave with brocading and skip plain weave, made in six strips
Size: 4.75m x 1.4m (full rug)
Origin: made by a weaver of the Peulh, nomadic tribes in West Africa, Niger Bend area, used by Tauregs

(Loaned by Kahlenberg Associates)

Berber woman wearing a *moucht'iya*. (Drawing by Nicole Gespi)

Blanket, men's weave
Warp: single-ply wool
Weft: single-ply wool, possibly with some hair
Technique: warp-faced plain weave, weft-float and warp brocade, made in six panels
Colors: black, white, brick red, some yellow
Origin: Fulani tribe, Nigeria, West Africa
Size: 2.52m x 1.3m

Some stripes include tiny geometric figures. The wider white stripes have traditional motifs. Similar weavings, known as *kassa,* have been made for centuries as rugs, blankets, and covers for drums and fetish bowls in the area of the Niger that is now part of Mali and Nigeria. They were an important item of trade.[21] (Loaned by UCLA Museum of Cultural History, gift of Dr. and Mrs. Joel Berman)

ETHIOPIA

The central highlands provide cool grazing land for sheep, goats, and other animals. Flat-woven rugs of wool and animal hair are made in traditional geometric designs. They are called *dessye* after the provincial capital and market center where they are traded. In recent decades pictorial designs such as the lion of Judah have been introduced. The Ethiopian weavers shown here, photographed in 1911, inhabit a hotter lowland area and use cotton. They are probably weaving fabric for the white cotton garments called *gabi* and *shamma*.

10

the near east

Ride upon a beetle rather than walk upon a carpet. —Near
Eastern proverb

The areas of the Near East included here are the valleys of the Tigris and Euphrates Rivers, the coastal areas of the Fertile Crescent, and the deserts and oases of the Nile, all birthplaces of ancient civilizations. The names of the modern countries of the region are: Egypt, Israel, Yemen (Yemen Arab Republic, Southern Yemen), Saudi Arabia, Oman, United Arab Emirates, Qatar, Bahrain, Kuwait, Jordan, Lebanon, Iraq, and Syria.

EGYPT

Egypt, a major meeting place of ancient cultures, has always occupied parts of the northeast corner of Africa and the Sinai Peninsula, which is in Asia. Its borders are the Mediterranean Sea on the north, the Red Sea on the southeast, Israel on the northeastern border of the Sinai peninsula, the Sudan in the south, and Libya in the west.

The valley of the Nile River, which runs between large deserts that stretch across the continent, was the site of one of the greatest of ancient civilizations. Detailed hieroglyphs and wall paintings found in Egyptian tombs show aspects of textile making: the preparation of flax, the spinning and weaving of cloth, the shape of the loom, and something about the weaver's life. Wall paintings in the tombs of Beni Hasan (2380–2167 B.C.) show a horizontal loom. Textiles have survived in such tombs from early periods due to the dry climate.

Early Egyptian history from 3400 B.C. to 332 B.C. has been divided into thirty periods. Alexander the Great entered Egypt in 332 B.C. and founded Alexandria. The country subsequently thrived under the Ptolemies, with the Hellenistic Greek culture of the period as its model. The period from the 3rd to the 7th century A.D. is referred to as Coptic. The Copts are now a remnant of those Christians living in Egypt who were not converted to Islam in the centuries of Moslem culture that started with the Hegira of Mohammed the Prophet to Mecca in 618 B.C.

Coptic textiles represent a milestone in the tapestry technique. Most existing examples date only from the 3rd to the 8th century A.D. due to a change of burial customs. The dead were now buried in their daily clothing, and other wrappings were used as burial cloths.[1] Egyptian fabrics had been woven of linen. Some wool was introduced in the Middle Kingdom (2050–1780 B.C.). Coptic fabrics were woven of wool (weft) and linen (warp). Flat-woven pieces (tufted or looped weaves were also woven during this period) included the panels (*clavi*) that bordered the garments of the time. In the form of roundrels or squares many examples of this work still exist.

Many of the designs were based on ancient wall paintings and other ancient Egyptian themes and were treated in a naturalistic style, going back to ancient roots and native culture and rejecting the "high style" court art of the conquerors, represented by the Hellenistic style. The favorite Old Testament character of Joseph was a recurring figure in textile design. Many Coptic fragments now in museums show part of the Joseph story. Other themes include domestic animals, flowers, and portrait heads such as those found in mummy portraits of the early Egyptian dynasties.

The most characteristic flat-woven technique was slit tapestry weaving with outlining. (Silks and silk twills were woven in a similar technique.) In addition to garments wall hangings and covers were made. Flat-woven rugs were known to have been used. There is a jump of 1,300 years between the first and second flat-woven rugs shown here. There must have been a continuing tradition of folk weaving in the towns, villages, and countryside of Egypt. Knotted rugs of distinctive geometric design, called *mamluk,* have been preserved from the 15th century. After the Ottoman occupation (1517) the knotted carpets made in Cairo began to show naturalistic designs. Many such high-style designs exist in museum collections around the world.

The Egyptian kilim is woven for local use. Designs vary from simple stripes to organized floral patterns. Characteristic of these kilims are the use of undyed wool in the three natural colors occurring in the delta; a pleasing, almost square format (5'' x 7'', 9'' x 11''); and the slit-tapestry-weave technique. They are made in one piece and are reversible. They are called *bisats,* or *busuts;* it is interesting to note that the word *búsut,* meaning a kind of carpet (not specified), is mentioned by an Arab writer in 903 A.D. in a description of textiles and household objects in the Tigris district of Iraq.[2] Makdisi, another early Arabic writer, used the word *búsut* to describe "excellent carpets" from southern Persia and the phrase *al-búsut al sani'* to describe certain weaving from the Persian province of Fars.[3]

The *bisats* are used in village homes, city homes, and public places. In an old Coptic church in the Old Town in Cairo they cover the floors and the corridors.

Rug (fragment)
Warp: hair
Weft: hair
Technique: plain weave with brocading, 3 selvages
Colors: dark brown field with pale green, orange, and mustard
Size: .86m x .47m
Origin: Egypt, Coptic period
The end panel shows a complex cross in an arch between swastikas. No information survives as to the design of the complete rug, but its width, simple design, and coarseness indicate that it could have been a sack or bag. (Collection of Los Angeles County Museum of Art)

Bisat
Warp: 2-ply cotton
Weft: wool
Technique: slit tapestry weave
Colors: natural beige, dark brown, medium brown
Size: 1.65m x 2.6m
Origin: Village-made, near Cairo (Lower Egypt), c. 1930
This is an art-deco design, perhaps copied from a magazine of the period. *Bisats* were also traditionally made and used in the Delta and in Upper Egypt.

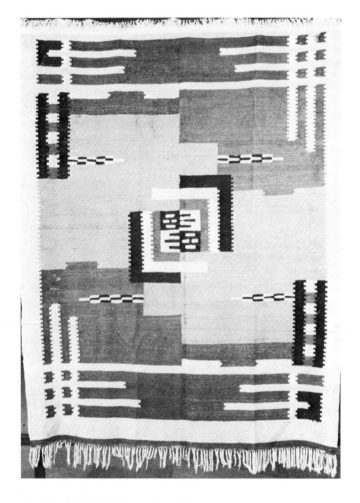

Bisat
Warp: cotton
Weft: wool
Technique: slit tapestry weave
Colors: natural undyed beige, two browns
Origin: Lower Egypt, c. 1930
Size: 3.03m x 3.72m
A center cartouche medallion and four small geometric figures are the only design elements on the field, which has serrated edges on all sides. Each village uses its own designs. This design is seen in contemporary rugs sold in Cairo.

Mat making in Egypt, early 1900s. Throughout the world in areas where suitable leaf fibers are abundant mats were made for many uses. In Egypt rushes of palm fibers are used, split longitudinally and dampened for weaving.

Egypt has a large Bedouin population whose nomadic pastoral life is similar to that of its brethren throughout Arabia. Egypt's Bedouins are found in the eastern desert (particularly in northern Sinai), parts of the Nile Valley, and in the western desert (Libyan desert). It is interesting to note that weaving in the western desert is generally weft-faced and made on a relatively wide loom, like North African weaving, while the loom products of the eastern desert are warp-faced and are made on a narrow loom like the Arabian weaving shown later in this chapter.

Camel with a Bedouin woven saddlebag of a type familiar throughout the area, Giza, Egypt. (Photo: Suad Cano)

ISRAEL

Some historians cite Mesopotamia as the original home of the Semites, while others favor Arabia or Africa.[4] It was in Mesopotamia that Abraham the Patriarch, who represents the covenant of God to the Jews and who is "the friend of God" to the followers of Islam (the appellation of Abraham in the Koran), started his wanderings. His father had apparently brought his family from far up in the valley of the Tigris and Euphrates Rivers to the ancient Sumerian capital of Ur (near Basra, now Iraq).

Abraham led his clan up the green valleys of the Euphrates River and down into the Judean highlands (now Jordan). He grazed his flocks in the Negev (now Israel). He crossed the vast desert (now southern Syria and the northern part of Saudi Arabia). In a time of drought he went into the green delta of the Nile in Egypt. Abraham's migrations were those of a pastoral nomad leading his tribe to areas where good pastures and water were available.

The Code of the Covenant (Exodus 20:22–23:19) describes a community that is no longer the nomadic one of Abraham the Patriarch. This code suited Israel as a community of shepherds and peasants evolving toward nationhood, adopting an agricultural way of life. An interest in beasts of burden, farming, and houses showed a predisposition to settlement indicating that the period of nomadism was at an end.

In the Book of Exodus Yahweh's instructions to Moses for making the tabernacle and its furnishings specify that sheets of goat hair be made to form a tent over the tabernacle. Eleven of these goat-hair sheets were to be made, each 30 cubits long by 4 cubits wide (the right dimensions for pieces made on the narrow nomad's loom). The tabernacle was then to be fitted with a variety of sumptuous textiles and finished with carved acacia wood; the tent over the tabernacle was woven of the same stuff and in the same way as is the tent used today by the nomads inhabiting the same desert.[5] Every version of the Old Testament details the making of the tabernacle by listing the work performed by the most skilled craftsmen. Knowing as we do the division of labor among the people of that period, we can assume that the craftsman who made the sheets of goat hair to form the tabernacle might have been a craftswoman.

Israel is now a modern, westernized state, becoming the dreamed-of Jewish homeland in 1948. It borders Egypt in the Sinai in the south and southwest, Syria and Jordan in the east, and Lebanon in the north. Its population in 1970 was 3,010,000. Israelis speak Hebrew, the revived national language. Arabic is widely spoken, as is English. Other languages were brought with them by immigrants.

Of its total 1972 population of 3,147,683, 85.3% was urban. Bedouin tribesmen around Jerusalem in the Negev, near Beersheba, and the Galilee, numbering 53,000, or 9.6% of the population, live a traditional pastoral life, and some still weave for their tents, as do the Bedouins of neighboring lands. Many textiles, including saddlebags, flat-woven rugs and finely made costumes are in Israeli museums, many brought by immigrants.

ARABIA

Arabia, the peninsula lying between mainland Africa and Asia, contains a great desert, which is a continuation of the Syrian desert in the north. In the desert are spotted a number of oases, where palm trees, particularly the famous date palms of Arabia, and tamarisks provide shade. The land west of the desert is particularly fertile, an area known as Arabia Felix.

Towns and cities with sedentary populations and oil-producing areas near the Persian Gulf make up less than half the population of Saudi Arabia. In 1965 two-thirds of the population (7,200,000) was nomadic. The nomadic people of Arabia, Semites, consider themselves the only true Arabs. They are referred to by others as Bedouins, based on the Arabic word for the desert inhabited by nomadic people, *al badia*. The lives led by the nomadic peoples of Arabia form a direct link to the biblical past of Christians, Jews, and Moslems and give us an opportunity to look back at a lifestyle that has changed little in 3,000 years.

Saudi Arabia was the birthplace of the Prophet Mohammed and the starting point of the Arab empire. Mohammed was born in Mecca and took his famed flight (*hegira*) to Medina. These two holy cities of Islam remain the pride of Saudi Arabia to which pilgrims from the Moslem world gravitate yearly. After the death of the Prophet and the zealous expansion of Islam cultural centers were founded in other converted areas, and Saudi Arabia faded into the background of world history for over a thousand years.

The major language is Arabic; the religion is Sunni Moslem. The Bedouin language is considered the purest of Arabic tongues, isolated as it has been from outside influences and remaining closest to the language as it was spoken by the Prophet.

In their life in the desert, in their direct day-to-day knowledge of the stars and the terrain, the Bedouins are the living memory of times past. The Ruwala, for example, are a powerful tribe of the Anazah confederation. They migrate extensively each year from near Damascus in Syria to the an-Nafud desert. When the star Canopus appears in the autumn sky, they leave their summer pastures in the cultivated areas and begin moving into the desert. Once in the open plains, they divide into subtribes and spread out depending on the availability of pastures and water. As Douglas L. Johnson pointed out in his study *The Nature of Nomadism,* the dispersal of nomadic tribes during migration gives the appearance of aimlessness and has been misinterpreted. Like others encountered in previous chapters, they have a regular but flexible movement, changing when patterns of rainfall and pasture growth change.[6] They move in order to sustain themselves and their flocks; they are by necessity in touch with the sky above and the earth below; they value above all their independence; they would not exchange all the worldly goods for their freedom.

Among the Bedouin tribes the lives of women are circumscribed. Arab women are less free than their Berber neighbors (Berbers are usually monogamous), and their activities are carefully governed by tribal traditions.

An oasis town near the Persian Gulf, 1950s. (Photo: Aramco)

Women of many tribes observe *purdah* (the concealment or veiling of adult women) in differing degrees. A sheik referred to by H.R.P. Dickson as "His Majesty Bin Sàud" said that he had had about 400 wives during his life but had never seen the face of any of them. Four is the legal number of wives set by the Koran.[7]

The women's portion of the tent contains cooking utensils, provisions, and family belongings. The bedding (rugs and mattresses) is stacked against the tent (in the same manner as in Iran and Central Asia) and covered by quilts (*lihaf*). In this area are the spindles (*maghzal*) and looms (*nati*). The loom is a horizontal ground loom on which is produced the strips of fabric that make the tent (wealthy Bedouins now purchase tent strips from urban weaving workshops). The Bedouin woman also weaves the *gata* (*sahah*), the dividing curtain that separates the men's portion of the tent from the women's portion. The *gata* is made of several strips that are sewn together, the pattern varying from tribe to tribe. Also made on the narrow loom is the *ruwag* (the back curtain of the tent), the *mizwad* (cushion), and the *khurj* (saddlebag).[8]

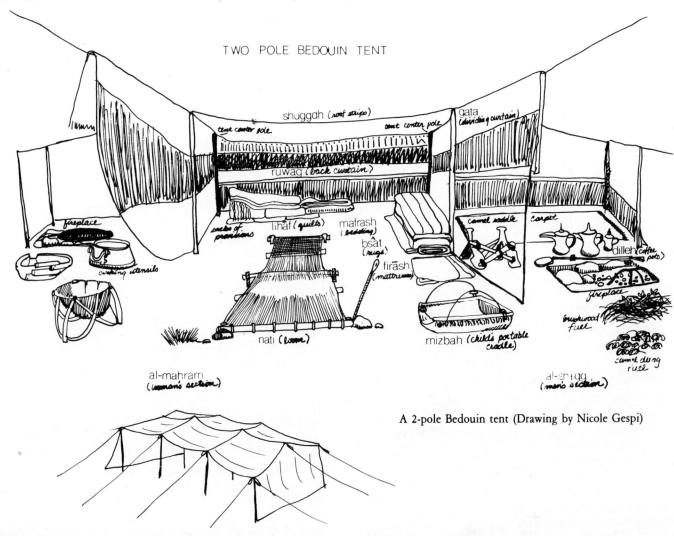

A 2-pole Bedouin tent (Drawing by Nicole Gespi)

In the men's portion of the tent the paraphernalia of coffee making is prominent, since the ceremony of making and serving coffee to guests is a function of the head of the family. Guests are always well received, and their safe conduct is ensured. The men's portion is furnished with carpets, mattresses for seating, and cushions for leaning.[9] The strength of the geometric design in these weavings is striking, and the weavings perhaps represent the most developed decorative craft of these people.

Tent rug (*bisat*)
Warp: wool
Weft: wool
Technique: dovetailed tapestry weave, made in two parts, warp ends grouped and wrapped to make tassels of varying colors
Colors: maroon, red, brown, black, dark blue, white, orange
Origin: Saudi Arabia
Size: 4.1m x 1.7m
Overall connected medallions make a pattern that can be read diagonally or horizontally. (Collection of the UCLA Museum of Cultural History)

Tent strip (*shuggah, flidj*)
Warp: undyed goat hair
Weft: undyed goat hair
Technique: heavy balanced plain weave
Color: dark gray
Origin: Arabia
Size: .51m x 7.2m
These pieces are often 10 yards long. They are sewn together to make the tent.

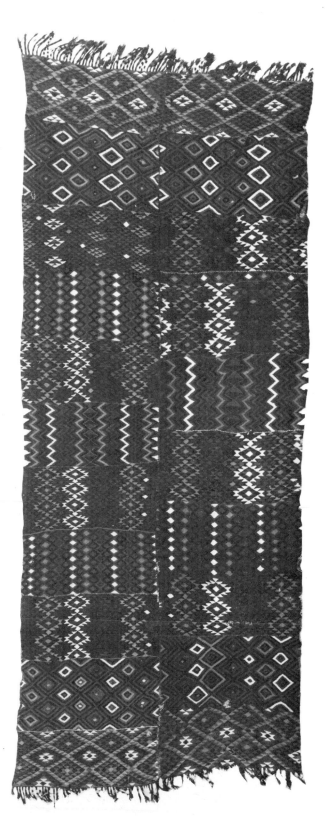

IRAQ

Iraq has been an independent country since 1932. It had been under British mandate as a result of World War I. Its boundaries are Turkey to the north, Iran to the east, Saudi Arabia and Kuwait to the south, and Jordan and Syria to the west. Its 1965 population was 8,261,527. Its languages are the official tongue, Arabic, southern Kurdish, and Turkish. In ancient times it was known as Mesopotamia. It centers on the great south-flowing rivers, the Tigris and the Euphrates, which come together in the Shatt El Arab.

Bisat (*b'sat* in Jordan)
Warp: 2-ply wool
Weft: 1-ply wool
Technique: slit tapestry weave, made in two parts
Colors: warm medium brown, blackish blue, white, orange, light green
Size: 1.5m x 2.18m

Ascending serrated diamonds, each with a typical Iraqi medallion, fill the field. The figures in the end border (called *nakelia*) are another typical Iraqi geometric motif. The names assigned to the motifs are derived from geometry.

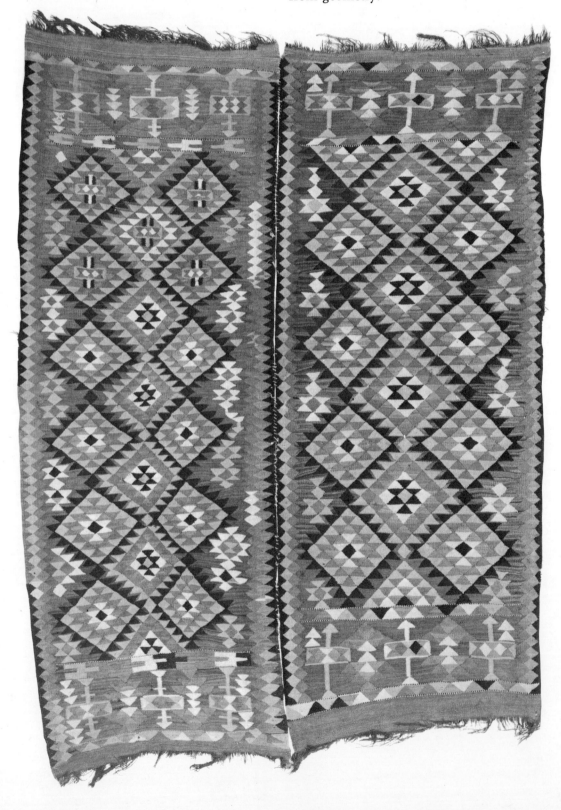

Woman's saddlebag
Warp: wool
Weft: wool
Technique: warp-faced plain weave, rows of
twined-weft patterning, tassels and loops added
Colors: brown, white, black; green, yellow, pink
(brocading); red, white, green, purple (tassels);
black, white (loops)
Origin: Bedouin
Size: 1.03m x .46m
Brown or black and white or red and black with bright-
colored tassels and stripes are seen in saddlebags
throughout the Bedouin weaving areas. Men's saddlebags are of the same design but larger and sometimes
more heavily tasseled.

Cushion
Warp: wool
Weft: wool
Technique: slit tapestry weave
Colors: pink, orange, light green, yellow, brown
Size: .46m x .65m
Plain bands are separated by bands with geometric
figures. The row of three triangles in diagonal progres-
sion is called a *majela.*

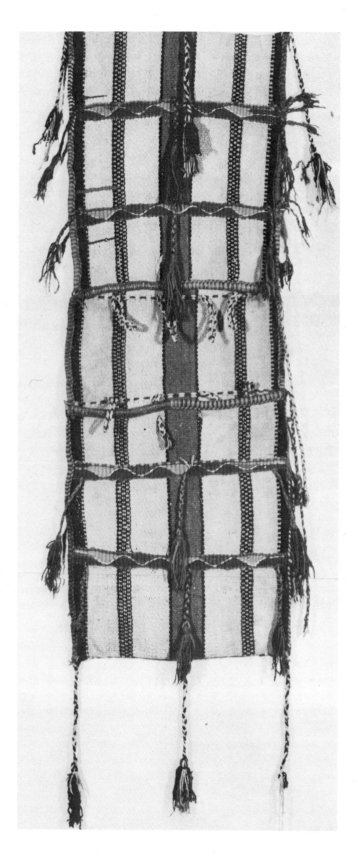

In the rug shown in color plate 33 (page 220) two strands, twisted together, are embroidered onto a plain-weave ground. The twisting creates three-dimensional areas. Four patterns are traditional—Kurdish (usually animal and human motifs), Assyrian (ancient geometric symbols), Babylonian (garden scenes), and Samawah (religious symbols). Some of these embroidered rugs are made as dowry rugs. Some are used in tents. They are prized possessions. Men sometimes participate in the embroidering.

Embroidered rug (*shef*)
Warp: wool
Weft: wool
Embroidery: wool
Technique: plain weave with coils of chain-stitch embroidery sewn on
Origin: Samawah, Iraq, c. 1930
Size: 2.57m x 1.75m

SYRIA

Syria, an Arab Republic, is bounded by Turkey, Iraq, Jordan, Israel, Lebanon, Turkey, and the Mediterranean. In 1970 Syria had a population of 5,900,000. Its official language is Arabic. Armenian, Kurdish, Turkish, and Syrian are secondary languages.

In the North kilims were woven in villages. In the South in the great Syrian desert Bedouin tribeswomen weave rugs and cushions for their tents and saddlebags for their animals, similar to those shown in Iraq and Saudi Arabia. Druses living in Syria, Lebanon and Israel weave saddlebags and cushions of similar design and technique.

Many fine textiles have been made in Syria; others have been traded in the great marketplace of Damascus. With the arrival of Armenians from Turkey in the early years of this century Syria gained master kilim weavers whose work was known for its delicacy of design and materials.

Kilim (section)
Warp: 2-ply white wool
Weft: 1-ply wool
Technique: slit tapestry weave, some brocaded detail, made in two pieces, braided, tasseled warp ends
Colors: white (undyed), red, orange, light green, blue, gray, lavender
Origin: northern Syria or southern Turkey
Size: 3.43m x 1.5m (entire rug), 1.16m x 1.5m (section shown)

Bands of varying colors with rows of small medallions make up the field. The border design contains running figures (called scorpions by weavers in various countries).

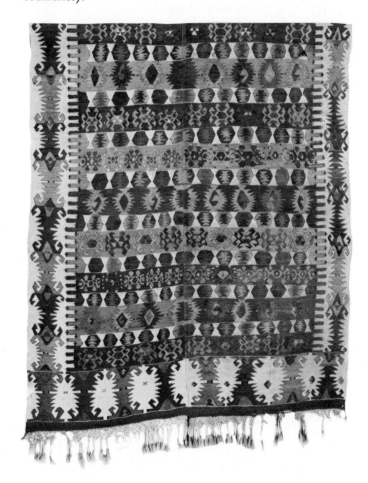

india and pakistan

A mother and daughter are like the handle and stick of a spinning wheel.—Kashmiri proverb

India is a subcontinent of Asia, about half of which is a peninsula with a coastline of 3,500 miles on the Arabian Sea on the west and the Bay of Bengal on the east. The population of India in 1970 was 550,370,000 (more than twice that of the USSR). The 1970 population of Pakistan was 55,000,000. Pakistan was formed in the Partition of 1947 from the predominantly Moslem areas of India. It is divided into two geographically separate parts, one on India's west, made up of the former Indian provinces of Baluchistan, West Punjab, the Northwest Frontier, Bahawalpur, and Khairpur, and one on India's east, Bangladesh (formerly East Bengal).

FLAT-WOVEN RUGS OF INDIA AND PAKISTAN

1. Kilims, brocaded rugs, and saddlebags, made by the Baluchis, were covered in Chapters 5 and 6. Some similar pieces are made in Baluchistan in western Pakistan by Baluchi nomads and settled Baluchi tribespeople.

2. *Druggets* are flat weaves of mixed materials made in simple patterns.

3. *Durries,* traditionally cotton but commercially wool, are made in widely diverse areas.

4. Folk *durries* are made for village use.

5. *Namdas,* felt rugs, are made particularly in Kashmir.

DRUGGETS

The Indian *drugget* is a handwoven flat rug decidedly in the low style. The weave is not finely textured, and the materials are coarse. It is made for a poor domestic and export market. Nonetheless, these large woven rugs serve their function as a floor covering and a decorative function as well. They are bold and simple in design, with appeal to contemporary taste.

Drugget
Warp: cotton
Weft: wool and unspun plant fiber
Technique: plain weave, adjacent areas of color changes sewn together
Colors: tan (field), orange, forest green, black
Size: 2.7m x 3.6m
Origin: India
The design is typically art deco.

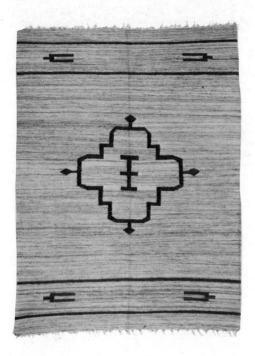

Drugget
Warp: cotton
Weft: twisted wool and plant fiber
Technique: weft-faced plain weave, dovetailed tapestry weave
Colors: tan (field), red
Size: 2.7m x 3.6m
The tapestry weave occurs where pattern areas of different colors meet.

DURRIES

A *durrie* (*dhurrie, dari* in Hindi) is a flat-woven cotton rug that is indigenous to India and the surrounding area (eastern Afghanistan, Pakistan, and Burma). A *durrie* can be woven "from jute, coir, sisal and even aak plant fiber, or from waste wool and cotton mixture . . . but the true durrie is a flat-weave of all-cotton warp and weft."[1]

In 1913 Walter Hawley described kilims from Dera Ghazi Khan (a town in what is now Pakistan near Lahore). They were wool, woven by women in their own homes, with stripes separated by designs that were "originally copied from the robes of the Pharaohs of Egypt."[2] The rugs Hawley saw were probably durries.

Although they became popular in the United States only in the 1970s, *durries* have been made continuously for centuries. According to Sir George Birdwood, "They illustrate the most ancient ornamental designs in India."[3] They were used in many ways: as floor coverings for palaces and village huts, as ground coverings for ceremonial occasions, as eating clothes for public events and lavish parties given by maharajahs. For the larger population they served as sleeping mats, prayer rugs, wagon covers, and carrying cloths. In the 15th century an Italian traveler observed that the Indian merchants were very rich: "these alone use tables at their meals with tablecloths and silver vessels as we do; the inhabitants of the rest of India eat on carpets spread on the ground."[4] These carpets referred to were *durries,*

since fine knotted carpets made in the "high style" of the 16th century were beyond the means of those inhabitants.[5]

In 1900 Mumford wrote that the lack of wool had always been a drawback to carpet weaving in India: "In fact, the only carpets made there prior to the Mohammedan domination [in the 16th century by Akbar] were wholly of cotton or cotton mixed with silk."[6] Silk as well as gold and silver was added to the cotton *durrie* for special orders, which were common in certain areas.

The palaces of maharajahs in Rajastan held fine antique *durries*. Collections still exist in other once princely homes. Many were made to order during the colonial period for the English, who brought them back to England, where they were very popular. (The Great London Exhibition of 1851 introduced *durries* and other Indian crafts into Europe.) Due to the English influence and the custom orders from western-educated Indians a wide variety of non-Indian designs are seen in existing *durries* that date back to the 18th century.

With the recent American demand *durrie* making has become a very large industry. India's largest exported handicraft is now rugs, and India is almost at the top of the world market in terms of rug manufacture. In central India the rug-making "villages" of Bhadohi and Said Raja employ 250,000 weavers to make flat-weaves and knotted rugs.[7] The workshops in which these rugs are made are valuable assets to the Indian economy and certainly contribute to the welfare of the Indian weaver. The commercial product, however, is not the subject of this volume; folk weaving is. In India *durries* were also made in the folk-art tradition.

In some areas of Madhya Pradesh state—Jobat, for example—cotton *durrie* making was a cottage industry, encouraged by the Tribal Welfare Department. An Indian member of the All India Handicrafts Board said that "these have won distinction because of their sturdy character and their bright delightful colors, for the tribals love warm tints."[8] The *durries* of this area are made on a pit loom in the slit tapestry technique, which is called *tillis* (the word for the place in the rug where the color of the weft is changed). In other areas of India

dovetailed tapestry weave and interlocking tapestry weave are common techniques. Complex looms are used. Tribal patterns from village murals and other handicrafts were introduced in workshop-made *durries*. *Durries* to be used as floor coverings for particular festivals included appropriate designs.

In the Punjab, a western state part of which is now Pakistan, *durrie* making had been long established as a folk-art tradition. Girls learned embroidery and weaving from childhood in preparation for marriage. *Durries* were the direct expression of the weavers and incorporated motifs from everyday life into weavings that became a part of the dowry and brought beauty into the home. *Durries* made in this tradition were kept as treasured possessions and rarely found their way to market. Many older cotton *durries* from the Punjab have been imported to the West. These were mainly the product of a cottage industry. Materials were supplied by a trader, who distributed the finished work. Most of these Punjabi rugs were made in two contrasting colors with simple geometric patterns.

These village women in the Sind desert area of Pakistan are weaving a *durrie*. The loom frame is that of the ubiquitous *charpaie,* the bed-lounge seen indoors and outdoors throughout the area. In the village of Bahawalpur warping is played as a game. After tying a ball of handspun cotton to the frame the woman at one end rolls it to the other end, where a second woman stretches it around her side of the frame and rolls it back, securing the warp. Children participate by retrieving the ball of cotton if it falls. (Photos: Sylvia Seret)

The *durrie*-making tradition in Madras (Bhavani *durries*) can be traced back at least 200 years. Simple striped designs were made at first, but floral and geometric motifs were added later. Many were silk or silk and cotton.

In Mysore the *durries* (Navalgund *durries*) were based on carpet designs (knotted) brought from Bijapur when it was a court center. The existing examples of old *durries* made in Navalgund display varied and intricate patterns. At that time Navalgund *durries* were made in very large sizes for special orders. Later, when the *durrie* market was less successful, they were made in small sizes for the local trade. These designs were geometrical and floral, delicately drawn, with some animal and bird forms. An Indian board game, *chaupat,* is represented in the center of some *durries* "to enable players to indulge in the game, sitting on the *durrie.*"[9]

Darjeeling (West Bengal), produced designs influenced by the area's proximity to Tibet; Patna and Obra (Bihar); Sholapur (Maharashtra); Panipat; Rohtak; Mani Majra (Punjab); and Warangal (Andhra Pradesh) were other centers for *durrie* making. While *durries* were made throughout greater India, it appears that the largest centers were in Agra, Aligarh and other towns in the Northwest provinces.[10]

Ripley, writing in 1904, mentions jail-made rugs (in Lahore and Agra).[11] *Durries* as well as knotted rugs were made in jails by convict labor. Records in the Peshawar (northern Pakistan) jail, for example, showed *durrie* orders dating over four decades. The jail-made *durrie,* as well as the jail-made carpet, was a widespread product. Its purposes were to make work for the prisoners and to reduce the expense of the penal system; the eventual effect, however, was to create unfair competition for the weaver whose craft was a hereditary part of the Indian caste system and who then was forced to cheapen his product by working more rapidly and weaving simpler designs. This deterioration coincided with a loss of popularity among the English, who had earlier been large *durrie* consumers. Some of the centers of *durrie* making fell into bad times and bad repair. In the 1960s, when an increase in American demand occurred, some of the earlier weaving centers were abandoned but others became centers for the thriving new industry.

Folk *durrie*
Warp: cotton
Weft: cotton
Technique: tapestry weave
Colors: ivory (field), white, red, green, blue, black, red (border)
Origin: India, region unknown
Size: 1m x 1.8m

Hunters on foot and on horseback pursue startled animals. One hunter with a bow has already pierced a deer. Other animals cavort. A chained elephant plays with or is being teased by a small animal. Birds perch on flowers in flowerpots and on free-floating branches. This rug is dated and signed.

Durrie

Warp: handspun cotton
Weft: cotton; gold (metallic) thread
Technique: tapestry weave
Colors: blue (from indigo), white, gold
Origin: Agra (Utter Pradesh State). c. 1870
Size: 1.20m x 2.10m

The field is composed of blue and white stripes, changing into bands with small star motifs (some with gold centers) at both ends. Of all the *durries* of India the finely striped ones from Agra are probably the most renowned. (Collection of Sylvia and Ira Seret)

NAMDAS

The *namda* is a felt rug made in different parts of India for many centuries. Designs are laid on the background, pressed in as part of the felting process, or appliquéd with a tambour needle, a large needle with a hooked end. Those from Kashmir, traditionally made with floral and geometric designs, have been patterned in the 20th century in a folk style with animal figures for export.

12

china

China, with its huge population (787,180,000 in 1970),
does not loom large in the flat-weave-rug world. Its interest is based on the following factors.

1. Its geographic position lies at the eastern end of
the silk route.

2. It has an ancient tradition of silk textile weaving
in the slit tapestry technique, known as *k'o-ssu*.

3. Its western provinces, encompassing eastern
Turkestan, are populated by tribal oasis-dwelling people, who are historically associated with the development of all forms of rug making, tapestry weaving,
brocading, felt making, and knotting.

4. Felt rugs are made in eastern Turkestan.

5. One type of flat-woven rugs, relatives of
Southeast Asia's popular woven mats, is made in
China.

Silk was an ancient Chinese treasure; sericulture (the
culture of the silkworm) was a carefully guarded secret
for thousands of years. Death was the penalty for exporting silkworm eggs. The caravan route that brought
raw silk from China had been operating since 114 B.C.
The silk route was in reality two different routes, both
starting near what is now Peking, one veering to the
north of the great Asian desert, the other to the south.
Both were arduous and dangerous. Bactria, a great
kingdom in central Asia that had become an eastern
province of the Persian empire, prospered as a connecting link along the silk route. At the western end of the
silk route centers developed, particularly in Tyre and
Berytus (Beirut), which at that time possessed the prized purple dye, and where silk was dyed and sold.

The Chinese version of tapestry weave is called
k'o-ssu. Scholars differ as to the derivation and meaning of the word.[1] Other fine silk weaving in China is
warp-faced. All the weaves utilize the fineness of the

silk filament and its ability to curve and bend. The
earliest surviving examples were found in Turkestan
along the silk route, in Korea, and in Roman tombs in
Palmyra. Some found in Japan have been dated in the
8th century.

Through the centuries *k'o-ssu* weaving has reflected
the taste of the given age. "The cultivated subtlety
of Chinese taste of the Sung period," for example,
showed in the fine textiles produced at that time.[2] The
technique can reproduce brushstrokes, express mobility, and reflect light with astonishing brilliance. *K'o-ssu*
was woven into large screen panels, small squares (many
survive that were worn on garments to denote rank),
collars, sashes, and other components of costume such
as beautiful robes.

China's northwest border abuts western Turkestan
(SSR Kirgiztan, SSR Tadjikistan), the territory of *yurt*-dwelling horse nomads. The area is now Sinkiang, an
autonomous region of the People's Republic of China.
Khotan (a great Chinese Buddhist center), Kashgar,
and Yarkand (a part of East Turkestan that did not actually become part of China until the mid-18th century) were near the Indian branch of the southern
caravan route. Because of their locations they were
storehouses for East–West trade goods. All three cities
were weaving centers for the famed knotted rugs called
Samarkand in the West and *Kansu* in China after their
relative entry points into these areas.[4] This method of
naming shows a consistency in the behavior of western
and eastern merchants.

Knotting was an ancient tradition in eastern
Turkestan, which is considered the probable birthplace
of rug making. Loulan, where the earliest known existing rug fragments were found (see Chapter 4), is on
the caravan route northeast of Khotan. Brocaded rugs

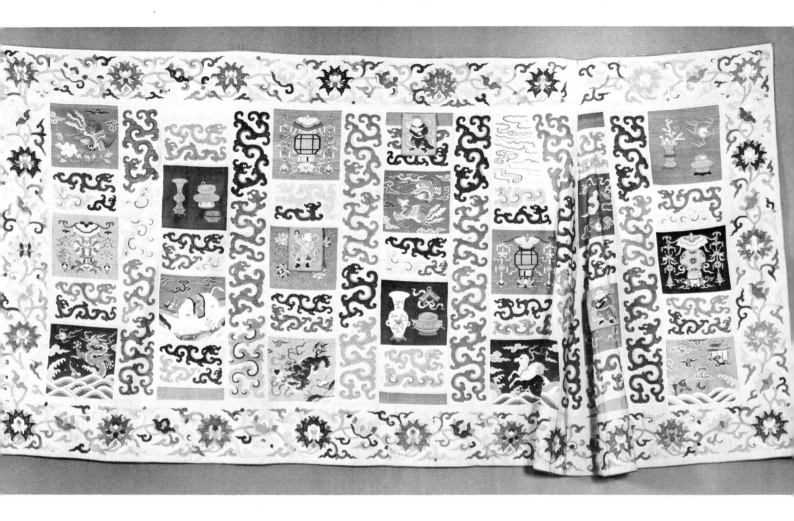

Buddhist priest's robe
Warp: silk
Weft: silk, gold decorative outlining
Technique: slit tapestry weave (k'ó-ssu), painted details
Colors: three blues, brown, ivory, red, pink, three greens, grey, mauve pink, aubergine brown, imperial yellow (ground)
Size: 1.08m x 2.18m
Date: 18th century
Many Buddhist symbols, including lanterns, beasts, a carp, fanged dragons, and cloud bands, are surrounded by a wide border of intertwined flower motifs and separated by cloud bands. Squares with costumed figures are attached. The sewing of the squares indicates that they might have been changed from their original position.[3] (Collection: Los Angeles County Museum of Art)

in the "high style" were made for the *yurts* of Mongol chiefs. Three Chinese scroll paintings from the 13th century represent knotted, brocaded, and tapestry-woven rugs, which were made throughout the area in what must have been a continuing tradition. They tell the same story of a Chinese lady, who was captured by raiders, taken to Mongolia as the wife of a chief, ransomed by a Chinese envoy, and returned to China. In the *yurts* rugs, saddlebags, saddle clothes, and cotton or straw mats are used, but in the Chinese scenes there are no rugs. Where Chinese and Mongolian figures appear together, the two are readily distinguished by their clothing and lifestyle. The Mongols, tent-dwelling oasis inhabitants, wore *chapans,* trousers, boots, and either furred or conical cloth caps; the Chinese, settled people living in well-built houses, wore flowing silk robes.[5]

Felt rugs were used in China (for cushion covers and as kneeling mats) 2,000 years ago. They were made by nomads and adopted by the Chinese, who exacted them as tribute from the wool-producing areas. Wool was associated with barbarians; silk and finer textiles were considered the proper fabrics for Chinese use. A similar differentiation took place in the Fertile Crescent area: Persian city dwellers wore elaborate silks and considered the people of Mesopotamia who wore wool as untutored, while the latter thought the Persians foppish.

Some 8th-century felt rugs survive (although there is some question about their exact origin) in the temple at Nara in Japan, donated as a memorial by the widow of the Emperor Shomu.[6] Patterns are characteristic of the Tang period (618–906): large floral rosettes, birds, bats, and clouds, symbols that would be used repeatedly in later Chinese rugs and in rugs shown in Chinese paintings of this and later periods. During the Mongol period (1260–1341) elaborate felt rugs were made for luxury use.

Felt rug
Rounded ornamentation is more frequent in eastern Turkestan, angular in western Turkestan. This rug, made in eastern Turkestan for nomadic use, shows a marked contrast with the intricate ones of earlier periods.[7]

Bamboo and grass mats have been used for sleeping and eating throughout Southeast Asia, particularly in humble surroundings. A style of flat-woven rug was made. They "have long been associated with riverboats," especially in the Yangtse region.[8] A pair in the Textile Museum (Washington, D.C.) was documented as originating in the French compound in Shanghai in 1909.[9]

Cotton weaving in a Chinese jail, early 1900s. (Photo: Le Tour du Monde)

Korean women spinning and weaving, 1910.

Rug (one of a pair)
Warp: cotton
Weft: wool, black hair
Technique: tapestry weave
Color: coral (field), aqua (birds), plum (combs)
Size: 1.2m x 3m
Date: 19th century
The large bird in the center of the plain field measures 1m. Four birds face inward. (Loaned by William H. Johnson, San Francisco)

Rug
Warp: cotton
Weft: wool, hair(?)
Technique: dovetailed tapestry, slit tapestry (*k'o-ssu*), eccentric weft beating
Colors: brown, white, rose, yellow, blue, green, tan
Origin: found in Mexico
Size: 1.83m x 1.34m
A center octagon holds a pagoda in a landscape. Groups of fans are symmetrically placed in the field. Block-printed branches fill the field. The block printing is on one side, which also has painted details. (Loaned by Sally Sirkin Lewis)

south america

When the rainbow enters the body of a man or woman, then the person becomes gravely ill. The sick person will be cured if he unravels a ball of yarn of seven colors.—Peruvian myth

The textiles of the Western Hemisphere are not referred to in books on oriental-style rugs. One of the reasons may be that the archaeological discoveries that led to the study of the former were made almost a century after the reawakened interest in antiquities that stemmed from Napoleon's Egyptian campaign in the early 19th century. Although explorations in Mexico and Peru were widespread, it was not until the discovery of Macchu Picchu in Peru in 1911 that the ancient civilizations of the Americas captured the world's imagination.

Like the weavers of the Middle East, the native weavers of the Americas made use of available natural materials and developed techniques that best suited these materials and the functions that their textiles served. The earliest textiles found in Peru (dating from 2500 B.C.) were made from a native cotton unique to this part of the world. It grew in two or more natural shades, enabling weavers to pattern without dyes.[1] The resulting techniques and fabrics depended in part upon the characteristics of the backstrap loom, the oldest South American loom, which is still in use.

The achievement of South American weavers, particularly of the Andean area, compares favorably in terms of design, use of color, and complexity of weaving, brocading, and embroidery methods with textiles made in any other part of the world at any time. Albers states that "In Peru where no written language, in the generally understood sense, had developed even by the time of the Conquest in the 16th century, we find—to my mind, not in spite of this but because of it—one of the highest textile cultures we have come to know." Albers makes the point that other parts of the world in

other periods achieved highly developed textiles, but none expressed itself as art directly through its textiles in the way that the ancient Peruvians did.[2] The elaborate fabrics of the Renaissance and the Far East served as giant illustrations and were considered decorative or minor art. Albers thinks that "regardless of scale, small fragment or a wall-size piece, a fabric can be great art if it retains directness of communication in

Double-weave bag, Inca, Central Coast, Peru. (Collection of Los Angeles County Museum of Art)

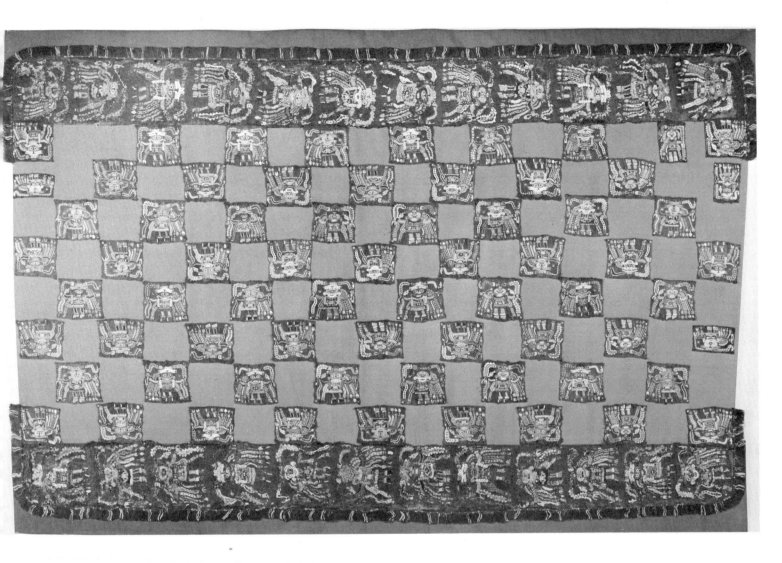

Mantle
Warp: unknown
Weft: unknown
Technique: details of ground weave unknown,
squares embroidered in stem stitch, fringed
borders
Origin: Paracas Culture, South Coast, 500–100
B.C.
Size: 1.5m x 2.66m
This piece has been restored. Only the embroidered
squares are original; they have been sewn to a cotton
backing. In each square a masked monkey holds a serpent whose mouth is filled with fruits and plants. A
weaver probably wove the plain ground, while em-
broiderers finished the piece. Some of these mantles
may have been used as hangings or coverlets, but most
were found wrapped between shrouds in the ruins of
the Paracas Necropolis. (Loaned by the Los Angeles
County Museum of Art)

153

its specific medium."[3] Albers' point seems to be that countries, like people, can be more visually than verbally oriented.

The ancient civilizations of South America inhabited the west coast in what is now southern Ecuador, Peru, and the northern part of Bolivia. The narrow coastal plains, the rugged Andean highlands, and the eastern slopes were areas in which diverse peoples built complex cities with rich cultures. The coastal area in particular, because of its arid, sandy environment, has yielded a remarkable store of archaeological material. Many textiles in almost perfect condition were found in coastal sites, while far fewer survived in the other areas.[4]

An early Peruvian civilization from which many textiles survive is the Paracas culture (1100–200 B.C.). Also leaving textiles were the Nazca culture (200 B.C.–600 A.D.), the Wari culture (600–1000 A.D.), and the Chimu Kingdom (1000–1470 A.D.). The Inca empire (1470–1532 A.D.) was the last and the most extensive of the indigenous preconquest South American cultures. The art of the Incas was rigidly prescribed, and artifacts of that period are readily identifiable.[5] The Incas wove fine ponchos, bags, and other articles of clothing for their officials, with patterns denoting rank and function.

Bag
Warp: wool, llama
Weft: wool, llama
Technique: dovetailed tapestry weave, selvages finished with herringbone stitch, heavily braided tassels
Colors: red, blue, white, black, green, yellow
Origin: Nazca, Wari, South Coast, Peru, 600–700 A.D.
Size: 41m x 16m
An abstract motif is framed by a step motif in alternating color sequence. (Loaned by the Los Angeles County Museum of Art)

Blanket
Warp: undyed cotton
Weft: wool, alpaca
Technique: plain-weave field, weft outlining (inner border), slit-tapestry weave (outer border)
Colors: red, yellow, tan (ground)
Origin: Peru, Inca, Central Coast, 12th–14th century
Size: 2.54m x 1.65m
The field holds twelve seated puma figures of different colors, all wearing weights. Narrow borders hold rows of bird figures. Alpaca wool is easily spun and takes dye well. It has many natural tones—ivory, buff, tan, several browns, and several grays. (Loaned by the Los Angeles County Museum of Art)

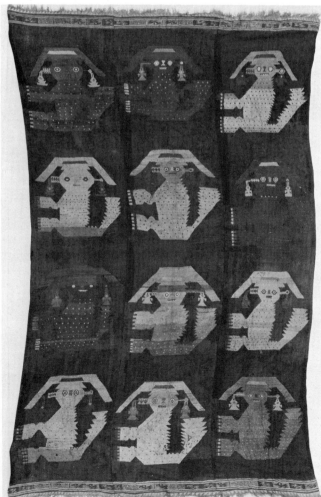

Pizarro landed in what is now the most northern part of modern Peru in 1532. Organized resistance was crushed, and soon almost all the native population (called Indians because of the belief at the time of Columbus that the Americas were the outermost of the East Indies) was subjugated.

The Spanish turned an Incan system of forced labor (in the form of occasional community service) into virtual slavery (known as the *encomienda*). Native men, for example, were forced to labor in weaving workshops (*obrajes*). The European floor loom introduced in these factories at that time is still used by men throughout South and Central America.[6] Women weave on the backstrap loom, also called the belt loom, commonly identified with South America. Sheep were also introduced. In Colombia, which had too wet a climate for the llamas and alpacas found in other South American areas, they provided a new weaving fiber.[7]

The indigenous population of the areas adapted to the Spanish presence by eventually separating into two strata: the *mestizo* and the *indio*. The *mestizo*, of mixed Spanish and Indian blood, "hispanicized" in language, clothing, and lifestyle, while the *indio* followed his tradition.

Carpet (one-quarter)
Warp: cotton, white
Weft: wool, one strand
Colors: red (background), light and dark blue, purple, light and dark gold, white, red
Technique: dovetailed tapestry weave, eccentric weft beating, woven in one piece
Origin: Peru, Spanish Colonial Period
Size: 6.48m x 3.89m (whole carpet)
The field contains stylized flowers with occasional birds; the four-sided border has a chain motif. This very large example is a floor rug, a carpet. Peruvian tapestries of the Colonial period were made for diverse purposes—to serve as portières, wall hangings, mantles, ponchos, and covers, as well as rugs. (Collection of Museum of Fine Arts, Boston, Charles Peter Kling Fund)

Cover or rug
Colors: red (field); mauve, dark red, beige, brown, cream, pink, yellow (inner guard); white, red, yellow, pink, mauve, purple (main border)
Technique: tapestry weave
Origin: Spanish-colonial Peru,[8] 17th century(?)
Size: 1.92m x 1.65m
The field holds two double-headed eagles from which sprout geometricized boughs with flowers and pairs of dovelike and black-headed birds. The main border consists of a continuing arabesque incorporating floral motifs. The format shows the influence of oriental rug design as filtered through European Renaissance tapestries. (Collection of the Victoria and Albert Museum, London)

155

The intricate textiles made for the Inca nobility and the tapestry-woven rugs and covers made after the conquest were "high-style" weavings, made by Indians but not for their own use. Indians living in isolation on Andean slopes and in the interior of the continent have retained native methods and designs. In diverse rural areas where the traditions of Indian culture have been preserved costumes for family wear and blankets for household use are woven. Among the far-flung surviving examples are the following.

1. The Araucanians in Chile (the only Indian tribe in that country with an intact native culture) weave striped rugs and saddle blankets from llama hair.

2. The Otavalos of northern Ecuador and the Guambiano and Páez of Colombia produce costumes that reflect a heritage of mother-to-daughter transmission of the techniques and designs of their cultures.

3. The Uro Indians at the edge of Lake Titicaca, near the ruins of the Tiahuanaco culture, weave warp-faced twill rugs. Every weaver makes a brocaded cover that is used to carry a baby or firewood. It is a special possession, as it was for their ancestors for centuries, rarely offered for sale.

4. The Aymara and Quechua of the Bolivian and south Peruvian highlands weave blankets in the same tradition as the following.

Blanket or rug
Warp: wool, 2 strands, twisted, handspun
Weft: wool, 2 strands, spun together, handspun
Colors: off-white, yellow, cranberry red, light green, dark blue
Size: 1.57m x 2.05m
Technique: interlocked tapestry weave, cut from loom, ends tucked back in one by one, and overcast with needle and yarn; made in two parts and joined together by removing last warp thread of each piece and interlocking the two pieces with additional yarn
Origin: Andean highlands, 1930s
Rows of eight-pointed stars, stacked diamonds (called *cocos*), and reciprocal mound shapes tipped with crosses and bands of stacked chevrons fill the field, which is bordered dynamically on the outer selvage edges by serrated triangles. This blanket was made by a now aged Peruvian Indian man who is directly descended from the Incas. His father was a weaver, as are others in his family. His blankets are distinctive and easily recognizable for their dynamic juxtapositions. (Collection of Joseph Fadish)

Blanket (*chamara*)
Warp: wool
Weft: wool
Colors: red, yellow, blue (indigo), green
Technique: tapestry weave
Size: 1.42m x 1.2m
Origin: Machiques, Lara state, Venezuela
(Loaned by Dennis Schmeichler Gallery, Caracas; photo: Charles Brewer)

In the 20th century rugs designed for local sale and the ever-increasing tourist trade are woven in villages, towns, and cities. They are based on motifs from ancient ceramics, architecture, and textiles. One town in Peru, San Pedro de Cajas, is a flourishing center for rug designs reproduced from the famed tapestries known as Mantas Paracas. Shaggy, flat-woven rugs woven of alpaca hair in simple designs are exported from Bolivia.

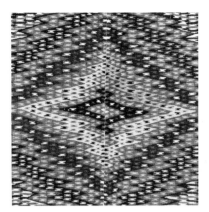

14

middle america

Middle America (or Mesoamerica when referring to the precolonial period) is bordered by the Pacific Ocean on the west and the Gulf of Mexico and the Caribbean Sea on the east.

The great pre-Columbian cultures of Middle America were the Maya, the Toltec, the Olmec, the Mixtec, and the Zapotec. The Aztec empire, the last of these cultures, with its capital at Tenochititlan in central Mexico, was conquered by Cortes and the Spanish in the early 16th century.

Information about the textiles of these people, one of their many highly developed arts, comes from decorations on ceramics, architectural and sculptural details, and Spanish accounts immediately following the conquest.[1] Examples, unfortunately, have not been preserved due to the damp climate.

Wool was introduced by the Spanish. Previous weaving materials had been cotton and a fiber from the century plant, the agave or American aloe. Under the Spanish taxes were exacted in woven products, as they had been under the Aztecs. Weavings based on European patterns were introduced. These designs became so intermixed with the former traditional designs that it is hard to separate the influences, but certain floral designs, for example, have a distinctly European feeling.

GUATEMALA

Guatemala, the most populous country of Central America (5,160,221 people in 1976) is bounded on the north and west by Mexico, on the east by British Honduras and the Caribbean Sea, on the southeast by Honduras and San Salvador, and on the southwest by the Pacific Ocean. Guatemala has two distinct regions, the tropical lowland areas and the temperate highlands.

Of the population 65% is Indian, most of whose cultural roots go back to the ancient Mayan civilization that flourished in Guatemala and whose high period fell from 300–900 A.D. The Indians of today live much as their forefathers did; they have kept their language, their style of dress, and their emphasis on the family. The western-oriented part of the population is of mixed Indian and European ancestry and favors western clothing and the Spanish language. Guatemala has two distinct regions, the tropical lowlands and the temperate highlands.

Wool is used for weaving in the Guatemalan highlands, which have a suitable climate for sheep grazing. Momostenango, a town in the department of Totonicapan, is the center for wool weaving. Its market day brings in raw wool and blanket sellers from far-outlying areas.

There are several blanket styles in the Indian tradition. A man's blanket worn as a kilt, called a *rodillera,* meaning "belonging to the knees," has been interpreted by some as a rug to kneel upon during religious observances.[2] The *rodillera* is worn in certain localities in the Guatemalan highlands. Other woven blankets are made for different uses. In Chichicastenango, for example, a man wears a shoulder blanket, sits on it, uses it as a shawl against the weather, and wraps it around his body to sleep. It serves an important function as a load cushion when he carries a load on his back. Additional blanket styles are the *capixay,* a waist-

or knee-length garment with a center slit accommodating the head, and the *tzute,* a rectangular or square head scarf. Most of the blankets, including those with household uses, are woven by men on Spanish-style floor looms.

The techniques used are plain weaves, tapestry weaves, and a variety of twill weaves. In one area a characteristic openwork border design is called "little windows." Long fringes are common. Many are made in two parts and later sewn together. Designs vary from

area to area; simple checks and stripes, bands of lozenges and chevrons, center diamonds or lozenges with small figures filling the field, and naturalistic or stylized animals, birds, and other figures are some of the motifs used.

Some blankets from the Momostenango area are made in an ikatlike tie-and-resist dyeing technique called *jaspe.*[3] This technique is not usually worked in wool; other fibers are used in this tedious work.[4] One old specimen of a ceremonial *capixay* from the Chimaltenango region shows a tie-dye technique called *plangi* not usually found in the western hemisphere.

Throughout Central America a plaited mat of reed or palm fiber called a *petate* is the main fitting of the Indian home. *Petates* are used for walls of houses, as they were when the Spaniards first saw them and called an area of Mexico Petatlan, "the land of mats."[5] In the Mexican state of Sonora Yaqui Indians still weave large numbers of heavy-twilled *petates.*

Blanket
Warp: cotton, 2 strands used as 1
Weft: single-ply wool
Colors: natural white, natural blackish brown (possibly overdyed with black to resist a tendency to become brown with age), blue, green, red, orange
Technique: interlocked tapestry weave, with wefts pulled from third row at both ends twisted to make a fringe
Size: 2.05m x 1.5m
Origin: Quechua-Maya, probably Monostenango; found in Tecpan, Chimaltenango, where it had been used for Cakchiquel Indians
The motifs seem to be very stylized animals, which are massed for a striking visual effect. (Gordon Frost Guatemalan Indian Folk Art Collection, Newhall, California)

When the weaving is completed, the blanket is taken off the loom for fulling and washed in natural hot springs. Water from the springs is poured onto the weaving as it is being pounded on the rocks. In other areas it is washed in hot water scooped out of heating pots and poured onto the weaving. The man seen in this photo from Nahuala (department of Solola) has devised a system in which canes are used for balance as he treadles on a plank. (Photo: Gordon Frost Guatemalan Indian Folk Art Collection, Newhall, California)

MEXICO

Mexico, with a 1976 population of 48,225,238, actually lies entirely in North America except for three of its states. Its Mesoamerican roots place it in this chapter. Its northern provinces do have indigenous populations that share much with the Indians of the southwestern United States.

Men weave on the Spanish floor loom, while women in rural Indian areas still use the backstrap loom for clothing, belts, and bags. Quite often the production of textiles for market is an extended family operation or the occupation of an entire village. In a village in Oaxaca Zapotec weavers with 25 looms make fine tapestry-woven floor rugs in both traditional designs and those ordered by American designers. When weather or crop conditions demand, the weavers stop their work and help in the fields.

Designs vary from area to area and from group to group, based on tradition mixed with a grab bag of influences, both local and external. Since a national reawakening in the early 1900s many designs have been based on motifs from clay stamps unearthed from earlier civilizations, religious figures (Aztec calendar stones, for example), and other patterns found in the pictorial records of the Aztec and Mayan cultures. Near Teotitlan delValle in Oaxaca ruins were found from a 1st-century A.D. Mixteca culture. The architectural details at the site, Mitla, provided inspiration for weaving designs. Other designs are striped, geometric, and floral. Common design features are the step motif, cross motifs (used by Indians and also brought by Catholic missionaries), eight-pointed stars, a fret motif similar to Greek-key patterns called *Grecas Aztecas* by the Spanish, and a variety of bird motifs. A central medallion is common to most weavings of blanket size from northern areas, and it provides a dramatic design element that is identifiably Mexican.

Poncho
Warp: single-ply wool
Weft: single-ply wool
Technique: interlocking tapestry weave (*vaciado*), a diagonal joining technique used in Mexico in which the weft advances one warp thread in each row, uncut twisted warp ends, woven in two pieces
Colors: natural undyed, off-white, dark brown, medium brown
Origin: Oaxaca, south-central Mexico, early 20th century
Size: 1.3m x .8m
A poncho is a waist-length wearing garment with a center slit accommodating the wearer's head. Wide stripes of lightning stripes alternate with plain weave and with bands of small boxed S and E shapes.

Blanket-rug
Warp: 1-ply wool
Weft: 1-ply wool
Technique: tapestry weave
Colors: natural, undyed white, tan, brown
Origin: Oaxaca, c. 1930
Size: .95m x 1.29m
The design is a repeated architectural detail from the ruins at Mitla.

Tapete
Warp: single-ply wool
Weft: single-ply wool
Technique: interlocking tapestry weave
(*vaciado*), woven in 2 pieces
Colors: white, black, turquoise, blue, orange,
rust, red
Origin: Mexico, possibly Toluca area, c. 1930
Size: 1.85m x 1.35m

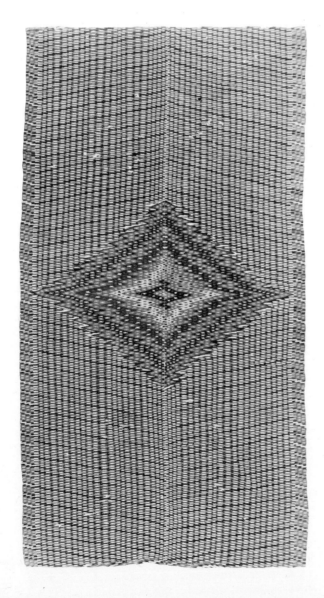

The center medallion, called *fundacion*, contains a serpent and an eagle, the Mexican national emblem. Spots (weft patterning using a number of wefts to make dots, eyes, or tails for animal figures while the ground weft continues from selvage to selvage around the insert, or spot) and *piqueteados* (a design technique in which spots are connected with a shot of weft) are included.[6] Large rugs of similar design were made during a period of national awakening in the 1910s, 1920s, and 1930s. Mexican homes were decorated in a local handicraft style in support of the concept of popular government. Stuart Chase gave this advice to Mexican villagers: "You have in your possession something precious; something which the western world has lost and flounders miserably trying to regain. Hold to it. Exert every ounce of your magnificent inertia to conserve your way of life. . . . Hold to your handicrafts and the philosophy of your handicrafts and watch them jealously in the face of tourists and ignorant exporters. When they debase the work of your hands they debase you. Remember the code of the craftsmen in the great civilization from which you descend. You have their honour to keep."[7]

The distinctive wearing blanket from the Saltillo region, the serape (sarape), has been celebrated since it was developed in the late 17th century. Artists "depicted it being utilized in all segments of Mexican society,"[8] and sailors and other travelers collected serapes as momentos. These serapes became known by the generic name *saltillo,* although many were actually woven in other centers throughout the ranches, mining towns, and growing fields of a vast area. The use of many-colored yarns to achieve a dazzling mosaic effect and a dynamically drawn center medallion were their most striking features. The serape could be worn dramatically as a cape or cloak; when a slit was made in the center, it was worn like a poncho, with the medallion forming a yoke on the wearer's upper body.

Serape
Warp: white, undyed 2-ply handspun linen
Weft: 1-ply handspun wool
Technique: tapestry weave, 12 warps, 60 wefts
per inch, made in two parts
Colors: white, black, red, pink, gold, blue,
green
Origin: Saltillo area, now state of Coahuila,
north-central Mexico, 1800–1850
Size: 1.23m x 2.41m
The sharply serrated, diamond-shaped center medallion holds a series of concentric medallions. The field is covered with a small repeating figure. Dyes used include cochineal and indigo. (Collection of the Maxwell Museum of Anthropology, University of New Mexico)

Solid-color stripes, spots, and striated-color stripes are separated by narrow red, white, and green rows (colors of the Mexican flag) in the blanket shown in color plate 34 (page 221). The center medallion is the *palmas* design.

Shoulder or throw blanket
Warp: silk
Weft: wool, white cotton, white silk
Technique: plain-weave stripes spot detail, tapestry weave (*vaciado*)
Colors: gradations of blue-green, ocher-brown, purples, reds, black, white
Origin: Saltillo
Size: .92m x .42m

Wedding blanket
Warp: cotton
Weft: wool
Technique: tapestry weave with spot patterning
Colors: white (field) undyed, indigo blue
Origin: Halisco(?), northern Mexico
Size: 2.14m x 1.52m
The central medallion, called *palmas,* is combined with spots and connected spots, called *pique teados.* In areas of Mexico and Guatemala fine serapes using the whitest and finest wool available are woven as wedding blankets.

Serape
Warp: wool
Weft: wool
Technique: interlocked tapestry (*vaciado*), spot details, woven in two pieces
Colors: red, black, gray, pink, blue
Size: 1.9m x 1.35m
Origin: northern Mexico
The central medallion is combined with butterfly (*mariposa*), palm (*palmas*), and chicken (*gallita*) details.[9] There is a striped border. A serape with a hole is called a *jorongo.*

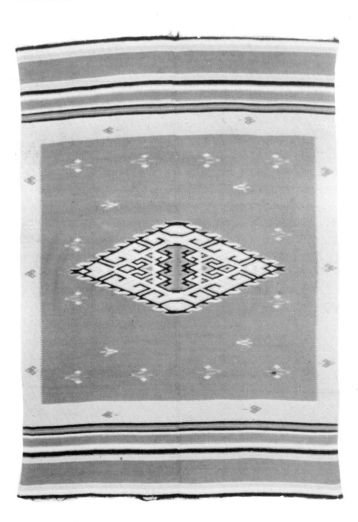

In the northern provinces of Mexico, which are geographically similar to the southwestern United States, live Indians whose language is related to that of Indian tribes in the Southwest. This area is a continuation of the mainland, with a similar arid climate. Until the mid 1800s it had been part of northwestern Mexico. It was divided by the treaty and acquisition that created the southwest border of the United States. The local tribes are the Tarahumara, Yaqui, and Mayo. The last two are closely related, with a rich heritage of religious drama and ritual dance.

As to weaving (the women are the weavers), the Mayos continue to weave traditional objects for their own use, making blankets (*cobijas*), belts, and sashes on horizontal looms. They do make rugs, the only northwestern Mexican Indians to do so. Aside from Mayo rug making, a development due to outside demand, the northwestern Mexican Indian arts are at the same stage as were southwestern American Indians 100 years ago: "They are making blankets, even as Hopi and Navajo and New Mexico Puebloan Indians once wove blankets . . . Nights are cold in the Sierra Madre. No one wants to wrap in a rug. One needs a heavy woolen blanket with its insulating air spaces." [10]

Blanket
Warp: natural handspun 1-ply wool
Weft: 1-ply wool
Technique: tapestry weave
Colors: dark brown, medium brown, beige, gold, medium blue, light blue
Origin: Yaqui-Mayo Indian
Size: 2.11m x 1.11m
Stripes are of consistent widths. The wide stripes near the ends contain small geometric designs. (Collection of the Maxwell Museum of Anthropology, University of New Mexico)

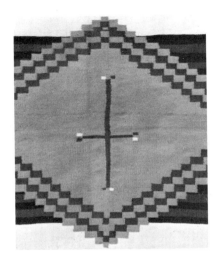

north america

Spider Woman instructed the Navajo woman how to weave on a loom which Spider Man told them how to make. The crosspoles were made of sky and earth cords, the warp sticks of sun ray, the healds of rock crystal and sheet lightning. The batten was a sun halo, white shell made the comb. There were four spindles: one a stick of zigzag lightning with a whorl of turquoise; a third had a stick of sheet lightning with a whorl of abalone; a rain streamer formed the stick of the fourth, and its whorl was white shell.—Navajo legend

RIO GRANDE

Coming north from Mexico into the United States is an area of New Mexico and southern Colorado where Spanish colonials from Mexico settled. Coronado had entered Cibola (a Zuni Indian settlement in what is now New Mexico) in 1540 but returned to Mexico after the expedition encountered too many obstacles. Interest in the Pueblo region grew in the following years, and an official colonization took place in 1598.

The weaving of these people is called Rio Grande, as it originated in villages near the river of that name. The loom used for Rio Grande weaving was a variation of the horizontal Spanish loom. The locally made Rio Grande version was massive, resembling a four-poster bed and canopy from which the harnesses (four or more) were hung (see Chapter 3). This loom can be warped for any length of textile as the finished portion is rolled onto a beam and cut later to take the weaving off the loom or to make individual pieces from the large piece, leaving loose warp threads that must be secured by knotting. On this loom the three basic textiles of colonial New Mexico were made: yardage of *bayeta* or *sabanilla* (homespun), serapes or *fresadas* (blankets), and *jergas* (carpets).

Jergas were heavy lengths of simple checks and plaids that were sewn together for the floor and animal coverings. They were spun with heavy yarn and woven in plain or twill weave (diagonal twill, herringbone twill, and a type of diamond twill called *ojo de perdiz*, or "partridge eye"). The word *jerga* has been used in recent years in Spanish New Mexico to refer to any floor covering.

Serapes were woven from undyed natural merino yarn in bands, stripes, and ticked lines. Some more complex designs with center medallions and overall patterns were woven; these elements seem to be the same as those used in old Saltillos, which later in the 19th century influenced Rio Grande and Navajo weavers. The early use of the central medallion and field filled with small design elements might have come from exposure to outside influence. It has been suggested that galleons bringing trade goods from Manila had brought other textiles from the Orient, from which the weavers of Saltillo, northern Mexico, and the Rio Grande weavers adopted lozenges and center medallions. Observers have noted a similarity to kilim rugs from Senna. Later serapes were made with the Saxony and Germantown yarns, which incorporated vivid color into the weaving, and after 1880 with handspun yarn dyed with newly available aniline colors.

In Chimayo, a small town near Santa Fe, a wider loom was introduced by a trader in the 1890s to accommodate the demand for wider weavings.[1] Due to the circulation of Chimayo textiles, early weavings from the entire area are often mistakenly attributed to Chimayo.

Blanket
Warp: white, undyed, 2-ply handspun wool
Weft: undyed 1-ply handspun wool
Technique: tapestry weave
Colors: brown, white, gold, yellow, blue (indigo), bluish green (indigo)
Origin: Rio Grande area, c. 1850–1870
Size: 2.13m x 1.3m

The design consists of stripes of varying widths. The blanket is woven in one piece with four warps in the center, a characteristic of Rio Grande weaving. The additional warps indicate double warping to make the piece wide enough to avoid later joining of separate sections. (Collection of the Maxwell Museum of Anthropology, University of New Mexico)

Throw
Warp: cotton
Weft: single-ply wool
Technique: dovetailed tapestry weave
Colors: white, pink, blue, gray, black
Origin: Chimayo, New Mexico
Size: .4m x .99m
A small center medallion and two larger medallions are on the pink field. The colors are typical of Chimayo weaving.

PUEBLOS

Weaving among the indigenous Pueblo Indians of the Southwest is a very old tradition. Their ancestors were known to have used the vertical loom as long ago as 800 A.D.[2] The narrow horizontal, or oblique, backstrap loom was also known to the Anazasi (as those ancestors of the Pueblo were called by the Navajos); it was brought from Mexico by Indians centuries before the arrival of the Spanish. The Pueblos whose villages were built in the Rio Grande areas of New Mexico include the Hopis (northern Arizona), the Zunis (New Mexico), and the Hohokam (southern Arizona). They wove blankets with fine striped designs and embroidered woven pieces for distinctive clothing.

The early textiles of the Pueblos were woven with vegetable fibers (into which some wild animal hair was often spun). Later they cultivated cotton, which gave them a strong, stable yarn and suited their sedentary lifestyle. Their weaving techniques were complex; all manner of twill weaves (herringbone, diamond pattern, eccentric twills), patterned weaves, weft-wrapped openwork, and variations of tapestry weave were included in their repertory.

Men were the weavers except among the Zuni. The era before the Spanish conquest was the high point of Pueblo weaving. The Hohokam wove sophisticated textiles in the period preceding the 17th century. That tradition died after the Spanish arrival, and few examples exist. Pueblo weaving also deteriorated after the Spanish conquest of the Southwest. Pueblos were taken as slaves and became accustomed to weaving on the horizontal Spanish loom. Whole villages were taken as the territory became a part of Mexico. The Spanish domination changed the texture of life of Pueblo Indian tribes and destroyed many aspects of their culture.

By the time of the Pueblo revolts in 1680–1695 and their subsequent resubjugation and emigration the weavings had simplified into the patterns seen in examples from the late 19th and early 20th centuries. The techniques were warp-faced and balanced plain weave, often finished off the loom with embroidery stitches (particularly identified with the Hopis). The Pueblos did not make rugs for their own use and did not turn their blanket-making tradition into a rug-making tradition, as did their former students and neighbors, the Navajos.

Hopi shawl-blanket
Warp: white native cotton
Weft: white native cotton, blue native wool, red Germantown yarn
Size: 1.2m x 1m
Date: 1937
The design is typical of the Hopi, with bands separating solid blocks of color. (Photo: Southwest Museum)

Hopi weaver in *kiva*. (Photo: Southwest Museum)

NAVAJOS

The Navajos, now the largest Indian tribe in the United States, are unique in the manner in which they and their culture have survived. To themselves they are The People, the Dineh (Tinneh and Déné are related Athapascan tribes from the far north from which the Navajos probably migrated). They have a feeling of unity with their environment, which is readily perceptible to any traveler who visits the Canyon de Chelly in Arizona, considered by The People as their heartland, the land enclosed by their four sacred mountains.

The beginnings of Navajo weaving are not completely established. Evidence seems to show that it coincided with the arrival of Pueblo refugees from Spanish territory, where they were suffering excess taxation (blankets were the tribute) and against which they revolted. The revolt of 1680 temporarily drove the Spanish from Mexico; the Spanish return in 1692 drove many Pueblos into what would later become the United States. The integration of those Pueblos into Navajo society brought new customs to the heretofore mobile Navajo. According to Berlant and Kahlenberg Pueblo husbands taught Navajo wives to weave, a fascinating example of cultural diffusion. Men were the weavers in the Pueblo culture, but weaving did not fit the role of men in the Navajo culture, as they had no domestic chores.[3] Weaving fell to the Navajo woman, who picked it up and carried it proudly upward and onward.

The Navajo blanket seemed to be an extension of the weaver, a part of the wearer, and a natural component of the landscape in which it appeared, so completely did it belong in its own culture: "In their blankets, the Navajo had a visual language that enabled them to show each other who they were. The blankets were self-portraits in which the Navajo manifested their place among people, their integration with the landscape and their oneness with the spiritual forces of life."[4]

Among the most aesthetically acclaimed and commercially valuable textiles of the contemporary world are those wearing blankets made by Navajo Indians in the Southwest in a tradition formed during the same span of history that formed the United States. There is perhaps a poetic or artistic connection between the drama of the Navajo blanket and the dynamics of pioneer America.

The history of the Navajo in the 19th century is a contradictory one. Amsden makes a fascinating analysis: "The tribal countenance of this time has two markedly different aspects . . . weaving was in its most brilliant stage . . . and the fame of the Navajo blanket grew like young corn in summer . . . for it we may thank the women of the tribe . . . When the activities of the men are scanned . . . we find that while the women sat peacefully at home plying spindle and batten to the ever-growing glory of their craft, the warriors were no less intent on a reputation in their own right. They were out pillaging the communal lands and herds of the Pueblos and the isolated farmsteads and small villages throughout New Mexico. . . . If one asked a chance acquaintance for an opinion of the Navajo, the tone of the reply would depend greatly on whether that person had just bought a blanket or lost a herd of sheep. The men managed to ravel the tribal repute much faster than the women could spin it, and it was generally agreed throughout the Spanish settlements of the Rio Grande valley . . . that the Navajo were the foremost scourge of a land that knew its scourging well."[5]

Manueleta, Navajo leader. (Photo: Southwest Museum)

(Photo: G. W. James, loaned by Southwest Museum)

Navajo weaver. (Photo: Southwest Museum)

Many of the tribal women whose weaving is shown in this volume would share, as do contemporary women and enlightened men, the painful memory of a like experience. The Navajos were powerful and feared. Mexico declared its independence from Spain in 1910. The Mexican areas were complexly involved in their own politics and vulnerable to Navajo raiding. The Mexican war brought the American army permanently into the area, and the desire to subjugate the marauding Navajo became a prime concern of those troops. In 1863 the campaign against the Navajo stepped up and finally terminated with their surrender and removal to a reservation called Bosque Redondo. There the destitute Navajos were expected to adapt to a meager farming existence. In 1868 a peace agreement was reached, and the Navajos were given a large reservation in their old tribal territory.

The Navajos may or may not have prospered on their reservation in later years. Their weaving helped sustain their economy, but the golden age of the Navajo blanket was over. In Amsden's touching words: "The con-

quest brought many changes in Navajo life which bore directly on the loom. It destroyed the old unthinking freedom, killed the joyous, prideful spirit in which fine blankets were woven and worn before Government-issue clothing set a lower standard of tribal dress . . . It opened a door, in short, through which flowed that mediocre flood of frontier civilization and petty officialdom from which the Navajo by a sure instinct had hitherto held themselves aloof. And as regards the Navajo blanket, the conquest of the Navajo commercialized that article for all time to come."[6]

In the Navajo language the word for "teach" is the same as the word for "show." Navajo women show their daughters how to weave when they are very young (as do the Turkmen women in Central Asia and the Yoruk in Asia Minor). The Navajo girl often starts weaving on a small loom of her own, practicing on designs of her own making or on pictorials.[7] Now women in different parts of the reservation weave regional designs developed by traders several decades ago.

The following are dates for some groups of Navajo weaving. Not all weavers conformed to the predominant style of the period.

1830–1860	classic period	
	early serape style	
	late serape style	
1850–1900	chief-style blanket	
1880–1890	late blankets	
	eye-dazzlers	multicolors from aniline dyes brought with the railroad
	pictorials	letters of the alphabet, railroad cars
1890s	vertical designs	
	regional styles	started as traders' designs
	poundage	blankets paid for by weight
1890–1910	revival-style blanket-rugs	Hubbell attempted to bring back classic style
1897	crystal style two gray hills	Moore's designs, some Navajo elements
1920	chinlee style	native dyes, simple striped designs

The 1870s brought the first trading post to the reservation, at which Navajos began to trade blankets; weaving was still primarily for the tribe's own use. The 1880s brought the railroad and additional trading posts: "the increasing ease with which white man's clothing and textiles were obtainable spelled ultimate doom for much of the hand-spun, hand-loomed garments, once deemed a necessity."[8] The Navajo blanket of the 19th century, with its powerful abstract designs, is prized by artists and collectors and is classed with those objects that have a lasting place in history.

Poncho-style classic blanket
Warp: 1-ply undyed light handspun wool
Weft: 1-, 2-, and 3-ply handspun wool
Technique: tapestry weave, tightly woven
Colors: blue (indigo), red, white (undyed)
Size: 2.12m x 1.4m
Date: 1840–1855
Bayeta (probably baize, as it is called in English) was raveled by Navajo wearers and spun into weft yarn.
(Collection of Southwest Museum, Los Angeles)

Chief blanket, 1st phase
Warp: handspun wool
Weft: handspun wool
Technique: tapestry weave
Colors: blue (indigo), white and brown (un-dyed)
Size: 1.4m x 1.77m
Date: c. 1800–1850
Chief blankets (chief-pattern blankets) were blankets of prestige but not a badge of chieftancy.[9] A broad stripe (of indigo) is a major characteristic known as Ute because neighboring Ute tribesmen favored it. (Collection of Anthony Berlant, Santa Monica)

The blanket shown in color plate 36 (page 223) is from the 2nd phase. (Collection of Anthony Berlant, Santa Monica)
Chief blanket
Warp: natural handspun wool
Weft: handspun wool
Colors: white, brown (undyed), blue (indigo), red (aniline)
Date: c. 1867–1870
Size: 1.62m x 1.7m

Chief blanket, 3rd phase
Warp: machine-spun cotton
Weft: 4-ply machine-spun wool
Technique: tight tapestry weave with lazy lines
Colors: white (undyed), purple, red, blue-black (aniline dyes)
Size: 1.63m x 1.81m
Date: 1890–1900
Wearing (shoulder) blankets are woven sectionally; the weaver stays at one side of the loom and reaches as far as she can in each row. The diagonal line of open slits left in the weaving as a result are called lazy lines. The geometric figures in a blanket were designed so that, when the corners were folded together, the four quarters formed one whole. When the blanket is worn a diamond is centered on the back and another on the front. (Collection of the Southwest Museum, Los Angeles)

Woman's blanket
Warp: 1-ply undyed handspun wool
Weft: 1- and 3-ply handspun and machine-spun, dyed and undyed wool
Technique: tapestry weave, some lazy lines
Colors: brown (undyed), blue (indigo), red (vegetal dyes)
Size: 1.57m x 1.37m
Date: c. 1870–1875
Saxony, a very fine vegetal-dyed European yarn that was brought in by some southwest traders, was probably used. According to Charles Amsden Saxony was much rarer than *bayeta*.[10] The size makes this a woman's blanket. It is in a chief pattern, 2nd phase. (Collection of the Southwest Museum, Los Angeles)

Blanket/rug
Warp: 1-ply white undyed handspun wool
Weft: 4-ply machine-spun wool
Technique: tight tapestry weave
Colors: salmon pink, green, dark blue, yellow, green-yellow (aniline dyes)
Size: .132m x .8m
Date: c. 1880

The Germantown yarn used here is the American aniline-dyed successor to the European vegetal-dyed yarns, named for the seat of manufacture, Germantown, Pennsylvania. It came into use among the Navajos around 1880 and was popular for perhaps 30 years. The center diamond pattern radiates outward to all four sides of this weaving, producing a powerful visual effect characteristic of the eye-dazzler style. (Collection of the Southwest Museum, Los Angeles)

Blanket/rug
Warp: handspun wool
Weft: handspun wool
Technique: interlocking tapestry weave, lazy lines
Colors: dark blue, light blue (indigo), red, white
Size: 1.75m x 2.18m
Date: c. 1900

Design elements are similar to those of chief patterns, but are vertically oriented, as in Mexican and Rio Grande serapes, while the chief-pattern blanket is woven with the design reading horizontally. The blue and black stripes derive from Pueblo weaving. Hopis and other Pueblo weavers continued to use the simple stripes of earlier periods. Navajos added bold elements from their chief-blanket design. This style is called "Moki," the name used by the Navajo for the Hopi.

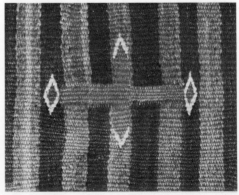

Saddle blanket
Warp: 4-ply cotton
Weft: single-ply handspun wool
Technique: interlocking tapestry weave, lazy
lines
Colors: red, black, white, gray
Size: .87m x .65m
Center stripes and corner medallions characterize this
smaller-scaled version of a wearing blanket.

Saddle blanket
Warp: single-ply handspun wool
Weft: single-ply wool
Technique: interlocking tapestry weave, lazy
lines
Color: white, 3 browns, red
Size: .75m x .73m
Date: 1930s
The center field contains stacked rectangular figures.
The four-sided border is stepped on two sides. After the
blanket-making period borders were added to Navajo
weavings. The presence of a border on a transitional
piece (between blanket-making and rug-making
periods) helps identify it as a rug, not a blanket. Early
saddle blankets were often simply striped.

Charles Amsden wrote that "Navajo saddle blankets were in general use through the latter days of the cowboy's glory, all over the West. In color, pattern, workmanship and material, the saddle blanket was often one of the finest products of the Navajo loom."[11]

Rug
Warp: single-ply wool
Weft: single-ply wool
Technique: interlocking tapestry weave, lazy lines
Color: white (ground), black-brown, khaki green, taupe
Size: 2.6m x 1.51m
Date: 1849
Lightning motifs form half medallions at each end. Four spread wings of birds lie in the four corners of the field. The center border is edged with a continuing terraced motif. Reichard, analyzing Navajo symbolism, calls the terraced triangle a secular cloud symbol and stacked triangles sacred cloud symbols.[12] (Collection of William Playter)

Rug
Warp: single-ply wool
Weft: single-ply wool
Technique: interlocking tapestry weave, lazy lines
Colors: white, light gray, dark gray, brown, red
Size: 2.62m x 1.58m

Rug
Warp: single-ply wool
Weft: single-ply wool
Technique: interlocking tapestry weave, lazy lines
Colors: red, dark brown, white, gray
Size: 2.54m x 1.43m
These rugs are also shown in Color Plate 35 (page 222).

Rug
Warp: 1-ply handspun wool
Weft: 1-ply wool
Technique: interlocking tapestry weave
Colors: tan, brown, black, white
Origin: Two Gray Hills, Arizona, c. 1925
Size: 2.25m x 1.3m
The weavers of this area rarely use red. Two Gray Hills rugs use natural colors and are known for finely spun wool and precise execution of design. (Collection of the Southwest Museum, Los Angeles)

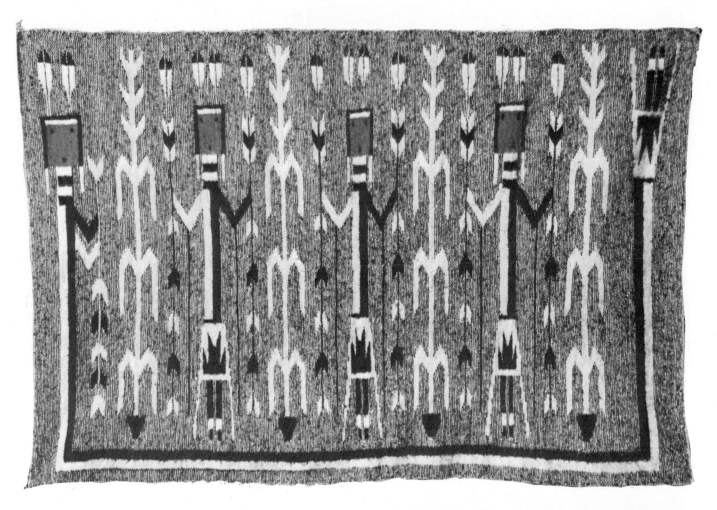

Yei
Warp: wool
Weft: undyed wool
Technique: interlocking tapestry
Colors: brown, light brown, white
Size: .88m x 1.26m
Origin: Lukachukai, Shiprock area, 1975
Weaver: Rachel Makai

In the late 19th century the Yei blanket was commercially developed by a reservation trader. The Yei figures are ritual supernatural beings in the Navajo religion used in their sand paintings. Although the use of the Yei figure in commercial products is considered to be sacrilegious, the blankets are woven by Navajo weavers. In a related weaving, *Yeibichai,* a line of Navajo dancers drawn as human figures impersonate Yeis. The Shiprock–Red Rocks area of the reservation is known for them. Four Yei figures facing forward alternate with tall cornhusks. The extension of the dancer at the right continuing around the rug is this weaver's interpretation of the stylized rainbows that enclose Navajo sand paintings. Sand paintings themselves are made by sprinkling colored sand onto the ground during ritual sings. The rug was woven sideways on the loom so that the figures would be viewed horizontally when on the loom. Alternating rows of brown and white create a tweed ground.

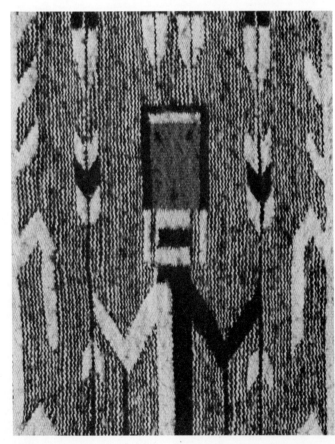

A

B

A, B. Bicentennial flag weavings
Warp: wool
Weft: wool
Technique: dovetailed tapestry weave, tasseled ends on four sides
Colors: red, white, blue (aniline dyes)
Size: (A) .68m x 1.28m, (B) .92m x 1.35m
Origin: Lukachukai, 1976
Weaver: Mary Bahé

(A) is a 1976 commissioned version of the Betsy Ross American flag, with 13 stripes and 13 stars in a circle and the date "1976" inside. (B) has 15 stripes and 12 stars arranged in a square around the date. It is the weaver's own interpretation. "The American flag had a special appeal to the Navajo for its striking similarity to the Chief blanket."[13] These flags were awarded a ribbon by Women Artists of the American West. In the exhibit The American Indian/The American Flag eight flag weavings were shown as well as a picture of Juanita, wife of Navajo leader Manuelito, with a small flag weaving on her loom.[14]

Interior of the Will Rogers home as it was decorated in the 1930s. In addition to the use of a chief-pattern blanket on a couch and two large rugs and one small rug on the floor, other Navajo weavings are draped over banisters and used as pillow faces and chair covers. Mexican weavings are also in evidence (a blanket covers a second couch), as is a pillow face from Chimayo. (Will Rogers State Park, Pacific Palisades, California; photographs: Herm Falk)

footnotes

FOREWORD

1. Phyllis Ackerman, *Tapestry the Mirror of Civilization* (Oxford University Press, 1933), Chapter 1. I paraphrase her idea.

2. Marcel Griaule, *Conversations With Ogotemmeli: An Introduction to Dogon Religious Ideas* (Oxford University Press, 1965), p. 39. The Dogon religion in Mali assigns an entire set of symbols to the weaving process: "Weaving, like smithing, is daytime labour, for warp and woof symbolize a being of light and language, while the spinner's spindle turns on a skin sun, and her calabash of white ash is a fertilized sun. It is only fitting, therefore, that the sun should shine on the craft. Weaving by night would produce a web of silence and shadow. A weaver who worked after sunset, when God shuts the door of the world, would become blind."

3. Chloe Sayer, *Crafts of Mexico* (London: Aldus Books Ltd., 1977), p. 35.

4. W. Fritz Volbach, *Early Decorative Textiles* (London: Paul Hamlyn, 1969), p. 18.

5. G. Schaefer, "The Loom of Ancient Egypt," *CIBA Review* 16 (1938): 546.

6. E. Vogt, "Woven Fabrics," *CIBA Review* 54 (1947): 1955.

7. Arthur Urbani Dilley, *Oriental Rugs and Carpets* (New York: Charles Scribner's Sons, 1931), p. 250. Dilley describes the kilim's relationships in this way: "Khilim- 'the earliest kind of oriental rug weaving' . . . 'The rugs of Babylon and Persepolis are their remote great-grandparents and all European tapestries their first cousins.' "

8. R. B. Serjeant, *Material for a History of Islamic Textiles Up to the Mongol Conquest* (Beirut: Librairie du Lebanon, 1972), p. 19. Among the many occurrences of the word *bisat* (carpet) are words of a courtier in Samarra in the 9th century A.D.:"Poetry is a carpet (*bisat*) of wool (*suf*) and when goat hair (*sha'r*) is mixed with pure wool, its beauty is evident through the combination, and its luster through the composition."

9. A. E. Edward, "Persian Carpets" (Chapter 9), in *The Legacy of Persia*, ed. A. J. Arberry (Oxford: Clarendon Press, 1953). The author cites Hudud al-Alam, who wrote in A.D. 892 about rugs woven in Fars, a province of Persia and makes a case for an existing Persian rug-weaving tradition at the time.

10. Alexander Speltz, *The Styles of Ornament* (New York: Dover Publications, 1951), p. 1.

11. Charles Grant Ellis, *Near Eastern Kilims,* exhibition catalog (Washington D.C.: Textile Museum Journal, 1965), p. 1.

INTRODUCTION

1. Walter B. Denny, "Anatolian Rugs: An Essay on Method," *Textile Museum Journal,* Vol. 3, No. 4 (1973) p. 20. Denny suggests using the words "carpet" and "rug" interchangeably, citing Schuyler Cammann in "Symbolic Meanings in Oriental Rug Patterns," Part 1, *Textile Museum Journal,* Vol. 3, No. 3 (1972). Other authors use "carpet" to denote a large rug.

2. A. E. Edward, "Persian Carpets" (Chapter 9), in *The Legacy*

of Persia, ed. A. J. Arberry (Oxford: Clarendon Press, 1953), p. 230.

3. Kurt Erdmann, *700 Years of Oriental Carpets,* ed. Hanna Erdmann, trans. M. H. Beattie and H. Herzog (Berkeley: University of California Press, 1970), p. 7.

4. Anthony N. Landreau and W. R. Pickering, *From the Bosporous To Samarkand: Flat-Woven Rugs* (Washington D.C.: The Textile Museum, 1969), p. 12.

5. Anthony N. Landreau, "Kurdish Kilim Weaving in the Van-Hakkari District of Eastern Turkey," in *Textile Museum Journal,* Vol. 3, No. 4 (1973).

6. May H. Beattie, "Some Weft-Float Brocaded Rugs of the Bergama-Ezine Region," in *Textile Museum Journal* Vol. 3, No. 2 (1971).

7. Belkis Acar, *Kilim ve Duz Dokuma Yaygilar* (Istanbul: Ak Yayinlari Turk Susleme Sanatlari Serisi: 3, 1975).

8. Walter B. Denny, "Anatolian Rugs: An Essay On Method."

9. Amadeo de Franchis and John T. Wertime, *Lori and Bakhtiyari Flat Weaves* (Tehran: Tehran Rug Society, 1976).

10. Jenny Housego, *Tribal Rugs* (London: Scorpion Publications Ltd., 1978).

11. Anthony N. Landreau, ed., *Yörük: The Nomadic Weaving Tradition in the Middle East* (Pittsburgh: Pittsburgh Museum of Art, Carnegie Institute, 1978).

12. F. Lewis Hinckley, *A Directory of Antique Furniture* (New York: Bonanza Books, 1953), preface. Hinckley emphasizes the need to classify antique furniture according to a comparison with properly attributed pieces and to understand and correct mistakes of attribution caused by the dispersion of craftsmen and pieces.

13. Landreau and Pickering. *Bosporus to Samarkand.* They were the first to divide flat weaving into these six categories.

CHAPTER 1

1. Kurt Erdmann, *700 Years of Oriental Carpets,* ed. Hanna Erdmann, trans. M. H. Beattie and H. Herzog (Berkeley: University of California Press, 1970), p. 27.

2. Arthur Upham Pope and Phyllis Ackerman, *Oriental Rugs As Fine Art* (International Studio, 1976) p. 322.

3. Bert Flint, *Tapis, Tissages, Formes et Symboles Dans Les Arts du Maroc,* Tome 2 (Tangier-Maroc: EMI, 1974), unpaged.

CHAPTER 2

1. Irene Emery, *The Primary Structure of Fabrics* (Washington D.C.: Textile Museum, 1966), p. 4. Emery divides usable animal fibers into (1) external fibers—skin products such as wool, hair, strips of hide, and fur; (2) internal fibers—split, shredded, or spun sinews; (3) secreted filaments—silk from caterpillars, spiders, mollusks, and so on.

2. Margaret Seagroat, *A Basic Textile Book* (New York: Van Nostrand Reinhold, 1975), p. 17. The author refers to linen fragments found in archaeological deposits from the Neolithic period in

Switzerland and to Egyptian records dating from 4500 B.C.

3. Emery, p. 5. Her plant classifications are: (1) seed and fruit hairs—"Fibers and floss surrounding and attached to the seeds of certain trees and shrubs"; (2) leaf fibers; (3) bast fibers (stem structures); (4) bark and root fibers; (5) miscellaneous (including palms, reeds, and grasses).

4. Anthony N. Landreau, "Kurdish Kilim Weaving in the Van-Hakkari District of Eastern Turkey," in *Textile Museum Journal* Vol. 3, No. 4 (December 1973): 32. Landreau observed weavers using metal-wrapped wefts, which were common in older pieces. He believed that they might be Lurex, available in a nearby village.

5. Élisée Réclus, *The Earth and Its Inhabitants* (sometimes entitled *The Universal Geography*), 19 vols. (New York: D. A. Appleton & Co., 1884) 6: ch. 5.

6. F. H. Bowman, *The Structure of the Wool Fibre* (London: Macmillan & Co., 1908), p. 111.

7. Bowman, p. 111.

8. W. T. Blanford, *Eastern Persia: An Account of the Journeys of the Persian Boundary Commission* (London: Macmillan & Co., 1876) 2: 87.

9. Isabella L. Bird Bishop, *Journeys in Persia and Kurdistan* (New York: G. P. Putnam's Sons, 1891).

10. H. R. P. Dickson, *The Arab of the Desert* (London: Geo. Allen & Unwin, 1949), p. 399.

11. Landreau, p. 33.

12. Alfred Leix, "Turkestan," in *CIBA Review* 40 (1941): 1454.

13. John Kimberly Mumford, *Oriental Rugs* (New York: Charles Scribner's Sons, 1900), p. 37.

14. Mumford, p. 37.

15. Gladys A. Reichard, *Navajo Shepherd and Weaver* (Glorieta, New Mexico: Rio Grande Press, 1968), p. 185.

16. Interview with Jeanine Brinkman, who has worked with Zapotec weavers in Mexico for many years.

17. Anthony Berlant and Mary Hunt Kahlenberg, *Walk In Beauty* (Boston: New York Graphic Society, 1977), p. 47.

18. Leix, "Turkestan," p. 1454.

19. Mumford, p. 42.

20. Mumford, p. 42.

21. Elizabeth Chesley Baity, *Man is a Weaver* (New York: Viking Press, 1942), p. 33.

22. A. Juvet-Michel, "Dyeing and Knotting of Oriental Carpets," in *CIBA Review* 15 (1938): 512.

23. Mumford, p. 52.

24. R. B. Serjeant, *Material for a History of Islamic Textiles Up to the Mongol Conquest* (Beirut: Librairie du Lebanon, 1972), p. 207.

25. Juvet-Michel, p. 513.

26. Juvet-Michel, p. 514.

27. Alfred Leix, *Turkestan and Its Textile Crafts*, reprint from *CIBA Review* 1941 (Wales: Crosby Press, 1974), p. 28.

28. Robert de Calatchi, *Tapis d'Orient* (Paris: Bibliothèque des Arts, 1967), p. 27.

29. Cheryl Plumer, *African Textiles: Outline of Handcrafted Sub-Saharan Fabrics* (East Lansing: Michigan State University, 1971), p. 51.

CHAPTER 3

1. Henry Harald Hansen, *Kurdish Woman's Life* (Copenhagen: National Musset, 1961), p. 58.

2. Charles Masson, *Narrative of Various Journeys in Baluchistan, Afghanistan, the Punjab and Kalât*, 4 vols. (London: R. Bentley, 1844), described in David Black, *Rugs of the Wandering Baluchi* (London: David Black Oriental Carpets, 1976), p. 9.

3. Cheryl Plumer, *African Textiles: Outline of Handcrafted Sub-Saharan Fabrics* (East Lansing: Michigan State University, 1971), pp. 116-119.

4. John Kimberly Mumford, *Oriental Rugs* (New York: Charles Scribner's Sons, 1900), p. 35.

5. Alfred Leix, "Turkestan," in *CIBA Review* 40 (1941): 1454.

6. The "mother of all" is the base on which the components of the spinning mechanisms, including the bobbins, spindle, and flyer, sit. It can be adjusted for tension.

7. Walter A. Hawley, *Oriental Rugs, Antique and Modern* (1913, reprint ed. New York: Dover Publications 1970), p. 44.

8. Reinhard G. Hubel, *The Book of Carpets* (New York: Praeger, 1970), p. 24.

9. Anthony N. Landreau, "Kurdish Kilim Weaving in the Van-Hakkari District of Eastern Turkey," in *Textile Museum Journal* Vol. 3, No. 4 (1973): 34.

10. Gladys A. Reichard, *Navajo Shepherd and Weaver* (Glorieta, New Mexico: Rio Grande Press, 1968), p. 82.

11. Plumer, p. 74.

12. Annie Albers, *On Weaving* (Middletown, Conn.: Wesleyan University Press, 1965), p. 23.

13. Irene Emery, *The Primary Structure of Fabrics* (Washington D.C.: Textile Museum, 1966), p. 79.

14. Landreau, p. 28.

CHAPTER 4

1. *United Nations Statistical Yearbook 1975*. Unless otherwise noted, statistics are from this edition.

2. *United Nations.*

3. Ignaz Schlosser, *The Book of Rugs, Oriental and European* (1960, reprint ed. New York: Crown Publishers, 1963), p. 32.

4. Marco Polo, *The Book of Marco Polo, the Venetian*, ed. Geo. B. Parks (New York: Book League of America, 1929).

5. Kurt Erdmann, *700 Years of Oriental Carpets*, ed. Hanna Erdmann, trans. M. H. Beattie and H. Herzog (Berkeley: University of California Press, 1970).

6. Erdmann, p. 95.

7. My use and definition of the words *çiçim* and *zili* are based on Belkis Acar, *Kilim ve Duz Dokuma Yaygilar* (Istanbul: Ak Yayinlari Turk Susleme Sanatlari Serisi: 3, 1975).

8. Douglas L. Johnson, *The Nature of Nomadism*, Department of Geography Research Papers #118 (Chicago: University of Chicago, 1969), p. 17. Johnson discusses the complexity involved in classifying nomads: "It would seem desirable to leave the term 'semi-nomadism' in abeyance and to classify groups on the basis of broad general criteria, setting nomads off from groups that are essentially sedentary. A group does not cease to be nomadic unless it gives up migration totally."

9. Daniel G. Bates, *Nomads and Farmers: A Study of the Yörük of Southeastern Turkey*, Museum of Anthropology Anthropological Paper #52 (Ann Arbor: University of Michigan, 1973), pp. 121-141. It is interesting that the Yörük tribes that Bates studied took twice as long to return to winter quarters (2 months). Bates explains that at this time of year there was more grazing and thus little concern that flocks would cause crop damage (a worry for pastoral nomads), since crops had already been harvested, and that the downward trek is generally easier and more pleasant.

10. Thomas Athol Joyce, *Women of All Nations*, 2 vols. (London: Cassell & Co., 1911) 1: 669.

11. The Kurds are defined as Yörüks in Ralph S. Yohe, "Gone to the Yayla: Rugs of the Yörük Triangle," in *Yörük: The Nomadic Weaving Tradition of the Middle East*, ed. Anthony N. Landreau (Pittsburgh: Pittsburgh Museum of Art, Carnegie Institute, 1978), p. 36.

12. Isabella L. Bird Bishop, *Journeys in Persia and Kurdistan*, 2 vols. (New York: G. P. Putnam's Sons, 1891), 1: 376.

13. *Statistical Yearbook of Turkey* (State Institute of Statistics, 1973), p. 75.

14. Louise W. Mackie, *The Splendor of Turkish Weaving*, exhibition catalog (Washington D.C.: Textile Museum, 1973), p. 17.

15. According to Ursula Reinhard, "The name *sili* is always connected with the stacked prayer niche-like motifs called 'saddle tree' (*egher kast*) or *catmah ala* ('stacked in colors')." Ursula

Reinhard, "Turkic Nomad Weaving in the Doshemealti (Antalya) Area of Southern Turkey," in *Yörük: The Nomadic Weaving Tradition of the Middle East,* ed. Anthony N. Landreau (Pittsburgh: Pittsburgh Museum of Art, Carnegie Institute, 1978), p. 34.

16. May H. Beattie, "Some Weft-Float Brocaded Rugs of the Bergama-Ezine Region," in *Textile Museum Journal,* Vol. 3, No. 2 (1971): 24.

17. The finds in eastern Turkestan made by Sir Aurel Stein and others, including those at Loulan, established the routes taken in Asia by the famed silk caravans as early as the 2nd century B.C.

18. Belkis Acar, "Yuncü Nomad Weaving in the Balikesir Region of Western Turkey," in *Yörük: The Nomadic Weaving Tradition of the Middle East,* ed. Landreau, p. 31.

19. Yohe, p. 39.

20. Walter B. Denny, "Anatolian Rugs: An Essay on Method," in *Textile Museum Journal,* Vol. 3, No. 4 (1973): 15.

21. Albert Achdjian, *Un Art Fondamental: Le Tapis* (Paris: Editions Self, 1949), p. 31.

22. Yohe, p. 38. Yohe points out that the latch-hook motifs are called "geese heads" by Turkish weavers. "Watch out for geese" is a common admonishment to drivers on the back roads of Turkey, who must wait for flocks of geese to cross the path in single file. This motif is popular with Yörük weavers.

23. Mackie, Plates 36 and 43.

24. Walter A. Hawley, *Oriental Rugs, Antique and Modern* (1913, reprint ed. New York: Dover Publications, 1970), p. 280.

25. Hawley, p. 175.

26. Anthony N. Landreau, "Kurdish Kilim Weaving in the Van-Hakkar District of Eastern Turkey," in *Textile Museum Journal,* Vol. 3, No. 4 (1973): 27.

CHAPTER 5

1. Marco Polo, *The Book of Marco Polo, the Venetian,* ed. Geo. B. Parks (New York: Book League of America, 1929).

2. Percy Sykes, *A History of Persia,* 2 vols. (London: Macmillan & Co., 1951). This passage is quoted: no publication information is given.

3. May H. Beattie, *Carpets of Central Persia* (Kent, Eng.: World of Islam Festival Publishing Co., 1976). Beattie shows the Doistau kilim, lists four exhibitions in which it was shown, and cites its inclusion in twelve publications.

4. *The Qashqa'i of Iran,* exhibition catalog (Manchester, Eng.: Whitworth Art Gallery, University of Manchester, 1976), p. 11.

5. H. W. Bailey, "The Persian Language," in *The Legacy of Persia* ed. A. J. Arberry (Oxford: Clarendon Press, 1953), p. 175.

6. John Wertime, Parvis Tanavoli, *Tribal Animal Covers from Iran* (Tehran: Iran America Society, 1975), introduction.

7. Statistical Yearbook of Iran (June 1976), table: Settled and Unsettled Population by Divisions, unnumbered.

8. The Qashqa'i count must include sedentary members as well as nomadic ones. The following quote from *The Qashqa'i of Iran,* p. 12, explains the differentiation between tribalism and nomadism: "Tribalism is predominantly associated with an organizational form; a political means of defining populations. Nomadism on the other hand is primarily associated with adaptation to environmental conditions, through a particular type of resource management. The nomad, the villager and the city dweller can belong to the same tribal group."

9. Henry Field, *Contributions to the Anthropology of Iran,* Anthropological Series, Field Museum of Natural History, Vol. 29, #1 (Chicago: Field Museum of Natural History, 1939), p. 159. In his section on the people of Iran Field used tribal information from official and nonofficial sources who chose to remain anonymous: "Under the policy of His Imperial Majesty Riza Shah Pahlavi, the tribes are being disbanded, so that within a relatively short span of time tribal divisions will no longer exist and the possibility of tracing the interrelationships of these people will be lost beyond recall. It is important, therefore, to record their present distribution and estimated numerical strength. Reliable census figures on nomadic peoples are not available and so far no serious attempt of this character has been made." .

10. Peter Collingwood, *The Technique of Rug Weaving* (New York: Watson-Guptill Publications, 1969), p. 122.

11. Sykes, vol. 2, p. 176.

12. Jenny Housego, *Tribal Rugs* (London: Scorpion Publications, 1978), Plate 7.

13. Ulrich Schurmann, *Central-Asian Rugs* (Frankfort: Verlag Osterrieth, 1969), Plate 16.

14. Edward J. Linehan, "Old-New Iran, Next Door to Russia," in *National Geographic,* (Jan. 1961): 81. The author is quoting Jikhanizdah.

15. Henry Harald Hansen, *Kurdish Woman's Life* (Copenhagen: National Musset, 1961).

16. Elisée Réclus, *The Earth and Its Inhabitants* (sometimes entitled *The Universal Geography*), 19 vols, (New York: D. A. Appleton & Co., 1884).

17. Reinhard G. Hubel, *The Book of Carpets* (New York: Praeger Publishers, 1970), p. 33.

18. J. H. Iliffe, "Persia and the Ancient World," in *The Legacy of Persia,* ed. A. J. Arberry (Oxford: Clarendon Press, 1953), p. 4.

19. Mark Aurel Stein, *Old Routes of Western Iran* (London: Macmillan Co., 1940), Plates I-XXIII.

20. Oliver Garrod, "The Nomadic Tribes of Persia Today," in *Journal of the Royal Central Asian Society* (January 1946): 32.

21. Garrod, p. 43.

22. Murray Eiland, *Oriental Rugs* (New York: New York Graphic Society, 1973), p. 88.

23. Stein, *Old Routes of Western Iran,* p. 303.

24. J. V. Harrison, in *Geographical Journal* (London), Vol. LXXX No. 3 (September 1932).

25. *London Daily Telegraph,* quoted in "People of the Wind," a film by Anthony Howarth on the Bakhtiyari.

26. Isabella L. Bird Bishop, *Journeys in Persia and Kurdistan,* 2 vols. (New York: G. P. Putnam's Sons, 1891), 2: 112.

27. G. Reza Fazel, "Social and Political Status of Women Among Pastoral Nomads: The Boyr Ahmad of SW Iran," in *Anthropological Quarterly* (April 1977).

28. Amadeo de Franchis and John Wertime, *Lori and Bakhtiyari Flatweaves* (Tehran: Tehran Rug Society, 1976). This book gives detailed information about tribal use of bags and supplies a glossary.

29. *The Qashqa'i of Iran,* tribal map of Fars Province on inside cover.

30. Marie-Therèse Ullens de Schooten, *Lords of the Mountain* (London: Chatto & Windus, 1956), p. 116.

31. Ullens de Schooten, p. 85.

32. Eiland, p. 69.

33. *Kilim* (London: OCM Publication, 1977), Plate 31.

34. David Black, *Rugs of the Wandering Baluchi* (London: David Black Oriental Rugs, 1976), Jack Jackson interview, p. 14.

35. Robert Pehrson, *The Social Organization of the Marri Baluchi* (New York: Viking Fund Publication in Anthropology, 1965).

36. William Irons, *The Yomut Turkmen: A Study of Social Organization Among A Central Asian Turkic Speaking Population,* Museum of Anthropology Anthropological Papers, No. 58 (Ann Arbor: University of Michigan, 1975), p. 34.

CHAPTER 6

1. Elisée Réclus, *The Earth and Its Inhabitants* (sometimes entitled *The Universal Geography*), 19 vols. (New York: D. A. Appleton & Co., 1884) 3: 166.

2. Arminius Vambéry, *The Story of My Struggles* (London: T. Fisher Unwin, 1904), p. 471.

3. The population estimate of Kuchi nomads is from Thomas J. Abercrombie, "Afghanistan: Crossroad of Conquerors," in *National Geographic* (September 1968).

4. Andrei Andreyovich Bogolyubov, *Carpets of Central Asia*, 2 vols. (1908 and 1909, reprint ed. Wales: Crosby Press, 1973), Plate 44.

5. Ulrich Schurmann, *Central Asian Rugs* (Frankfurt: Verlag Osterrieth, 1969), p. 28.

6. Conversation with Don Bell, a seasoned Central Asian trader.

7. Schurmann, p. 61.

8. Bogolyubov, Plate 21.

9. Bogolyubov, J. M. A. Thompson's Introduction.

10. Attributions by Don Bell.

11. Percy Sykes, *A History of Persia*, 2 vols. (London: Macmillan & Co., 1951) 2: 203.

12. Richard Kassow in David Black, *Rugs of the Wandering Baluchi* (London: David Black Oriental Rugs, 1976), p. 6.

CHAPTER 7

1. Elisée Réclus, *The Earth and Its Inhabitants* (sometimes entitled *The Universal Geography*), 19 vols. (New York: D. A. Appleton & Co., 1884) 1: 226. The author quotes Kasovsky on population.

2. Veronica Gervers, "Felt in Eurasia," in *Yörük: The Nomadic Weaving Tradition of the Middle East*, ed. Anthony N. Landreau (Pittsburgh: Pittsburgh Museum of Art, Carnegie Institute, 1978), p. 17.

3. Examples were shown in an exhibit at the Metropolitan Museum of Art, *From the Land of the Scythians: Ancient Treasures from the Museums of the USSR 3000 B.C.–100 B.C.* (New York: New York Graphic Society, 1975), Catalogue Plates 23–25.

4. Gervers, p. 18.

5. Alfred Leix, *Turkestan and Its Textile Crafts* (Hampshire, Eng.: Crosby Press, 1974), pp. 41–42.

6. Gervers, p. 16.

7. Andrei Andreyovich Bogolyubov, *Carpets of Central Asia*, 2 vols. (1908 and 1909, reprint ed. Wales: Crosby Press, 1973), p.233.

8. Alfred E. Hudson, *Kazak Social Structure* (New Haven: Yale University Press, 1938).

9. Among wealthier tribespeople in some cultures women have separate tents. In some instances different wives of the same husband have individual tents.

10. David Lindahl and Thomas Knorr, *Uzbek*, exhibition catalog (Basel: Verlag AG, 1975), p. 23.

11. John Kimberly Mumford, *Oriental Rugs* (New York: Charles Scribner's Sons, 1900), p. 39. Mumford quotes Robinson in *Eastern Carpets*.

12. Lindahl, p. 23.

13. Lindahl, p. 22.

14. Nikolay Murav'yov, *Journey To Khiva Through The Turkoman Country* (1922, reprint ed. London: Oguz Press, 1977), p. 252.

15. L. Beresneva, ed. *The Decorative and Applied Art of the Turkmen* (Leningrad: Aurora Art Publishers, 1976), p. 9.

16. Réclus, 1: 33.

17. Réclus, 1: 73.

18. Jon Bell of Antermone, *Travels from St. Petersburgh in Russia to Various Parts of Asia*, 2 vols. (Edinburgh: 1788), 2: 464.

19. Richard E. Wright, "Some Notes on Travel to the Caucasus" (chapter 3), in *The Warp and Weft of Islam*, exhibition catalog (Seattle: University of Washington, 1978). Wright discusses locations where Caucasian rugs were observed by 19th- and early 20th-century travelers and opens questions about Caucasian rug attributions.

20. The beautiful colors of Caucasian rugs were prepared by professional dyers. The weaver spun the amount of wool needed for the work at hand and took it to the dyer (usually Jewish, sometimes Armenian), who dyed the wool with vegetable dyes prepared according to his own recipes. Conversation with Albert Ouzounian.

21. Charles Grant Ellis, "A Soumak-Woven Rug in a 15th Century International Style," in *Textile Museum Journal*, Vol. 1, No. 2 (1963): 3.

22. Maurice S. Dimand and Jean Mailey, *Oriental Rugs in the Metropolitan Museum of Art* (New York: New York Graphic Society, 1973), p. 264.

23. Ignaz Schlosser, *The Book of Rugs: Oriental and European* (1960, reprint ed. New York: Crown Publishers, 1963), p. 58.

24. State Museum of Ethnography, Ukraine SSR, *Ukranian Applied and Folk Art* (Kiev: Mistetstvo Publishers, 1976), unpaged, Plate 2.

CHAPTER 8

1. David Black and Clive Loveless, *The Undiscovered Kilim* (London: David Black Oriental Carpets, 1977), unpaged. A section of the book is devoted to kilims from Thrace, which is defined geographically as northeastern Greece, southern Bulgaria, and the European part of Turkey.

2. Black and Loveless, Plate 1.

3. George Oprescu, *Peasant Art in Roumania* (London: The Studio, Ltd., 1929), pp. 103–111.

4. Marcela Focsa, *Scoarte Românesti: Carpets of the Folk Art Museum of the Socialist Republic of Romania* (Bucarest: Muzeuleri de Arta Populara al R.S., 1970), p. 352.

5. Gheorghe Nistoroaia, *Romanian Folk Rugs*, exhibition catalog (Bucarest: Muzeuleri de Arta Populara al R.S., 1975).

6. Oprescu, p. 1.

7. Elisée Réclus, *The Earth and Its Inhabitants* (sometimes entitled *The Universal Geography*), 19 vols. (New York: D. A. Appleton & Co., 1884), 1: 146.

8. M. Matthews, "Greek Contemporary Handweaving," in *CIBA Review*, Vol. 2 (1969): 3–34.

9. Violetta Thurstan, *A Short History of Decorative Textiles and Tapestries* (London: Pepler and Sewell, 1934), p. 103.

10. Réclus, 1: 119.

11. Melville Chater, "Albania, Europe's Newest Kingdom," in *National Geographic* (February, 1931): 2.

12. Magda Gabor, *Hungarian Textiles* (Leigh-On-Sea, England: F. Lewis, 1961), p. 13.

13. Margaret Lathrop Law, "The Polish Kilim," in *House Beautiful* (September 1930): 256.

14. Jeanne G. Weeks and Donald Treganowan, *Rugs and Carpets of Europe and the Western World* (Philadelphia: Chilton Book Co., 1969), p. 133.

15. Janice S. Stewart, *The Folk Arts of Norway* (1953, reprint ed. New York: Dover Publications, 1972), pp. 149–180.

16. Cornelia Bateman Faraday, *European and American Carpets and Rugs* (Grand Rapids, Michigan: Dean Hicks, 1929), p. 77.

17. W. Fritz Volbach, *Early Decorative Textiles* (1966, reprint ed. London: Paul Hamlyn, 1969), p. 86.

CHAPTER 9

1. Thomas Athol Joyce, *Women of All Nations*, 2 vols. (London: Cassell & Co., 1911), 1: 222. "Some authorities say there are 1,200 divisions or clans of the Berber race."

2. E. W. Bovill, *The Golden Trade of the Moors* (London: Oxford University Press, 1968), p. 50.

3. Lucien Golvin, *Les Tissages Decores D'El-Djem et de Djebeniana* (Tunis: Bacone & Muscate, 1949), p. 96.

4. Bert Flint, *Tapis, Tissages, Formes et Symboles Dans Les Arts du Maroc*, Tome 2 (Tangier-Maroc: EMI, 1974), unpaged. Flint uses Prosper Ricard's definition. Ricard documented the rugs of Morocco in his *Corpus des Tapis Marocains* (1923–1934).

5. Sally Forelli and Jeanette Harries, "Traditional Berber Weaving in Central Morocco," in *Textile Museum Journal*, Vol. 4, No. 4 (1977): 41. The authors describe three knots used in Berber weaving. The Turkish knot in this example is called the Zaian knot by the weavers of Zemmour.

6. Eugene Fodor, *Fodor's Morocco* (New York: David McKay,

1974), p. 133.

7. Peter Collingwood, *The Techniques of Rug Weaving* (New York: Watson-Guptill Publications, 1969), p. 122. Collingwood defines skip plain weave used extensively by the Baluchi and the Berbers.

8. Flint, Plate 12.

9. Fodor, p. 158.

10. R. V. C. Bodley, *Algeria From Within* (Indianapolis: Bobbs-Merrill Co., 1927), p. 192.

11. Jean Gallotti, "Weaving and Dyeing in North Africa," in *CIBA Review*, Vol. 21 (May, 1939): 755.

12. R. P. G. Giacobetti, *Les Tapis et Tissages du Djebel-Amour* (Paris: Libraire Ernest Leroux, 1932). References are from the Introduction and Chapters 1 through 4.

13. Will Grohmann, *Klee* (New York: Harry N. Abrams, 1954), p. 74.

14. *The Diaries of Paul Klee: 1898-1918* (Berkeley: University of California Press, 1968), p. 297.

15. Jacques Revault, *Designs and Patterns From North African Carpets and Textiles* (1950-1957, 4 vols., reprint ed. New York: Dover Publications, 1973), p. x.

16. Revault, p. xii.

17. Golvin, p. 80.

18. Golvin, p. 132.

19. Roy Sieber, *African Textiles and Decorative Arts* (New York: Museum of Modern Art, 1972), p. 127. This book includes an extensive bibliography.

20. Cheryl Plumer, *African Textiles: Outline of Handicrafted Sub-Saharan Fabrics* (East Lansing: Michigan State University, 1971), p. 30-31.

CHAPTER 10

1. Elfriede Praeger, *Ancient Egypt: A Survey* (San Francisco: Gregory & Falk, 1975), p. 26.

2. R. B. Serjeant, *Material for a History of Islamic Textiles Up to the Mongol Conquest* (Beirut: Librairie du Lebanon, 1972), p. 35.

3. Serjeant, p. 58.

4. Isidore Singer, ed., *The Jewish Encyclopedia*, 12 vols. (New York: Funk and Wagnalls, 1916), 11: 184-187. This book summarizes the position of those who support Mesopotamia, Arabia, or Africa as the home of the Semites.

5. Exodus 20: 1 et seq.

6. Douglas L. Johnson, *The Nature of Nomadism*, Department of Geography Research Papers #118 (Chicago: University of Chicago, 1969), pp. 38-53.

7. H. R. P. Dickson, *The Arab of the Desert* (London: Geo. Allen & Unwin, 1949), p. 162.

8. Shelagh Weir, *The Bedouin: Aspects of the Material Culture of the Bedouin of Jordan* (London: World of Islam Festival Publishing, 1976). Weir documented groups of Huwaytāt Bedouins in south Jordan. I have used Weir's spellings of Bedouin objects. Weir describes a technique called twined weft patterning, which is used in many Bedouin rugs and bags.

9. Dickson, pp. 66-107.

CHAPTER 11

1. John Loring, "Durrie Rugs: New Direction for Collectors," in *Architectural Digest* (May-June 1976): 130.

2. Walter A. Hawley, *Oriental Rugs, Antique and Modern* (1913, reprint ed., New York: Dover Publications, 1970), p. 281. Hawley quotes *Carpet Weaving in the Punjab* by C. Latimer.

3. George C. M. Birdwood, *The Industrial Arts of India* (1880, reprint ed. London: The Reprint Press, 1971), p. 285.

4. Bracciolini, *The Indies Revisited*, 1380-1459 (Cambridge, Mass.: Harvard University Press, 1963), unpaged. The reference is to the part of the volume called "Travellers in Disguise."

5. Ananda K. Coomeraswamy, *The Arts and Crafts of India and Ceylon* (London: T. N. Foules, 1913), p. 208. Coomeraswamy claims that the "familiar cotton *dari* is the true indigenous carpet, much cooler to the bare foot than any wool-pile rug could be."

6. John Kimberly Mumford, *Oriental Rugs* (New York: Charles Scribner's Sons, 1900), p. 254.

7. Figures are from a correspondence with Cary Wolinsky, a photographer who has worked extensively in Central Indian villages.

8. Kamaladevi Chattopadhyaya, *Carpets and Floor Coverings of India* (Bombay: Taraporevala, 1969), p. 51.

9. Chattopadhyaya, p. 47.

10. T. N. Mukharji, *Art Manufacturers of India* (1888, reprint ed. New Delhi: Navrang Publishers 1974), p. 397.

11. Mary Churchill Ripley, *The Oriental Rug Book* (New York: Fred A. Stokes Co., 1904).

CHAPTER 12

1. Jean Mailey, *Chinese Silk Tapestry K'o-Ssu*, exhibition catalog (New York: China House Gallery, 1971), pp. 10-12.

2. Mailey, p. 18.

3. Mailey, p. 45. The example from the Metropolitan Museum of Art shown in Plate 26 has squares in the inside corners. Those in the Los Angeles robe were probably changed from a similar position.

4. Hans Bidder, *Carpets from Eastern Turkestan* (New York: Universe Books, 1964), p. 28.

5. Maurice Dimand and Jean Mailey, *Oriental Rugs in the Metropolitan Museum of Art* (New York: New York Graphic Society, 1973), pp. 22-24.

6. Dimand and Mailey, p. 298.

7. Veronica Gervers, "Felt in Eurasia," in *Yörük: The Nomadic Weaving Tradition of the Middle East*, ed. Anthony N. Landreau (Pittsburgh: Pittsburgh Museum of Art, Carnegie Institute, 1978), pp. 16-22. The author discusses the decline of felt making from an art produced for a nomadic aristocracy to the recent mass production.

8. Dimand and Mailey, p. 307. A pair of rugs in the Metropolitan shown in this book contains a design of wild geese.

9. Correspondence with Anthony N. Landreau, director of the Textile Museum, at the time that he documented the two weavings.

CHAPTER 13

1. Junius Bird, *Paracas Fabrics and Nazca Needlework: Catalogue Raisonné* (Washington D.C.: The Textile Museum, 1954), p. 91. Bird mentions white, tan, dark brown and light gray.

1a. Lilly de Jongh Osborne, *Indian Crafts of Guatemala and El Salvador* (Norman, Okla.: University of Oklahoma Press, 1965), p. 30. Legends of Central American Indians cited mention cotton in several colors of the rainbow.

2. Annie Albers, *On Weaving* (Middletown, Conn.: Wesleyan University Press, 1965), p. 68.

3. Albers, p. 68.

4. Alan R. Sawyer, *Mastercraftsmen of Ancient Peru*, exhibition catalog (New York: Solomon R. Guggenheim Foundation, 1968), introduction.

5. Sawyer, p. 93.

6. Frank Salomon, "Weavers of Otavalo," in *Peoples and Cultures of Native South America*, ed. Daniel R. Gross (New York: Doubleday for the American Museum of Natural History, 1973).

7. Lynn Meisch, *A Traveler's Guide to El Dorado and the Inca Empire* (New York: Penguin Books, 1977), p. 197.

8. Adolph S. Cavallo, *Tapestries of Europe and of Colonial Peru in the Museum of Fine Arts, Boston*, 2 vols. (Boston: Museum of Fine Arts, 1967), p. 187. Cavallo points out that these tapestries were woven "somewhere in the Viceroyalty of Peru but not necessarily in the territory associated with modern Peru. In 1544 the Viceroyalty of Peru included all the Spanish territory in South America from Panama to the southern tip of Chile."

CHAPTER 14

1. Sylvanus G. Morley, *The Ancient Maya* (Stanford, Calif.: Stanford University Press, 1946), pp. 380–384.

2. Lila M. O'Neale, *Textiles of Highland Guatemala* (Washington D.C.: Carnegie Institution, 1945), p. 208.

3. Jack Lenor Larsen, Alfred Bühler, and Garrett Solyom, *The Dyer's Art: Ikat, Batik, Plangi* (New York: Van Nostrand Reinhold, 1976), p. 129. This book gives a basic definition of ikat.

4. Larsen, Bühler, and Solyom, p. 192. A fine example of a wool blanket in the jaspé technique is shown.

5. P. Westheim, "Textile Art in Mexico," in *CIBA Review*, Vol. 70 (September 1978): 31–40.

6. Joanne Hall, *Mexican Tapestry Weaving* (Helena, Montana: J. Arvidson Press, 1976), p. 48.

7. Stuart Chase, *Mexico: A Study of Two Americas* (New York: The Macmillan Co., 1931), p. 318.

8. James Jeter and Paula Marie Juelke, *The Saltillo Serape*, exhibition catalog (Santa Barbara, Calif.: New World Arts, 1978), p. 7.

9. Hall. The descriptions of Mexican techniques and designs given in this chapter are in Hall's words.

10. Bernard L. Fontana, Edmond J. B. Faubert, and Barney T. Burns, *The Other Southwest*, exhibition catalog (Phoenix, Ariz.: Heard Museum, 1977), p. 31.

CHAPTER 15

1. Marian E. Rodee, *Southwestern Weaving* (Albuquerque, N.M.: University of New Mexico and Maxwell Museum of Anthropology, 1977), p. 155. Rodee's reference is to the trader J. S. Candelario (from the unpublished journal of Mrs. Richard Wetherill).

2. Rodee, p. 115. The dating of the loom is from J. B. Wheat, *Patterns and Sources of Navajo Weaving* (Denver: The Printing Establishment, 1975).

3. Charles Avery Amsden, *Navaho Weaving: Its Technic and Its History* (1934, reprint ed., Glorieta, New Mexico: The Rio Grande Press, 1969), pp. 31–32. In this authoritative work Amsden arrives at the conclusion that the Navajo loom was borrowed from the Pueblos. He also rejects the possibility that the Navajos were weavers prior to the introduction of domestic European sheep.

4. Anthony Berlant and Mary Hunt Kahlenberg, *Walk In Beauty* (Boston: New York Graphic Society, 1977), p. 36.

5. Amsden, p. 153.

6. Amsden, p. 170.

7. Gladys A. Reichard, *Navajo Shepherd and Weaver* (New York: J. J. Augustin, 1936), p. 3. Reichard learned about Navajo weaving while living with a Navajo family from 1930–33. The book gives detailed technical weaving information.

8. Mary Hunt Kahlenberg and Anthony Berlant, *The Navajo Blanket*, exhibition catalog (Los Angeles: Praeger Publishers in association with the Los Angeles County Museum of Art, 1972), p. 25. In discussing the design influence of the traders on blanket designs that would find greater acceptance with their eastern clientele the authors say, "A wearing blanket was not precisely what Eastern ladies needed."

9. Amsden, p. 100. The author describes the wearing of the blanket and the wearers.

10. Amsden, p. 183.

11. Amsden, pp. 103–104.

12. Reichard, p. 181.

13. Berlant and Kahlenberg, Plate 50.

14. Richard A. Pohrt, *The American Indian/The American Flag*, exhibition catalog (Flint, Michigan: Flint Institute of Arts, 1976). The exhibition showed the quillwork, beading, leatherwork, basketry, painting, and weaving of 35 tribes.

APPENDIX A

credits

Below is a list of plates reproduced in other publications or shown in exhibitions.

Page 37. *Saph* (multiple prayer kilim). Published: Hajji Baba Society, *Turkish Rugs,* Plate 68.

Page 39. Prayer kilim. Published: David Black and Clive Loveless, *The Undiscovered Kilim,* Plate 27.

Page 42. Silk kilim (the Doisteau kilim). Exhibited: 1903, Paris, Musée des Arts Decoratifs, L'Exposition des Arts Musulmans. 1935, New York, Metropolitan Museum of Art, Oriental Rugs and Textiles. 1937, Chicago. 1938, Paris, Bibliotheque Nationale. Published: May H. Beattie, *Carpets of Central Persia.* p. 42. The author refers to 12 publications in which this kilim appears, along with its attributions. Other English-language publications: A. F. Kendrick and C. E. C. Tattersall, *Hand-Woven Carpets, Oriental and European,* Plate 26. M. S. Dimand, *A Guide to an Exhibition of Oriental Rugs and Textiles,* New York: Metropolitan Museum of Art, 1935, p. 21, No. 10. Arthur Upham Pope and Phyllis Ackerman, *A Survey of Persian Art,* Pl. 1262. Richard Ettinghauen, "The Boston Hunting Carpet in Historical Perspective," *Boston Museum Bulletin* LXIX:355 and 356, pp. 70–81.

Page 51. Animal cover. Exhibited: 1978, Boston Museum of Fine Arts, From Turkey to Turkestan.

Page 92. Kilim. Published: Sotheby Parke Bernet, *Catalogue,* sale #224, Los Angeles, March 1978, p. 122.

Page 94. Soumak rug. Published: The Textile Museum, *Journal,* Vol. 1, No. 2 (Dec. 1963), Figure 1.

Page 98. *Verneh* (cover). Sotheby Parke Bernet, *Catalogue,* sale 4106, New York, 1978, Plate 67.

Page 102. Kilim. Exhibited: 1978, Los Angeles, Craft and Folk Art Museum, Romanian Folk Textiles. Published: exhibition catalogue, Joyce Winkel, *Romanian Folk Textiles,* Los Angeles, Craft and Folk Art Museum, 1978.

Page 106. *Scoarte.* Published: George Oprescu, *Peasant Art in Romania,* pp. 125 and 121.

Page 107. *Scoarta.* Exhibited: 1978, Los Angeles, Craft and Folk Art Museum, Romanian Folk Textiles.

Page 108. *Scoarta.* Exhibited: 1978, Romanian Folk Textiles. Published: exhibition catalogue, Winkel, *Romanian Folk Textiles,* p. 39: "A classically beautiful example of this type of rug, it shows the ordered yet charmingly exuberant style of Oltenian design."

Page 113. Cover. Exhibited: 1969, Washington, D. C., The Textile Museum, From the Bosporus to Samarkand: Flat-Woven Rugs. Published: Anthony N. Landreau and W. R. Pickering, *From the Bosporus to Samarkand: Flat-Woven Rugs,* Plate 84.

Kilim. Exhibited: 1969, From the Bosporus to Samarkand: Flat-Woven rugs. Published: Landreau and Pickering, *From the Bosporus,* Plate 7.

Page 149. Buddhist priest's robe. Published: Los Angeles County Museum of Art, *Quarterly,* Los Angeles, Summer 1954, No. 31.

Page 160. Serape. Published: Marian E. Rodee, *Southwestern Weaving,* Plate 7, p. 151.

Page 162. Blanket. Published: Rodee, *Southwestern Weaving,* Plate 14, p. 154.

Page 164. Blanket. Published: Rodee, *Southwestern Weaving,* Plate 18, p. 158.

Page 169. Chief blanket. Published: Joseph Ben Wheat, *Navajo Blankets from the Collection of Anthony Berlant,* Tucson, University of Arizona Press, 1974, Plate 1.

Page 175. Flag weaving. Exhibited: 1976, Los Angeles, Museum of Science and Industry, American Crafts Festival. 1976, Los Angeles, Museum of Science and Industry, Women Artists of the American West, awarded ribbon.

Page 203. Prayer kilim. Exhibited: 1974, Washington, D.C., Textile Museum, Prayer Rugs. 1975, Montclair, New Jersey, The Montclair Art Museum, Prayer Rugs. Published: The Textile Museum, *Prayer Rugs,* Washington, D.C., 1975, Plate XXVIII.

Page 216. Kilim. Published: John Loring, "Kilim Rugs, Fabled Craftsmanship in Flatweave," *Architectural Digest,* Los Angeles, Jan./Feb. 1978, p. 121.

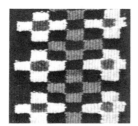

weaving references

Examples of weavings similar in technique, design, and function to plates in this text are listed below. Also listed are some examples similar in only one aspect, accompanied by an explanation.

Page 32. Célal Esad Arsevan, *Les Arts Décoratifs Turcs*, Plate 23, a 19th-century kilim listed under Inventory #200 in the Turk-Islam Eserleri Museum, Istanbul, Turkey.

Page 34. Reinhard G. Hubel, *The Book of Carpets*, Figure 48, a Kuba knotted rug with similar design elements. David Black and Clive Loveless, *The Undiscovered Kilim*, Plate 16.

Page 36. J. Iten-Maritz, *Turkish Carpets*, p. 248.

Pages 38–39. Black and Loveless, *The Undiscovered Kilim*, Plate 26, identified as Central Anatolian; Murray Eiland, *Oriental Rugs*, Plate 101, Konya region suggested; Arsevan, *Les Arts Décoratifs Turcs*, Figure 670, Kirchehir; Elizabeth Dunn, *Rugs In Their Native Land*, p. 140, Malatya; Ignaz Schlosser, *The Book of Rugs*, Plate 163, Karabagh, 19th-century: "woven woolen carpet (kilim) . . . pile short or medium length. Ghiordes or Turkish knot." Since the rug is a kilim, there can be no pile; the description is wrong.

Page 37. Belkis Acar, *Kilim ve Düz Dokuma Yaygilar*, plate 26.

Page 39. Franz Bausback, *Alte Orientalische Flachgewebe*, plate 27.

Page 40. Anthony N. Landreau (ed.), *Yoruk, the Nomadic Weaving Tradition of the Middle East*, Plate 26, attributed to Sinan village, purchased in the bazaar at Malatya, early 20th century.

Page 47. Housego, *Tribal Rugs*, Plate 32, a bag with the two-headed bird motif in its border; Anothy N. Landreau and W. R. Pickering, *From the Bosporus to Samarkand: Flat-Woven Rugs*, Plate 48, attributed to the Caucasus.

Page 48. Housego, *Tribal Rugs*, Plate 9 and book jacket.

Page 50. Hubel, *The Book of Carpets*, Plate 78, an example of a Senna-knotted bag face.

Page 53. John Wertime and Parvis Tanavoli, *Lori and Bakhtiyari Flat Weaves*, 21 bags, all with soumak fronts, plain-weave backs, and a pile area at the bottom. Wertime and Tanavoli, *Lori and Bakhtiyari Flat Weaves*, Plate 40, *boteh* and design of central field similar.

Page 54. Housego, *Tribal Rugs*, Plate 141, central motif knotted.

Page 55. Housego, *Tribal Rugs*, Plate 55, attributed to Shushtar in the winter territory of the Bakhtiyari; Wertime and Tanavoli, *Lori and Bakhtiyari Flat Weaves*, Plate 52.

Page 57. Housego, *Tribal Rugs*, Plate 91.

Page 58. Landreau (ed.), *Yoruk*, Plate 72.

Page 62. Housego, *Tribal Rugs*, Plate 145.

Page 64. Housego, *Tribal Rugs*, Plate 134.

Page 65. Landreau and Pickering, *From the Bosporus to Samarkand*, Plate 36.

Page 70. International Hajji Baba Society, *The Ersari and Their Weaving*, Plate 48.

Page 71. International Hajji Baba Society, *Rugs of the Yomud Tribes*, Plate 33.

Page 78. Black and Loveless, *The Undiscovered Kilim*, Plate I.

Page 85. David Lindahl and Thomas Knorr, *Uzbek*, Plate 12.

Page 87. Lindahl and Knorr, *Uzbek*, Plate 4, late 19th century; Sotheby Parke Bernet, Los Angeles, *Catalogue, Sale #209*, Plate 30.

Page 88. Ulrich Schurmann, *Central-Asian Rugs*, Plate 58, 18th-century: Lindahl and Knorr, *Uzbek*, p. 23, attributed to Uzbeks; Bogolyubov, *Carpets of Central Asia*, Plate XLI/1, attributed to Ersari tribe.

Page 90. International Hajji Baba Society, *Rugs of the Yomud Tribes*, Plate 33, attributed to Jafarbai, Yomud subtribe.

Page 92. Black and Loveless, *The Undiscovered Kilim*, Plate 33, second half of 19th century; Maurice S. Dimand and Jean Mailey, *Oriental Rugs in the Metropolitan Museum of Art*, Figure 241, 19th century; Bausback, *Alte Orientalische Flachgewebe*, p. 42, called Kazak, 18th century; Murray Eiland, *Oriental Rugs*, Plate 178, called Shirvan kilim, 19th century.

Page 97. Schlosser, *The Book of Rugs*, Plate 167; Landreau and Pickering, *From the Bosporus to Samarkand*, Plate 16; Dimand and Mailey, *Oriental Rugs*, Plate 244; Hubel, *The Book of Carpets*, Plate 66; Lucien Coen and Louise Duncan, *The Oriental Rug*, Plate 78; many other examples published.

Page 98. Hubel, *The Book of Carpets*, plate 65.

Page 99. Landreau and Pickering, *From the Bosporus to Samarkand*, Plate 49, attributed to the Caucasus; Housego, *Tribal Rugs*, Plate 16, attributed to northwest Iran or south Caucasus.

Page 100. Lviv State Museum of Ethnography and Crafts, *Album of the Lviv State Museum;* Plate 9, attributed to Vikno village, Ternopil region; *Ukrains'kyi Radians'kyi Kylym* (Kiev: Naukova Dumka, 1973).

Page 101. George Oprescu, *Peasant Art in Roumania,* p. 145.

Page 107. Cecil Lubell, ed., *Textile Collections of the World,* Volume I, p. 90, detail of a Carpatho-Ukrainian wall hanging dated 1870 from the Ukrainian Arts & Crafts Museum, Saskatoon, Canada.

Page 108. Marcela Focsa, *Scoarte Românesti,* Plate 65.

Page 109. Dimitar Stamkov, *Carpettes et Tapis,* Plate 306, attributed to Pirot, 19th century.

Page 110. Black and Loveless, *The Undiscovered Kilim,* Plate 6, attributed to Sarkoy, similar overall figure in center field and square format; Stamkov, *Carpettes et Tapis,* Plates 256, and 257, 18th century.

Page 115. Janice S. Stewart, *The Folk Arts of Norway,* Plate 102.

Page 120. Bert Flint, *Tapis, Tissages, Maroc,* Plates 34 and 35, attributed to Siroua, Haut-Atlas, called *mangeoire.* Flint, *Tapis, Tissages,* Plate 12, attributed to Beni Mguild tribe.

Page 122. Flint, *Tapis, Tissages,* Plate 8. J. P. Bernes and Alain Jacob, *Meubles, Zellidjs, Tapis, Arts et Objets du Maroc,* Paris: C.P.I.P., 1974, Plates 76, 77, tent hanging; Flint, *Tapis, Tissages,* Plates 36, 37, called *sac de mariage.*

Page 128. Jacques Révault, *Designs and Patterns from North African Carpets and Textiles,* Plate 74.

Pages 130–131. Lucien Golvin, *Les Tissages Décorés D'El-Djem et de Djebeniana,* p. 80.

Page 133. Roy Sieber, *African Textiles and Decorative Arts,* p. 190, Woga, Nigeria; Venice and Alastair Lamb, *West African Weaving,* p. 43, Goundam, Mali.

Page 139. Thomas J. Abercrombie, ''Saudi Arabia,'' *National Geographic* (Jan. 1966), p. 33, photograph of veiled woman holding similar rug and surrounded by other examples.

Page 141. Iraqi Ministry of Information, Folklore Center, *Rug Weaving in Nassirya and Gharraf.*

Page 151. Dimand and Mailey, *Oriental Rugs in the Metropolitan Museum,* Figure 264 and p. 337, 19th century.

Page 155. Anne Rowe, *Warp-Patterned Weaves of the Andes,* Figure 21, shape, use of borders, and some design elements similar in this example, called a cover; Mary Hunt Kahlenberg, *Fabric and Fashion,* Plate 13, poncho with similar format.

161. Lubell, ed., *Textile Collections,* Vol. 1, p. 278, attributed to Texcoco, Mexico, from American Museum of Natural History, New York.

Page 173. Lubell, ed., *Textile Collections,* Vol. 1, Figure 6.

Page 175. Anthony Berlant and Mary Hunt Kahlenberg, *Walk In Beauty,* Plate 50, 9 birdlike stars and 11 stripes; Richard A. Pohrt, *The American Indian / The American Flag,* Plate 85, 48 stars (crosses) and 13 stripes, made in 1915; Pohrt, Plate 117, 54 stars, 21 stripes, made in 1950; Pohrt, Plate 61, 48 stars (diamond shaped), 21 stripes, made in 1955; Pohrt, Plates 85, 173, 174 (55 stars), 175.

Page 197. Louise W. Mackie, *The Splendor of Turkish Weaving,* 1, Plate 43, an 18th-century knotted rug with similar field and borders; Plate 36, a 17th-century knotted rug with similar design and color; Jean Lefevre, *Turkish Carpets,* Plate 11, an antique knotted rug with similar design.

Page 199. Sotheby Parke Bernet, New York, *Catalogue, Sale #4106,* Plate 66.

Page 202. Jenny Housego, *Tribal Rugs,* Plate 11.

Page 206. Wertime and Tanavoli, *Lori and Bakhtiyari Flat Weaves,* Plate 50.

Page 210. Landreau and Pickering, *From the Bosporus to Samarkand,* Plate 73; Andrei A. Bogolyubov, *Carpets of Central Asia,* Plates 21, 44; Landreau (ed.), *Yoruk,* Plate 89.

Page 212. Black and Loveless, *The Undiscovered Kilim.* Plate 36, Northern Caucasus, 19th century.

Page 213. Jos. V. McMullan and Donald O. Reichert, *The Smith collection of Islamic Rugs,* Plate 42, a Caucasian pile rug of similar design.

Page 215. Stamkov, *Carpettes et Tapis,* Plate 290.

Page 216. Cornelia Bateman Faraday, *European and American Carpets and Rugs,* Plate 6, attributed to Podolia.

Page 218. Flint, *Tapis et Tissages,* Plate 10, attributed to Zaian, tribe of Beni M'tir; Sally Forelli and Jeanette Harries, ''Traditional Berber Weaving in Central Morocco,'' *Textile Museum Journal, Vol. 4. No. 4,* Figure 6, called *Ahbl* by Ait Mguild, *Ahnbl* by Zemmour tribe.

Page 220. Similar rugs in the Museum of Ancient Art, Baghdad, Iraq.

bibliography

Abercrombie, Thomas J. "Afghanistan: Crossroad of Conquerors." *National Geographic* (Sept. 1968): 297-345.

———. "Saudi Arabia: Beyond the Sands of Mecca." *National Geographic* (Jan. 1966): 1-53.

Acar, Belkis. *Kilim ve Duz Dokuma Yaygilar*. Istanbul: Ak Yayinlari Turk Susleme Sanatlari Serisi: 3, 1975.

Achdjian, Albert. *Un Art Fondamental: Le Tapis*. Paris: Editions Self, 1949.

Ackerman, Phyllis. *Tapestry the Mirror of Civilization*. Oxford University Press, 1933.

Albers, Annie. *On Weaving*. Middletown, Conn.: Wesleyan University Press, 1965.

Amsden, Charles Avery. *Navaho Weaving: Its Technic and Its History*. 1934. Reprint. Glorieta, New Mexico: The Rio Grande Press, 1969.

Anderson, Marilyn, *Guatemalan Textiles Today*. New York: Watson Guptill, 1978.

Arseven, Celal Esad. *Les Arts Decoratifs Turc*. Istanbul: 1950.

Atwater, Mary M. *Guatemala Visited: Feb.-Mar. 1946*. Reprint. Shuttle Craft Guild Monograph #15.

Azadi, Siaviosch. *Turkoman Carpets*. Wales: Crosby Press, 1975.

Babayan, Levon. *Romance of the Oriental Rug*. Toronto: Babayan's Ltd., 1925.

Bacharach, Jere L. and Bierman, Irene A., eds. *The Warp and Weft of Islam: Oriental Rugs and Weavings from Pacific Northwest Collections*. University of Washington, 1978.

Barnes, Alexander. *Travels Into Bokhara*. 3 vols. 1834. Reprint. London: John Murray, 1973.

Bates, H. W. *Illustrated Travels: A Record of Discovery, Geography and Adventure*. London: Cassell, Petter and Galpin, 1869.

Beattie, May H. *Carpets of Central Persia*. Kent, England: World of Islam Festival Publishing Co., 1976.

Beaumont, Roberts. *Carpets and Rugs*. London: Scott, Greenwood and Son, 1924.

Bell, John (of Antermone). *Travels from St Petersburgh in Russia to Various Parts of Asia*. 2 vols. Edinburgh, 1788.

Bennett, Ian., ed. *Complete Illustrated Rugs and Carpets of the World*. New York: A & W Publishers, 1977.

Berlant, Anthony and Kahlenberg, Mary Hunt. *Walk In Beauty*. Boston: New York Graphic Society, 1977.

Beresneva, L., ed. *The Decorative and Applied Art of the Turkmen*. Leningrad: Aurora Art Publishers, 1976.

Bidder, Hans. *Carpets from Eastern Turkestan*. New York: Universe Books. Reprint from 1964 German edition.

Bird, Junius Bouton. *Paracas Fabrics and Nazca Needlework*. Washington D.C.: National Publishing Co. for the Textile Museum, 1954.

Bishop, Isabella L. Bird. *Journeys in Persia and Kurdistan*. New York: G. P. Putnam's Sons, 1891.

Black, David and Loveless, Clive. *Rugs of the Wandering Baluchi*. London: David Black Oriental Carpets, 1976.

———. *The Undiscovered Kilim*. London: David Black Oriental Carpets, 1977.

Bogolyubov, Andrei Andreyovich. *Carpets of Central Asia*. 2 vols. 1908 and 1909. Reprint. Wales: Crosby Press, 1973.

Boyd, E. *Popular Arts of Spanish New Mexico*. Santa Fe: Museum of New Mexico, 1974.

Bryan, Nonabah G. *Navajo Native Dyes*. Lawrence, Kansas: U.S. Department of Interior, Bureau of Indian Affairs, 1940.

Calatchi, Robert de. *Tapis d'Orient*. Paris: Bibliothèque des Arts, 1967.

Campana, Michele. *Oriental Carpets*. Translated by Adeline Hartcup. Feltham, Middlesex, Eng.: Hamlyn Publishing Group, 1969.

Canadian Museum of Carpets and Textiles. *The Mysterious East: Puzzles of Origin, Authenticity and Function in Oriental Rugs and Embroidery*. Toronto: Canadian Museum of Carpets and Textiles, 1977.

Cavallo, Adolph S. *Tapestries of Europe and of Colonial Peru in the Museum of Fine Arts, Boston*. 2 vols. Boston: Museum of Fine Arts, 1967.

Cerny, Charlene. *Navajo Pictorial Weaving*. Santa Fe: Museum of New Mexico Foundation, 1975.

Chattopadhyaya, Kamaladevi. *Carpets and Floor Coverings of India*. Bombay: Taraporevala, 1969.

Coen, Lucien and Duncan, Louise. *The Oriental Rug*. New York: Harper and Row, 1978.

Collingwood, Peter. *The Techniques of Rug Weaving*. New York: Watson-Guptill Publications, 1969.

Coon, Carleton S. *Caravan: The Story of the Middle East*. New York: Holt Rinehart and Winston, 1951.

Cooper, Marian C. *Grass*. New York: G. P. Putnam's Sons, 1925.

Denny, Walter B. "Anatolian Rugs: An Essay on Method." *Textile Museum Journal*, Vol. 3, No. 4 (1973): 7-25.

Dimand, Maurice S. *A Handbook of Mohammedan Decorative Arts*, New York: Metropolitan Museum of Art, 1930.

———. *Peasant and Nomad Rugs of Asia*. New York: Asia House, 1961.

——— and Mailey, Jean. *Oriental Rugs in the Metropolitan Museum of Art*. New York: New York Graphic Society, 1973.

Dickson, H. R. P. *The Arab of the Desert*. London: Geo. Allen and Unwin, 1949.

Dilley, Arthur Urbani. *Oriental Rugs and Carpets*. New York: Charles Scribner's Sons, 1931.

Doughty, Charles M. *Wanderings in Arabia*. London: Duckworth, 1908.

Dunn, Elizabeth. *Rugs in Their Native Land*. New York: Dodd, Mead and Co., 1910.

Edward, A. E. "Persian Carpets." *The Legacy of Persia*. Edited by A. J. Arberry. Oxford: Clarendon Press, 1953.

Eiland, Murray. *Oriental Rugs.* New York: Graphic Society, 1973.

Ellis, Charles Grant. "A Soumak Woven Rug in a 15th Century International Style." *Textile Museum Journal,* Vol. 1, No. 2 (Dec. 1963): 3–18.

Emery, Irene. *The Primary Structure of Fabrics.* Washington D.C.: The Textile Museum, 1966.

Erdmann, Kurt. *Oriental Carpets.* 1960. Reprint. Wales: Crosby Press, 1976.

———. *Seven Hundred Years of Oriental Carpets.* Edited by Hanna Erdmann, translated by M. H. Beattie and H. Herzog. Berkeley: University of California Press, 1970.

Fairservis, Walter A. (Jr.). *Costumes of the East.* New York: American Museum of Natural History, 1971.

Faraday, Cornelia Bateman. *European and American Carpets and Rugs.* Grand Rapids, Mich.: Dean Hicks, 1929.

Fertig, Barbara C., ed. *Turkish Rugs from Private Collections.* Washington D.C.: The Textile Museum, 1973.

Flint, Bert. *Tapis, Tissages. Formes et Symboles Dans Les Arts du Maroc,* Tome 2. Tangier-Maroc: EMI, 1974.

Focşa, Marcela. *Scoarţe Româneşti: Din Colectia Muzeului de Arta Populară al R.S.* Bucarest: Muzeului de Artă Populară, 1970.

Fontana, Bernard L.; Faubert, Edmond J. B.; and Burns, Barney T. *The Other Southwest.* Phoenix, Ariz.: Heard Museum, 1977.

Forelli, Sally and Harries, Jeanette. "Traditional Berber Weaving in Central Morocco." *Textile Museum Journal,* Vol. 4, No. 4 (1977): 41–60.

Franchis, Amadeo de and Wertime, John T. *Lori and Bakhtiyari Flat Weaves.* Teheran: Teheran Rug Society, 1976.

Franses, Jack. *Tribal Rugs from Afghanistan and Turkestan.* London: Ditchling Press Ltd., 1973.

Fraser, James B. *Narrative of a Journey Into Khorasan.* London: Longman, 1825.

Gabor, Magda. *Hungarian Textiles.* Leigh-on-Sea, Eng.: F. Lewis Ltd., 1961.

Gallotti, Jean. "Weaving and Dyeing in North Africa." *CIBA Review* (May 21, 1939): 738–761.

Gans-Ruedin, E. *Connoisseur's Guide to Oriental Carpets.* Translated by Valerie Howard. Rutland, Vermont: Charles E. Tuttle, 1971.

Gardiner, Roger F. and Allen, Max. *Oriental Rugs from Canadian Collections.* Toronto: Oriental Rug Society, 1975.

Giacobetti, R. P. G. *Les Tapis et Tissages du Djebel-Amour.* Paris: Libraire Ernest Leroux, 1932.

Hackmack, Adolf. *Chinese Carpets and Rugs.* Tientsin: Le Libraire Française, 1924.

Hall, Joanne. *Mexican Tapestry Weaving.* Helena, Mont.: J. Arvidson Press, 1976.

Harris, Nathaniel. *Rugs and Carpets of the Orient.* London: 1977.

Hawley, Walter A. *Oriental Rugs, Antique and Modern.* 1913. Reprint. New York: Dover Publications, 1970.

Hedin, Sven. *Through Asia.* London: Methvin and Co., 1898.

Holt, Rosa Belle. *Rugs: Oriental and Occidental, Antique and Modern.* Chicago: A. C. McClurg, 1927.

Hopf, Albrecht. *Oriental Carpets and Rugs.* 1961. Reprint. London: Thames and Hudson, 1962.

Housego, Jenny. *Tribal Rugs.* London: Scorpion Publications, 1978.

Hubel, Reinhard G. *The Book of Carpets.* New York: Praeger Publishers, 1970.

Jeter, James and Juelke, Paula Marie. *The Saltillo Sarape.* Santa Barbara, Calif.: New World Arts, 1978.

Johnstone, Pauline. *A Guide to Greek Island Embroidery.* London: Victoria and Albert Museum, 1972.

Jones, H. McCoy and Boucher, J. W. *Baluchi Rugs.* Washington D.C.: International Hajji Baba Society, 1974.

Juvet-Michel, A. "Dyeing and Knotting of Oriental Carpets." *CIBA Review* 15 (Nov. 1938): 512–521.

Kahlenberg, Mary Hunt. *Fabric and Fashion.* Los Angeles: Los Angeles County Museum of Art, 1974.

——— and Berlant, Anthony. *The Navajo Blanket.* Los Angeles: Praeger Publishers in association with the Los Angeles County Museum of Art, 1972.

Kendrick, A. F. and Tattersall, C. E. C. *Hand-Woven Carpets: Oriental and European.* London: Benn Bros., 1922.

Lamb, Venice. *West African Weaving.* London: Duckworth, 1975.

——— and Lamb, Alastair. *The Lamb Collection of West African Narrow Strip Weaving.* Washington D.C.: The Textile Museum, 1975.

Landreau, Anthony N. "From Mexico to Rumania to Sweden." *Textile Museum Journal,* Vol. 2, No. 4 (Dec. 1969): 37–40.

———. "Kurdish Kilim Weaving in the Van-Hakkari District of Eastern Turkey." *Textile Museum Journal* Vol. 3 No. 4 (Dec. 1973): 27–42.

———, ed. *Yörük: The Nomadic Weaving Tradition in the Middle East.* Pittsburgh: Pittsburgh Museum of Art, Carnegie Institute, 1978.

——— and Pickering, W. R. *From the Bosporus to Samarkand: Flat Woven Rugs.* Washington D.C.: The Textile Museum, 1969.

Larsen, Jack Lenor; Bühler, Alfred; and Solyom, Garrett. *The Dyer's Art: Ikat, Batik, Plangi.* New York: Van Nostrand Reinhold, 1976.

Lefevre, Jean. *Caucasian Carpets.* London: Lefevre and Partners, 1978.

———. *Central Asian Carpets.* London: Lefevre and Partners, 1976.

———. *Turkish Carpets.* London: Lefevre and Partners, 1977.

Leix, Alfred. *Turkestan and Its Textile Centers.* Hampshire, Eng.: Crosby Press, 1974.

Lewis, G. Griffin. *Practical Book of Oriental Rugs.* 6th ed., rev. Philadelphia: Lippincott, 1945.

Liebetrau, Preben. *Oriental Rugs in Color.* New York: Macmillan, 1962.

Lindahl, David and Knorr, Thomas. *Uzbek.* Basel: Verlag AG, 1975.

Linehan, Edward J. "Old-New Iran, Next Door to Russia." *National Geographic* (Jan. 1961): 44–85.

Lubell, Cecil, ed. *Textile Collections of the World.* 3 vols. New York: Van Nostrand Reinhold, 1976.

Lviv State Museum of Ethnography and Crafts. *Album of the Lviv State Museum of Ethnography and Crafts.* Lviv, Ukraine SSR: State Museum of Ethnography and Crafts, 1976.

McMullan, Joseph V. *Islamic Carpets.* New York: Near Eastern Art Research Center, 1965.

———. *Rugs from the Jos. V. McMullan Collection.* Washington D.C.: Smithsonian Institution, 1966–1968.

Mackie, Louise W. *The Splendor of Turkish Weaving.* Washington D.C.: The Textile Museum, 1973.

Mailey, Jean. *Chinese Silk Tapestry K'o-ssu.* New York: China House Gallery, 1971.

Matthews, Washington. *Navajo Weavers and Silversmiths.* Palmer Lake, Colorado: The Filter Press, 1968.

Maxwell, Gilbert S. *Navajo Rugs: Past Present and Future.* Palm Desert, Calif.: Best-West Publications, 1963.

Meisch, Lynn. *A Traveler's Guide to El Dorado and the Inca Empire.* New York: Penguin Books, 1977.

Mera, H. P. *Navajo Textile Arts.* Santa Barbara, Calif.: 1975.

Metropolitan Museum of Art. *From the Land of the Scythians: Ancient Treasures from the Museums of the USSR.* New York: New York Graphic Society, 1975.

Morley, Sylvanus G. *The Ancient Maya.* Stanford, Calif.: Stanford University Press, 1946.

Mumford, John Kimberly. *Oriental Rugs.* New York: Charles Scribner's Sons, 1900.

Murray, G. W. *Sons of Ishmael: A Study of the Egyptian Bedouin.* London: George Routledge and Sons, 1935.

Museum of International Folk Art *Indigo.* Santa Fe: Museum of New Mexico, 1962.

O'Neale, Lila M. *Textiles of Highland Guatemala.* Washington

D.C.: Carnegie Institution, 1945.

Oprescu, George. *Peasant Art in Roumania*. London: The Studio Ltd., 1929.

Osborne, Lilly de Jongh. *Indian Crafts of Guatemala and El Salvador*. Norman, Okla.: University of Oklahoma Press, 1965.

Philby, H. St. J. B. *Arabian Highlands*. Ithaca, N.Y.: Cornell University Press, 1952.

Plumer, Cheryl. *African Textiles: Outline of Handicrafted Sub-Saharan Fabrics*. East Lansing: Michigan State University, 1971.

Pohrt, Richard A. *The American Indian/The American Flag*. Flint, Michigan: Flint Institute of Arts, 1976.

Pope, Arthur Upham. *Masterpieces of Persian Art*. New York: The Dryden Press, c. 1945.

———. *A Survey of Persian Art from Prehistoric Times to the Present*. 6 vols. London: Oxford, 1939.

——— and Ackerman, Phyllis. *Oriental Rugs as Fine Art*. International Studio, 1976.

Praeger, Elfriede. *Ancient Egypt: A Survey*. San Francisco, 1975.

Pronun, Alexander and Barbara. *Russian Folk Arts*. New York: A. S. Barnes, 1975.

Reath, Nancy Andrews. *The Weaves of Hand-Loom Fabrics*. New Haven: Yale Univ. Press for Pennsylvania Museum of Art, 1927.

Réclus, Elisée. *The Earth and Its Inhabitants* (sometimes entitled *The Universal Geography*). 19 vols. New York: D. A. Appleton, 1884.

Redfield, Robert and Rojas, Alfonso Villa. *Chan Kom: A Maya Village*. 1934. Reprint. Chicago: University of Chicago Press, 1962.

Reichard, Gladys A. *Navajo Shepard and Weaver*. 1936. Reprint. Glorieta, New Mexico: Rio Grande Press, 1968.

Revault, Jacques. *Designs and Patterns from North African Carpets and Textiles*. 4 vols. 1950–1957. Reprint New York: Dover Publications, 1973.

Riefstahl, R. M. "Primitive Rugs of the Konya Type in the Mosque of Beyshehir." *Metropolitan Art Bulletin*, Vol. 13, No. 2 (1931): 15–16.

Ripley, Mary Churchill. *The Oriental Rug Book*. New York: Fred A. Stokes, 1904.

Rodee, Marian E. *Southwestern Weaving*. Albuquerque, New Mexico: University of New Mexico Press and the Maxwell Museum of Anthropology, 1977.

Roth, H. Ling. *Studies in Primitive Looms*. Halifax: Bankfield Museum, 1918.

Rowe, Anne. *Warp Patterned Weaves of the Andes*. Washington D.C.: The Textile Museum, 1977.

Sawyer, Alan R. *Mastercraftsmen of Ancient Peru*. New York: Solomon R. Guggenheim Foundation, 1968.

Sayer, Chloe. *Crafts of Mexico*. London: Aldus Books, 1977.

Schlosser, Ignaz. *The Book of Rugs, Oriental and European*, 1960. Reprint. New York: Crown Publishers, 1963.

Schooten, Marie-Therese Ullens de. *Lords of the Mountain*. London: Chatto & Windus, 1956.

Schorch, Anita. ed. *The Art of the Weaver*. New York: Universe Books, 1978.

Schurmann, Ulrich. *Caucasian Rugs*. London: Allen and Unwin, 1968.

———. *Central-Asian Rugs*. Frankfurt am Main: Verlag Osterrieth, 1969.

———. *Oriental Carpets*. London: Paul Hamlyn, 1966.

Seagroat, Margaret. *A Basic Textile Book*. New York: Van Nostrand Reinhold, 1975.

Serjeant, R. B. *Material for a History of Islamic Textiles up to the Mongol Conquest*. Beirut: Librairie du Lebanon, 1972.

Sieber, Roy. *African Textiles and Decorative Arts*. New York: Museum of Modern Art, 1972.

Sirelius, U. T. *The Hand-Woven Rugs of Finland*. Helsinki: Helsingfors, 1930.

Soustelle, Jacques. *Daily Life of the Aztecs (on the Eve of the Spanish Conquest)*. Stanford: Stanford University Press, 1961.

Spicer, Edward H. *Cycles of Conquest*. Tucson: University of Arizona Press, 1962.

Stamkov, Dmitri. *Carpettes et Tapis*. Sofia: Bulgarian Academy of Sciences, 1975.

Stein, Mark Aurel. *Sand-Buried Ruins of Khotan*. London: Hurst and Blakett, 1904.

Stewart, Janice S. *The Folk Arts of Norway*. 1953. Reprint. New York: Dover Publications, 1972.

Sykes, Percy. *A History of Persia*. 2 vols. London: Macmillan and Co., 1951.

Thatcher, A. B. *Turkoman Rugs*. New York: E. Weyhe, 1940.

Thurstan, Violetta. *A Short History of Decorative Textiles and Tapestries*. London: Pepler and Sewell 1934.

Tschebull, Raoul. *Kazak: Carpets of the Caucasus*. New York: The Near Eastern Art Research Center and The New York Rug Society, 1971.

Turkhan, Kundret H. *Islamic Rugs*. New York: Frederick A. Praeger, 1969.

University of Manchester, Whitworth Art Gallery. *The Qashqa'i of Iran*. Manchester, England: World of Islam Festival, 1976.

Vambéry, Arminius. *The Life and Adventures of Arminius Vambéry*. New York: Frederick A. Stokes.

———. *The Story of My Struggles*. London: T. Fisher Unwin, 1904.

Volbach, W. Fritz. *Early Decorative Textiles*. 1966. Reprint. London: Paul Hamlyn, 1969.

Walker, Daniel S. *Oriental Rugs in Cincinnati Collections*. Cincinnati, Ohio: Cincinnati Art Museum, 1976.

Wheat, J. B. *Patterns and Sources of Navajo Weaving*. Denver: The Printing Establishment, 1975.

Weeks, Jeanne G. and Treganowan, Donald. *Rugs and Carpets of European and the Western World*. Philadelphia: Chilton Books, 1969.

Weibel, Adele. *Two Thousand Years of Textiles*. New York: Pantheon Books, 1952.

Weir, Shelagh. *The Bedouin: Aspects of the Material Culture of the Bedouin of Jordan*. London: World of Islam Festival Publishing, 1976.

Wertime, John and Tanavoli, Parvis. *Tribal Animal Covers From Iran*. Tehran: Iran America Society, 1975.

Yohe, Ralph S. and Jones, H. M. *Turkish Rugs*. Washington D.C.: Textile Museum, 1968.

index

C-1. See page 9.

C-2. See page 27.

1

2

3

C–3. 1–4. See page 29.

4

C–4. See page 32.

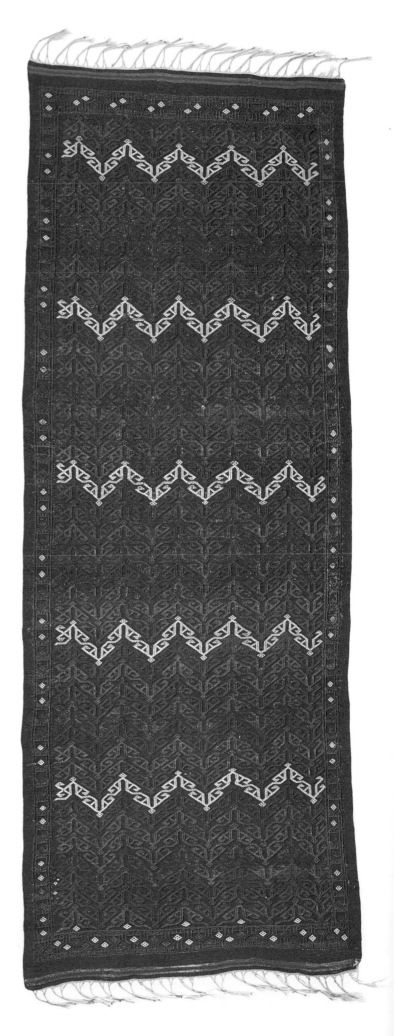

C-5. See page 33.

C-6. See page 33.

197

C-7. See page 35.

C–8. See page 39.

A

C–9. A–E. See page 43.

B

C

D

E

201

C-10. See page 44.

C-11. See page 47.

C–12. See page 49.

A

B

C

C–13. A–C. See page 53.

A

B

C–14. A–B. See page 48.

C-15. See page 56.

A

B

C

C–16. A–C. See page 56.

A

C–17. A–B. See page 65.

B

A

C–18. A–B. See page 65.

B

A

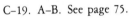

C-19. A-B. See page 75.

B

A

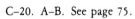
C-20. A-B. See page 75.

B

211

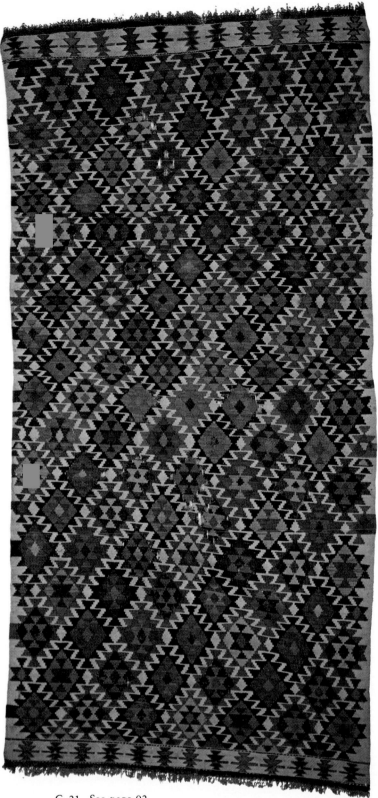

C–21. See page 92.

C–22. See page 92.

A

C–23. A–B. See page 95.

B

A

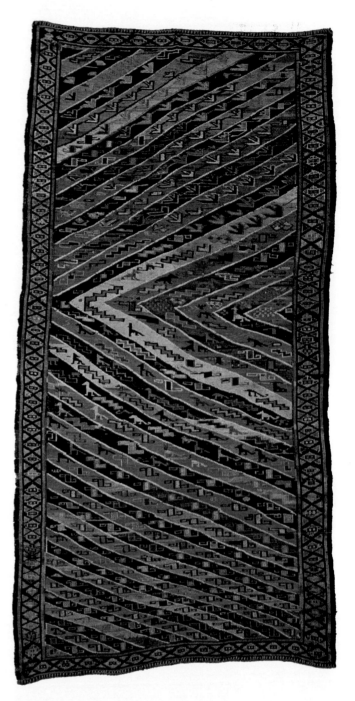

B

C–24. A–C. See page 95.

C

214

C-25. See page 109.

C-26. See page 109.

A

C–27. A–B. See page 114.

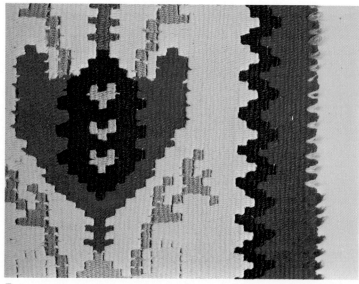

B

C–28. See page 119.

C–29. See page 119.

A

B

C

C-30. A–C. See page 124.

C–31. See page 127.

C–32. See page 127.

A

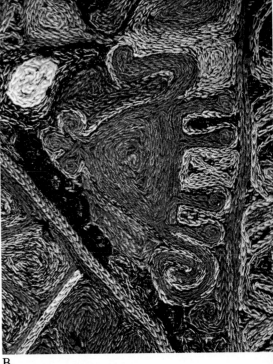

B

C-33. A–B. See page 142.

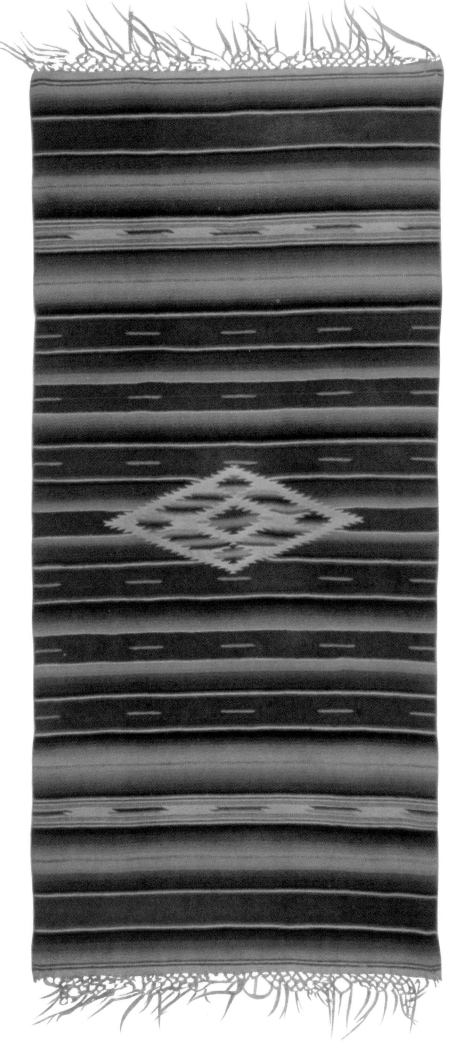

C–34. See page 161.

A

C–35. A–B. See page 173.

B

C–36. See page 169.

A

C–37. A–B. See page 9.

B

224